Dangerous Prayer

'Most Christians would agree that prayer is essential for mission. Darren Cronshaw goes a step further and argues that prayer – specifically the Lord's Prayer – impels us into mission. Cronshaw's earlier book, *Sentness*, articulated his deep passion for Christians to understand and engage with the mission of God. In *Dangerous Prayer* that same commitment shines out, with prayer as the foundation. I am thrilled that he has articulated and illustrated this important perspective so powerfully.'

Revd Dr Lynne M. Baab, author and Jack Somerville Lecturer in Pastoral Theology at University of Otago, New Zealand

'*Dangerous Prayer* by Darren Cronshaw is one of the few books that challenge both contemplatives and activists. It's a kind of manifesto meditation for those seeking to go deeper in this life as it collides with the next. Darren's gentle but articulate voice draws on the Jesus Prayer in ways I have never fully seen before and invited me into the flow of quiet, dangerous, risky, radical, committed actions. If prayer is taken up like this, then surely we and our world can be transformed. What a hopeful book!'

Dr Ash Barker, Founder and Director, Newbigin School for Urban Leadership, www.NewbiginHouse.uk

'In *Dangerous Prayer* Darren Cronshaw invites us on a journey to explore the prayer that Jesus taught us. This is the prayer he rightly terms 'dangerous' because he shows that when we engage with the Dangerous Prayer we come closer and closer to God's heart, God's plan and God's possibility. That's dangerous because it means not playing safe, not sticking with well-worn customs, looking past the complacent and comfortable, the conventional and convenient. Darren's gift for looking at something very familiar, and finding something that shines with new life and new possibility, is in full flight in this challenging, enlivening, engaging book.'

Revd Tim Costello, CEO World Vision Australia

'The majority of books on prayer and the deeper life understand the Lord's Prayer at a personal level. "Our Father" is often reinterpreted as "My Father"; "Give us this day our daily bread" becomes "Give my family what we need for today." *Dangerous Prayer* by Darren Cronshaw uniquely challenges us to pray the most famous prayer of all time in the context of social and global issues. Challenging and thought-provoking!'

Felicity Dale, author

'This book says it plain and true: the Dangerous Prayer will not support self-edification but will bring transformation, of us and our world. Do not read this if you want to stay comfortable or stay put. Read it if you are wanting to engage in God's world and, needing fuel for the missional journey, are ready for its storied challenge.'

Dr Rosemary Dewerse, missiologist

'What we're like in private places affects what we're like in public places. Prayer is one of those private places that can determine all. Sadly, prayer is one of the forgotten arts in activistic circles and therefore, not surprisingly, activistic Christians fall by the wayside after five to seven years of action. Darren rightly weds mysticism and activism. Without participation in Christ through prayer, imitation of Christ is nigh on impossible. This is a book that will have you deeply reflecting. For example, on one page alone Darren is quoting a diverse range of authors: Crossan, Hybels and Peterson. It's nice to read a book that drinks from many wells. This book is good for the soul . . . and the streets.'

Dr Mick Duncan, Minor Kiwi Prophet

'We have often thought of prayer only in personal, contemplative and formal liturgical ways, and of mission in active, corporate and entrepreneurial ways. We have also often separated them one from another. However, both prayer and mission are part of the Triune God's gracious and wonderful dealing with us, and of our responsive joy in being caught up in God's very purpose. Both prayer and mission are parts of the interrelated adventure in our being incorporated into the wonder of Christian existence. In this excellent book,

Darren Cronshaw shows us how these two interconnected parts of Christian existence can be expressed in the personal, social, public, political and global aspects of our Christian lives, both as individuals and in community. The book comes from deep reflection and wide experience. It, of course, points to being countercultural in much of our lives. However, it also is an invitation to the greatest adventure in our existence.'

Revd Professor James Haire AC, Research Professor, Australian Centre for Christianity and Culture, Charles Sturt University, Canberra, Australia

'Rooted in the reality of a world of pain, Darren Cronshaw's challenging book on Dangerous Prayer will inspire and motivate you to pray and live differently. Structured around the Lord's Prayer, the book is filled with profound and often overlooked insights, while always remaining readable and accessible. This is a book you will keep returning to. It is also ideal for small-group study and discussion. Risk reading it.'

Dr Brian Harris, Principal, Vose Seminary, Perth, Australia

'As the church in the West embraces its missionality or sentness, it needs to embrace missional practices. From new monasticism to the megachurch, *prayer* is the foundation of incarnational mission. God is at work and we join in with what God is doing. But how do we learn to begin with *prayer*? Why in the Western world do we go to action and service first before prayer? Why do we feel the contemplative is for a select few? When we feel overwhelmed by the world's needs, social problems and ethnic divisions, how can we pray for solutions, and be open to be the answer for our prayers? These questions of missional spirituality are central for the church in the West. Cronshaw's *Dangerous Prayer* points us wisely to rediscovering Jesus' pattern of prayer. I recommend you read this with an open heart from someone

I know lives this out every day and writes from a wealth of experience and conviction.'

Revd Kim Hammond, International Director, Forge Mission Training Network; Lead Pastor, CityLife Church Casey, Melbourne, Australia

'Darren has shown here that the very act of prayer itself is an orienting act that has significant implications for all Christian efforts to change the world. Prayer, learning to address God, is not a meaningless and passive activity; it is actually part of God's mission to change the world.'

Alan Hirsch, award-winning author; thought leader; founder of Forge Mission Training Network, 100Movements and Future Travelers; alanhirsch.org

'We all know that prayer is necessary in mission, it is the source of nourishment and, on occasion, a source of power to change situations that are deeply embedded in injustice. Power is dangerous and therefore the idea of Dangerous Prayer is both thought-provoking and inspiring. Darren has offered a reflection on a much-loved piece of scripture, possibly one of the few passages that most people in the West still retain in their memory. In doing so he brings together the great themes of mission as activism and mission as rooted in spiritual practices. Both are needed but hard to integrate. You will enjoy reading this rich and thoughtful approach to the Lord's Prayer.'

Revd Dr Martin Robinson, Principal, Springdale College, Birmingham, UK

'Familiarity with the Lord's Prayer can too easily lead us to domesticate its meaning. *Dangerous Prayer* gently but firmly returns us to the costly, radical and missional calling embedded in this most famous of prayers. But beware! Reading this book will change how you view yourself and God's desires for his world.'

Dr Perry Shaw, Professor of Christian Education and Acting Dean, Arab Baptist Theological Seminary

'For mission to be sustainable over a lifetime it has to be rooted in who we are, rather than just being one of the things we do as Christians. Darren Cronshaw's exposition of the Lord's Prayer is a welcome addition to the growing body of resources that explore a missional understanding of spirituality. Insightfully weaving Jesus' answer to the request 'Teach us to pray' with his own personal experience, the life of the church and the contemporary world, the result is a highly readable, thought-provoking and instructive engagement with this "dangerous prayer".'

Revd Dr Roger Standing, Principal, Spurgeon's College, London

Dangerous Prayer

Discovering a missional spirituality in the Lord's Prayer

Darren Cronshaw

First published 2017 by Paternoster
Paternoster is an imprint of Authentic Media Ltd
PO Box 6326, Bletchley, Milton Keynes MK1 9GG.
authenticmedia.co.uk

British Library Cataloguing in Publication Data

A catalogue record for this book is available from the British Library

ISBN: 978-1-84227-976-2
978-1-78078-277-5 (e-book)

Cover design by David Smart smartsart.co.uk
Printed and bound by CPI Group (UK) Ltd, Croydon CR0 4YY

Contents

Foreword

Karl Barth wrote, 'To clasp the hands in prayer is the beginning of an uprising against the disorder of the world.' In other words, prayer is subversive and dangerous. And when examined carefully it becomes obvious that the prayer our Lord taught us to pray is exactly that. From the seditious declaration of the pre-eminent kingship of God to the heartfelt yearning for the unfurling of God's alternative realm here on earth, those who pray the Lord's Prayer are calling forth trouble. We are expressing our desire for a new world, not at the mercy of presidents and prime ministers, czars and caliphs, dictators and demagogues, but under the rule of a parental God who hears our cries for daily bread, for endless forgiveness and for the strength to find a different way to be human.

In that ancient discipleship manual, the *Didache*, written in the first century, the earliest followers of Jesus were instructed to pray the Lord's Prayer three times a day. Those words were meant to take root in the lives of disciples, to become entwined around the rhythms of their daily lives, to inform their understanding of the universe, the empire, the village and their very existence.

Simone Weil said of the Lord's Prayer that it expressed every possible prayer or petition we could ever form. Advocating a similar daily rhythm of praying this prayer, she went on, 'It is impossible to say it once through, *giving the fullest possible attention to each word*, without a change, infinitesimal but real, taking place in the soul.'

Too bad that for many of us we grew up reciting these words by rote, memorizing them with the same absentmindedness with which we learned the lyrics to the theme songs of *The Brady Bunch* or *Friends*. But the words of the Lord's Prayer aren't mindless lyrics. They are a carefully crafted expression of the world made right. They express our hope of being restored to union with God and communion with others, in the context of a community for the good of others and the world.

In this book, missiologist Darren Cronshaw insists we do as Weil says we must and give the fullest possible attention to each word. He parses each line and reveals to us the dangerous implications of making such a series of petitions. Darren shows how this prayer, far from being merely a devotional device, is a manifesto for radical inclusion in God's family, for subversive justice and for a countercultural form of reconciliation, all under the guiding influence of the reign of the Triune God.

And how fitting that it be a missiologist who leads us down this road, for the Lord's Prayer is unquestioningly a missional prayer. As Barry Jones writes, 'In prayer our lives are turned outward from ourselves and toward God's name, God's kingdom, God's world. In praying the prayer that Jesus taught us, we find our voices and our lives swept up into the drama of what God is doing to rescue and renew his good but broken creation.'[1]

In other words, this prayer is concerned with the completion of God's purpose in the creation of the world. It's not a request for the redeemed ones to escape from history, but a plea to be used by God in the action of bringing history to its true end.

It is a dangerous prayer.

Pray it at your own peril.

Michael Frost, Morling College, Sydney, Australia
    author of *The Road to Missional, Surprise the World* and *Incarnate*

Preface

The heroes who have inspired me in mission and prayer are people to whom I owe a great debt. I would love to introduce you to some of them – people who have inspired me by fostering God's dreams among the school communities, homeless, mentally ill, refugees, addicted, youth and families in crisis across different neighbourhoods in the places I have lived and travelled.

I would love to invite you to share life and mission with the churches and tribes I have been privileged to serve, and with whom I shared some of these thoughts as they developed. These include Aberfeldie, Eastern Hills, West Preston, AuburnLife and Kew Baptist churches, and for the teams I have worked alongside with at Baptist Union of Victoria, Australian College of Ministries and Forge Mission Training Network. And I would love you to meet my family – my wife Jennifer, son Benjamin and daughters Jessie and Emily. My fellow travellers, church communities and family are precious to me, and it is in relationship with them that God has taught me so much about myself, about God and about genuine missional spirituality.

Thank you David Chatelier, Andrew Chua, Brad Coath, Benjamin Cronshaw, John Cronshaw, David Gallus, Gabriel Hingley, Maggie Kappelhoff, Lynette Leach and Anne Wilkinson-Hayes for reading drafts and offering invaluable feedback on one or more chapters. Well-deserved thanks also to Mike Parsons my commissioning editor, Reuben Sneller who took over the project as editor, Becky Fawcett as editorial administrator, Mollie Barker as copyeditor, and the rest of the team at Paternoster for believing in this project and adding value to it.

Chin and Karen migrants to Australia from Burma (Myanmar) have enriched the life of Victorian Baptist churches over the last decade.[1] They have opened my eyes to the struggle of groups like theirs for human rights and religious freedom, and the long road to asylum for refugees. Most of the 22,000 migrants to Australia from Burma have been displaced by persecution and injustice. Many others struggle for survival in Thailand and Malaysia. We live in a world of growing inequity between rich and poor, with growing numbers of people living in urban slums and squatter settlements. Yet the governments of many Western nations including Australia are looking at ways of cutting their aid and development budget. In this context, the work of non-government aid and development organizations is critically important. For example, Baptist World Aid Australia works with local partners in eighteen of the most vulnerable countries of the world in community development, child-centred community development and disaster management.[2] One of their programmes, the Chin Refugee Project, seeks to provide essential medical check-ups, health education and learning centres for the children of the estimated 45,000 Chin refugees in Malaysia. Author royalties for this book are donated directly from Paternoster to Baptist World Aid to provide daily needs and foster community development among refugees from Burma through the Chin Refugee Project, or other similar initiatives in years to come.

Darren Cronshaw
Hawthorn, Australia
July 2016

With appreciation for the inspiration of their faith and perseverance, I dedicate *Dangerous Prayer* to my Chin and Karen sisters and brothers
'of whom the world is not worthy'.

Introduction: 'Lord, teach us to pray *glocally*'

God help us to change. To change ourselves and to change our world. To know the need for it. To deal with the pain of it. To feel the joy of it. To undertake the journey without understanding the destination. The art of gentle revolution. Amen.

(Michael Leunig)[1]

What's in It for Me?

In the 2003 movie *Bruce Almighty*, TV reporter Bruce Nolan (Jim Carrey) takes the job of God (Morgan Freeman) while God goes on vacation. Bruce uses his newly acquired God-powers for himself a few times, then gets in the business of helping people by answering their prayers. He turns prayers into emails, saves time by automatically replying 'Yes' to all, and goes out to a party. Later on he notices that everyone in Buffalo has won the lottery, with the result that each person wins $17. This is a fair summary of many people's prayers: requests for their own enrichment.

Beth Barnett, who worked with me at Baptist Union of Victoria and now leads Victorian Council of Christian Education, introduced me to an app, 'Pray with me'. It puts all your prayer reminders in one place and shows who is praying for you (or at least virtually indicating they want to pray for you). As Beth warned me, it is designed for people who understand the latest technology, social media marketing, Christian guilt and first-world problems, but know little about prayer. You can download it onto your phone in a folder with all your other shopping list apps. You can add prayer requests to others who use the app. The prayers are even categorized neatly: Current Events, My Faith, My Finances, My Parents, My Children, My Church, My Marriage, None, My Health, My Friends, My Praise, My Family, My Relationships, Men's Issues, Forgiveness, My Loss. Can you see a pattern? Almost everything is about how prayer helps me. The samples I read under those categories included prayers for a worship leader's voice, healthy weight loss, a marriage partner, family troubles and dealing with financial debt. The Western world dream predominates. Global hunger and religious persecution, Afghanistan, Burma and Zimbabwe are noticeable by their absence. The app designer has one tab for issues beyond ourselves, Current Events, but when I looked, no one had posted anything under that category.

I find it easy to ask God for help with my concerns and issues. What I need is an app that lifts my vision beyond myself and those close to me. This is where the Dangerous Prayer is helpful. It guides me in prayer for my needs and my forgiveness, but also for God's dream to be outworked in my neighbourhood and the world around me.

The Dangerous Prayer has become for me the most important framework for prayer, and a framework for my broader spirituality and mission. As I look back over my prayer life over the last decade, it has radicalized my prayer. But it has also radicalized my approach to faith and mission. It challenges me that faith is not a consumer product that is only good as long as it adds to my sense of fulfilment. It reminds me to pray and live for God's missional purposes. Its radical inspiration draws me back to the core of what Christianity is about: the mission of God with which God invites us to cooperate.

That is why I feel this book is so important and why it has been refreshing to write. The Dangerous Prayer is a prayer that fuels and sustains mission. To have an effective mission we need to have a vibrant life of prayer. To have a vibrant prayer life we need an outlet for it in mission. Sustainability in mission is not possible without prayer. Vibrancy in prayer is not possible without mission.

At this time in church history and with the challenges of mission in the world, I am convinced there is nothing else that we need more to grapple with than prayer that engages the world and sustains mission.

As prayer is so essential to the missional life, missional prayer is an activity requiring urgent attention for all Christians. It takes us to the heart of our relationship with God. It is critically important for any of us who have begun to understand that all Christians are sent to our neighbourhoods and networks as missionaries.

That is why I urge us all to join the early disciples in asking Jesus to 'teach us to pray', to lead us to engage freshly with God and the world. My imagination is captured by a reading and application of the Dangerous Prayer that seeks to pray what God's dream is for the world (including that all be fed, forgiven and freed of oppression) and that seeks to live what we pray (to 'be the answer to our prayers' as Shane Claiborne and Jonathan Wilson-Hartgrove say).[2] The Dangerous Prayer is thus a seedbed for missional spirituality and radical discipleship. My imagination has also been grabbed by the way the Dangerous Prayer guides me to pray for local neighbourhoods and global needs. I urge you to ask God to teach you to pray for local and global issues: 'Lord, teach us to pray *glocally*.'

This is a very personal and spiritual journey for me. I wrote these reflections as a kind of spiritual autobiography. I wanted to rediscover a grace-based and life-giving invitation to pray actively and act prayerfully. The chapters are written to help missionaries cultivate a sustaining spirituality, to help contemplative types of people to develop missional practices, and to invite all of us into a deeper experience of spirituality and mission. We will examine some of the pressures and ideologies that compete with missional spirituality, including consumerism and violence. This is an ideal textbook for studying courses on spiritual formation and missional spirituality, but even more so an ideal guidebook for living your missional spirituality. I hope it draws your knees down to pray and your feet to step out in response. I pray it will motivate you in prayerful reflective and active response. Hopefully it draws one eye towards God and one eye towards the world, or – better yet – both eyes towards the world and God's activity in the world. I want us to get to know Jesus as the master pray-er and exemplar missionary, and explore the difference his prayer can make to our neighbourhoods and the broader world.

I have been teaching through the Dangerous Prayer for over a decade in different churches. At AuburnLife, the prayer is becoming not just something to pray in our Sunday gatherings, but a framework for reminding us how we follow Jesus. In the busyness of modern life and the disconnection of community, some of us at church have longed for common practices to adopt together that shape our spirituality and discipleship. The Dangerous Prayer is a primary practice we have gravitated to. It is becoming part of our 'Auburn Way'.

Prayer embraces the deepest and most personal cries from our hearts. Yet I find I can easily get caught in the same old rut. I need ways to pray that I can sustain and that keep me focused on what is on God's heart. Let's be honest about this. We know prayer is important. When we pray, we often acknowledge its importance and even experience its benefits. But it is challenging to keep at it. And when we do pray, it is all too easy to focus on the postmodern trinity – God for me, myself and I – rather than pleading with the Trinitarian God to transform the world.

My father John and brother Jason are in business together. They tell me that a key sales and marketing principle is to answer a question for people: 'What's In It For Me (WIIFM)?' The Dangerous Prayer is not firstly about WIIFM. The WIIFM equivalent in the Dangerous Prayer is about lifting our vision beyond ourselves as we pray. It's about WIIFGW – 'What's In It For God's World?' The Dangerous Prayer lifts our eyes beyond WIIFM and draws us irresistibly towards WIIFGW.

How Do You Pray?

I have a hobby – prayer collecting. I like collecting interesting and helpful and world-grasping prayers. But I also like collecting insights on what helps people to pray. I am curious about what motivates or enlivens people, and what drains or keeps us from prayer. How do you pray, I wonder?

When I look back over my prayer journals, they remind me of the diversity of prayer. My prayer spans praise and worship, tossing ideas around for guidance, handing anxieties over to God, pleading with God to change a situation for a friend or world tragedy, and asking for help when a situation is beyond me. But at times prayer has also included one or more of the following characteristics: dryness, self-ishness, repetitiveness or just plain weirdness! There have been some beautiful times of feeling close to God: when I came to faith in high school, when I discovered the richness of reading the Bible for myself, when I was involved in Christian camping in university years, when I felt God heal someone as I laid hands on them. There have been times I have prayed deeply and with perseverance for friends who were facing tough times and for drastic situations in the world. But I need to say there have been times when I felt no motivation to pray, practised minimal discipline in maintaining a life of prayer, and felt like my prayers bounced off the ceiling.

One of the most vibrant times was when I was living in Asia. I recall prayer never being so rich as I leaned deeply on God and sought God's blessing on the mission we were partnering with. In the 1990s I was preparing for missionary service, and recall realizing that unless I had a vibrant growing spirituality, I would have little to share with people of other religions who had deep and disciplined spiritual practices. Sri Lankan evangelist Ajith Fernando urges Christians to prioritize prayer for its own sake, but also so we have an authentic experience of God to share. He warns: 'Christians who do not know the joys of lingering in the presence of God will be at a loss to know how to respond when people speak of serenity through New Age disciplines like transcendental meditation.'[3] This leads me to ask: where have we experienced God? Where have we struggled and come through with the help of Jesus? Where is our spirituality growing and where does it have an outlet in mission?

What is your experience of prayer?

You might be wondering how to pray. Not knowing what to say, or how to frame our prayers, can limit our praying. It can also be hard in the midst of the busyness and noise of everyday life to find focused and quiet time to pray. Prayer as one more task to fit into the day is not very attractive and life-giving. I am eager to develop patterns of prayer that are simple enough for someone who is just starting to seek God, and accessible in the midst of everyday life.

You might be experiencing prayer as a delight of your life. If you can testify to God's goodness and faithfulness in answered prayer, and if prayer flows naturally for you, praise God. But you might long for more of God, and be eager to grow in prayer that impacts the world. Jesus had mountain-top experiences of being transformed. I picture Jesus inviting us to learn from him deeper things about God's heart. Jesus wants to teach us how to be changed ourselves, and how to embrace the world with our prayers.

Alternatively you might be well practised in prayer but feel dry and stretched in your spirit. Sometimes as people mature in faith, God does not necessarily 'feel' closer. In fact God can feel more distant. Saints have described such seasons as 'the dark night of the soul'. St John of the Cross first used that term, but many others before and since have had crises of faith and not felt as if God was the light of their life.[4] You might pray for months or years without evidence of God responding. Your heart for prayer may be cold and worn. If God seems inaccessible and your prayers feel like they are bouncing off the ceiling, let me assure you that I have been there. In fact, Jesus has been there. He who said to his heavenly Father, 'My God, my God, why have you abandoned me?' (Matthew 27:46), is the one we look to for our model of the Dangerous Prayer. Jesus had his fair share of demanding people and frustrating circumstances. This Jesus invites us, 'Let's go off by ourselves to a quiet place and rest awhile.' Mark tells us, 'He said this because there were so many people coming and going that Jesus and his apostles didn't even have time to eat' (Mark 6:31). It is this Jesus who offers to help us maintain connection with God and keep our heart open to the world.

What helps or motivates you to pray? Not just 'desperation prayers' in times of crisis, but what helps to develop an approach to communing and co-missioning with the Lord that will be consistent day by day, throughout the day, in the midst of life as well as at special times, with others as well as alone?

The Colorado-based poet Dorothy Walters wrote:

Something inside me
Constantly bleeds towards God.
That's why I keep writing,
Slipping messages under the door.[5]

Catholic sister and retreat leader Joyce Rupp comments on this poem, encouraging us to see prayer as natural and rhythmical as blood flowing from our heart to our body and back again, bringing life and cleansing from God.[6] Even if God seems behind a closed door, the poem encourages us to keep at it in prayer. If you could slip a message under the door, what would it be? What might God slip under your door?

Whether or not you struggle with what to say to God, the Dangerous Prayer is a profound framework for praying for yourself, your neighbourhood and the world. But before we dig deeper into the Dangerous Prayer and its transformational perspectives, I need to share an important background warning.

Warning, Warning, Warning

Lost in Space, a classic television series that I watched reruns of as a child, shows the Robinson family, a scientific friend and a trusty robot jetting around the galaxy on their rocket ship *Jupiter 2*, looking for a way back to Earth. As they discovered new worlds and encountered fresh adventures, all set in a convenient thirty-minute plot, the robot helped the Robinsons stay alive. The robot had a built-in detector for aliens, monsters and space cataclysms. It would pronounce 'Warning, warning . . . Danger, Will Robinson!' whenever a threat was imminent. The Robinson family would often embark on a course of action that they felt comfortable with, but the robot alerted them to the foolhardy nature of their actions.

Matthew has a warning of danger surrounding the Dangerous Prayer. Jesus counsels: 'Watch out! Don't do your good deeds publicly, to be admired by others, for you will lose the reward from your Father in heaven' (Matthew 6:1). He goes on to explain how this applies to the acts of justice/righteousness of giving, prayer and fasting. If you pray (or give or fast or do other good deeds) in order to appear good to others, then you already have your reward. People will give you attention or think of you as spiritual. The issue is not the action but the motive. Prayer is to be practised with a single eye on God, not a sideways glance at whoever might be impressed.[7]

Mark Sayers is an insightful cultural commentator and senior leader of Red Church in Box Hill, a neighbouring suburb close to our church, AuburnLife, in Melbourne. Sayers, in *The Vertical Self*, critiques our Western culture's obsession with evaluating ourselves horizontally according to the opinions of others.[8] He warns against trying to be cool, sexy and glamorous. But the warning is equally appropriate for trying to appear spiritual. Preoccupation with appearance is as rampant in the church as in society. Sayers sums up this thinking:

> Our moral choices do not matter. What does matter is being seen as having the right opinions. Instead of letting our actions show our convictions, we speak empty platitudes through our blogs, bumper stickers, and T-shirt slogans. In the age of the horizontal self, backing up our opinions with the right behaviour is seen as neither essential nor necessary. Because there is no authoritative story or deeper set of values, people are quite comfortable holding contradictory opinions within themselves. For hundreds of years the concept of holiness and sin in Western culture created a concern for doing good, for maintaining integrity. Today, however, we are not bothered when our actions do not match our rhetoric. This is because our basic understanding of what it means to be good has changed. It is not as important that we are good as it is that we appear good.[9]

The world is tired of the musician with a cause advocating for an end to global poverty but also wanting to sell more CDs. Scepticism equally leads us to point our fingers back at ourselves and question our own motivations for engaging in social justice and doing good. What is our motivation for missional prayer and activism?

Before we start on lessons in how to pray, it is helpful to reflect on why we pray. Nurturing our souls is more important than constructing an image. It is more important to change the world than impress the world. Everyone does well to take a dose of self-awareness about what drives them. We all carry around different motivations and degrees of selfishness. If we deny this, God has to deal with our dishonesty first and then the poor motivations. It is better to be honest and open – with ourselves and with friends and God. The more years I spend in ministry, the more I realize this is so important if I want to be authentically spiritual and last the distance. Robert Fryling, Vice-President of InterVarsity Christian Fellowship, taught me this in one of my favourite books on leadership and spirituality, *The Leadership Ellipse.* In modelling healthy self-awareness and pointing the finger at himself, Fryling helped me realize my posturing, impatience, control and denial. I journaled and wrote in my review:

> I have realized that sometimes when I appear at my best, it is just appearance. I have communicated vulnerability as a technique, been enthusiastic as a show to build momentum, performed to get people to like me, built my identity from my role, compulsively strived for significance, avoided service opportunities except where I can be in charge, and made decisions for what is best for my reputation rather than what is best for the people concerned. And what pride . . . now, in showing how self-aware I am? It is easy to get caught up in mental knots, but helpful to exercise self-examination about the tensions that direct us.[10]

Self-awareness applies to ministry but also to prayer – why are we coming to God to pray? Who are we seeking to impress? It boils down to asking ourselves 'Who is our audience?' Are we praying (and giving and loving and serving on mission) to please God, or to impress others? Our real audience to keep in mind is an audience of one. God is our proper audience.

There is another warning about 'public praying' that I draw from the actual words of the Dangerous Prayer. Jesus' words about not praying in public to get attention for ourselves are well worth hearing. But the public appropriateness of the prayer is well worth heeding too. This is a *public prayer*. Some commentators describe it as a model of 'devotional' or 'private' prayer.[11] But to label it as such is missing the point. Part of its dangerous nature is that it is a *public* prayer to its very core. It is a key text for engaged spirituality and public theology. It is not '*My* Father who art in heaven', but '*Our* Father . . .' The request is not 'Give *me my* daily bread', but 'Give *us our* daily bread.' We might pray it devotionally and privately, but it should never be limited to this. Matthew teaches against any tendency to see prayer as a public event that draws attention to our own spirituality or practice of mission, but rather to pray with an audience of one. Nevertheless, the prayer is not just about God for me, myself and I, but embraces the concerns of the world. It is a 'prayer that spans the world', as Helmut Thielicke titled his sermons on the Lord's Prayer.[12] John Dominic Crossan describes it as the greatest prayer because it is so world-embracing in its scope and interest.[13] The Dangerous Prayer is to be directed primarily to God, not to a *public audience*, yet it still has great *public significance*.

Contemplative Space

Jesus expanded on his warning about not drawing attention to yourself in prayer:

> When you pray, don't be like the hypocrites who love to pray publicly on street corners and in the synagogues where everyone can see them. I tell you the truth, that is all the reward they will ever get. But when you pray, go away by yourself, shut the door behind you, and pray to your Father in private. Then your Father, who sees everything, will reward you.

> When you pray, don't babble on and on as people of other religions do. They think their prayers are answered merely by repeating their words

again and again. Don't be like them, for your Father knows exactly what
you need even before you ask him!

Matthew 6:5–8

This preamble emphasizes a private, quiet and simple approach to
prayer. Prayer is not improved by a big audience, fancy language or
extended oratory. Although Jesus said these words to underline his
warning about praying to God, not people, the picture he paints of
prayer invites us in contemplative directions. This is a growing edge
for my walk with God – learning to be still and quiet.

The longer I explore faith and engage in mission, the more I realize
my desperate need for quiet and prayerful retreat space. An enriching
spirituality is essential for sustainability in mission, but it is also essential to maintain a relationship with God. Long-serving pastor and
widely loved spiritual theology writer Eugene Peterson contends that
effective mission begins in attentiveness to God: 'Anything creative,
anything powerful, anything biblical, insofar as we are participants in
it, originates in prayer. Pastors who imitate the preaching and moral
action of the prophets without also imitating the prophets' deep praying and worship so evident in the Psalms are an embarrassment to the
faith and an encumbrance to the church.'[14]

Contemplative practices provide helpful checks and balances for a
busy lifestyle. When we are too busy for some quietness and solitude
each day, we know we are too busy. Willow Creek Senior Pastor Bill
Hybels was right when he preached we are 'too busy *not* to pray'.[15]
But if we are not careful, that phrase can imply we fit a little prayer
into the middle of our busy agendas. Part of the gift of prayer and
contemplation is to deliver us from the compulsive feeling that we
have to be busy.

There are a variety of devotional practices for nurturing inner contemplation. A variety of common prayer practices have helped me,
including:

• Reading and praying through the Psalms
• Keeping a journal

- Reading prayer books
- Praying in tongues
- Silent retreats
- Fasting
- Centring prayer
- 'Every Day with Jesus' Bible-reading notes
- Family devotions over dinner or together as a family on Sunday night
- Ignatian *examen* prayer which considers what is life-giving and what is life-draining
- *Lectio Divina* contemplative reading of Scripture
- Biblical meditation
- Being present to the moment
- Enjoying a good rest and sleep
- Observing Sabbath.

These practices are life-giving when they slow us down, and make space for us to reconnect with God. They remind us that as much as our work is important and valuable, God does not expect us to be a slave to it. Contemplative prayer subverts the voices of our culture that say we have to be busy and justify ourselves with 24/7 activity. The world does go on without us, and we will be more attune to what God is doing in the world when we have practised being present to God in quiet times.[16]

More Than a Quiet Time

Spirituality is not, however, just about retreat and reflection. Worshipping God is more than just a quiet time. Staying indoors, being quiet and doing nothing has never particularly grabbed me as my most life-giving activity. I understand that quiet contemplation and slowing down is a helpful corrective to my driven and workaholic tendencies. But for morning prayer, I prefer a jog and a chat with God than a sit and a read. The best news for my worship of God in recent years was when my spiritual director said I was 'allowed' to use bushwalks and gardening as spiritual practices. Relationships, conversations, the outdoors, activism and even dancing are activities in which I discover and enjoy God. Quiet introverted ways are not the only way to encounter God. 'Praise God!' exclaims my extroverted and activist soul.[17]

I realized that spirituality can be engaged as well as contemplative when I read Nancy Reeves' *Spirituality for Extroverts*. I journaled after reading it:

> Like many evangelical Christians, I grew up with spirituality centring on family devotions and individual Bible-reading notes. As I went to college I discovered the gift of quiet contemplation for centring my soul. But I have also discovered we can engage with God in the midst of community and action. Engaged spirituality embraces ministry as well as retreating, relational interaction as well as soul work, loud advocacy as well as quiet prayer, worship outdoors in the bush as well as indoors in the chapel, and active mission as well as contemplative prayer.[18]

As well as desperately needing to grow in contemplative spirituality, I have also appreciated being able to cultivate missional spirituality with engaged practices, including:

- Seeing prayer as integrated with everyday life, or 'practising the presence of God' in the midst of work and everyday activities
- Prioritizing relationships
- Practising hospitality
- Engaging in discussion groups
- Advocating for justice
- Enjoying walking and recreation outdoors
- Stretching myself in sport (e.g. doing an Ironman Triathlon)
- Drinking coffee and getting to know friends
- Watching and reviewing movies with thoughtful themes
- Joining a book club and discussing the faith implications of novels.

I am drawn to action as well as contemplation, work and prayer, engagement and solitude. Missional spirituality is about expressing love for God and neighbour in active ways, as well as cultivating practices of contemplation.[19]

Do you feel as if you connect with God in those different ways? There is a long heritage of embracing both contemplation *and* action as essential aspects of a missional spirituality. This balance is important as we study and pray the Dangerous Prayer. It is a prayer to pray contemplatively but also to engage actively.

Inspiring Saints of Contemplation *and* Action

Lesslie Newbigin, legendary missionary strategist for the Western world, bemoaned the imbalance of spirituality that emphasized retreat on the one hand, or busy activism on the other. He suggested that some, perhaps most, Christians adopt the Pilgrim's Progress Model that seeks to flee from the threat of 'the world' in order to be spiritually nourished. Others go to the other extreme and follow the Jonah Model of, albeit sometimes reluctantly, going into the city and boldly taking the message of God into its turmoil. Both caricatures have biblical precedents but are unbalanced. Newbigin urges Christians to adopt that which is at the heart of their faith – the Cross Model. The path of the cross means inwardly disengaging and radical separation from the pressures of the world, while also entering into the world with total identification.[20]

David Bosch wrote the most significant mission text of the twentieth century, *Transforming Mission*. But he was also deeply committed to a thoroughgoing spirituality for mission. He prophetically challenged those involved in mission not to be preoccupied with organizational structures on the one hand, or on the other hand only *talking* to people about God, rather than also *listening* to God for one's self: 'Protestants, in particular, are challenged . . . with respect to their overly pragmatic mission structures, their tendency to portray mission almost exclusively in verbalist categories, and the absence of missionary spirituality in their churches, which often drastically impoverishes all their commendable efforts in the area of social justice.'[21] Bosch reminds us we need openness to hear words from God, as well as the availability to communicate words and deeds about God.

Michael Frost and Alan Hirsch's messianic spirituality maintains that active missional engagement is the best context for inner contemplative practices: 'one worships more fully, prays more deeply, and studies more diligently when all are done in the context of a life of action.'[22] They advocate for a distinctly missional approach to church, grounded in an engaged spirituality:

> [A]n alternative, missional approach to being and doing church is best supported by an alternative approach to Christian spirituality. Too much Christendom spirituality has been concerned with retreat and reflection. While we acknowledge the value of a rich interior life, as well as the value of solitude in interiority, we believe that retreat and reflection should be embraced as part of a broader spirituality that values engagement and action. We need to find a renewed framework and basis for understanding everyday life and our actions as a vital source of experience of God. We believe in the need for the recovery of a messianic spirituality, one rooted primarily in the life and teaching of Jesus himself.[23]

Jesus displayed this kind of spirituality of retreat and engagement, often ministering, teaching, healing and eating with all kinds of people, but regularly also seeking guidance and praying alone.[24]

The missional teaching and curriculum development I do with Forge Mission Training Network is developed around this premise. Forge is a grassroots training organization that aims to develop missionary identity and pioneering leadership skills. The residency training usually has three intensives. The central intensive course is called 'Missional Spirituality' or 'Beyond Consumerism: Spirituality, Sustainability and Discipleship'. Built into the rhythms of this course, and the overall Forge curriculum, is a combination of inner contemplation with outer missional engagement. This oscillating dynamic is consistent with reflective practice and a learning cycle that integrates action and reflection.[25] It is especially important for groups who engage in mission on the edges in poor communities, where they can be driven by an overwhelming sense of the needs and become overactive in trying to address the inequalities and injustice. There is a danger of burnout and cynicism if the rhythm of action/reflection is not adhered to.

My mission teacher at Whitley College, Ross Langmead, practised a 'theological reflection for mission' which guarded space for contemplation. As a bearer of good news he described how mission engaged him in difficult areas that need transformation, but warned:

> If mission were all action, with no reflection, we would go off the rails. We would 'hard sell' the gospel, organize our way to being an international brand name, manage the church and cram every living moment with mission activity. But it's mission with mystery, and waiting is as important as outreach, listening as speaking, responding as pro-active planning. The reflective and meditative dimension of mission is central.[26]

Langmead's reflective approach to mission arises out of committed action and advocacy for liberation, but still makes space for reflection, and then feeds back into ongoing missional action.[27] 'Contemplation' is not a separate, optional extra that we tack on to the important activity that we call 'mission'. It is an intrinsic, interdependent source and inspiration for all our missional activity.

The synthesis of contemplation and action is something we can learn from monasticism too. Father Richard Rohr, a Franciscan monk in New Mexico, runs the 'Center for Action and Contemplation'. He says the most important word in that title is 'and': '"And" demands that our contemplation becomes action; "And" insists that our action is also contemplative.'[28] Monasticism is not merely about retreat from the world, but giving due space for inner life *and* outer service and letting them both inform the other.

Thomas Merton, an American Catholic writer who was both a mystic and a social activist, affirmed the importance of deep soul-work, but for the purpose of deep engagement with the world: 'the monk abandons the world only in order to listen more intently to the deepest and most neglected voices that proceed from its inner depth.'[29] Whether inspired by old or new monasticism, or just driven to it by sheer need, retreat and contemplation is never for its own sake. But neither can we sustain activism without the balance of contemplative renewal.

Prayer in the Midst of Action

I enjoy watching my children play sport. One Saturday my two daughters, Jessie and Emily, were playing basketball and their coach could not be there. The parents nominated me as coach. I don't know much about basketball. But I rotated the girls so everyone got equal court time. At opportune moments I cheered. And I prepared myself for my most important moment as a coach – the half-time talk. An observer might not understand its importance. They might think that half-time is merely a break or diversion for kids to catch their breath and grab some sugary treats and oranges. But used wisely, it has the potential to reverse the game's direction. It is prime time for guiding the players to focus afresh on the game, recall the coach's game plan, and be refreshed for the next half. I mustered all my enthusiasm and rhetoric, and gave the girls fresh direction and encouragement. As a team they returned to the court and gave it their best shot, albeit losing 18–6. We needed more practice, especially me as coach, but the result does not undermine the difference a great half-time talk can make.

The Dangerous Prayer is a half-time prayer. It is not mainly about theory to prepare for the game. It is not about celebrating victory at the end of the game. It is for life and mission in the midst of play. It is a missional pep talk. The Dangerous Prayer offers us space to withdraw temporarily for reflection and renewal. It calls us to gather our thoughts, listen to the coach, and focus on the game plan.[30]

I confess I feel inadequate writing about this. In the life game of prayer, I sometimes feel like I am too long 'on the bench'. I have experienced my share of apathy, dissatisfaction and dryness. Some-times I play 'LRO' in prayer. LRO is the position I felt I sometimes played as a kid when sides were chosen. LRO is the 'Left Right Out' spot. It's not an 'outfield' position, but 'left right out' of being in-cluded. I would like to think my athleticism now makes that hard for you to believe, but it was the case. I have worked through the emotional scars that prove it. In prayer I sometimes feel unmotivated, commonly lack the words to say, and sometimes it just feels weird. I am being honest here. Repeating 'I am not an expert' is not the best way to promote a book. But what I do know is that the Dangerous Prayer has sustained me and given me a framework to pray. It is a framework to pray for ourselves, each other and for the world, and a framework not just to pray but to live.

I did final editing of this book while hiking in Tasmania. Wait-ing for my return flight, I met Father Jim McKeon who was reading Henri Nouwen's *Reaching Out*, which his parish was going to study in a book club. We discussed our approach to spirituality, and who we were learning from, and Jim kindly gave me his copy to read on the plane. Alongside Nouwen's teaching about the spiritual life reaching out to our innermost self, people and God, I was encouraged that he also felt hesitant to write personally about his spirituality. Nouwen resonated with the words of John of the Ladder, in which I also find consolation: 'If some are still dominated by their former bad habits, and yet can teach by mere words, let them teach . . . For perhaps, being put to shame by their own words, they will eventually begin to practice what they teach.'[31]

The disciples asked Jesus how to pray and he taught them how to live. They wanted a framework for prayer, and he gave them not just phrases for prayer but guideposts for missional living. The Dan-gerous Prayer is a highly practical but also deeply contemplative template for how Christians relate to God and what they do in the world. William Willimon and Stanley Hauerwas said that the early church instructed new Christians by teaching this prayer, and that 'a Christian is none other than someone who has learned to pray the Lord's Prayer'.[32]

In Search of a Pattern for Prayer

Jesus had lots of demands on his time and person. But we see in the gospels that Jesus prayed regularly and often. He retreated and sought God with extended periods of prayer and sometimes fasting, but was also attentive to God's voice in the midst of everyday activities. It was natural for the disciples to say, 'Lord, teach us to pray' (Luke 11:1). They knew he prayed missionally, and they wanted to learn how they could. So Jesus taught them this prayer we know as 'the Lord's Prayer'. It might be more correctly labelled 'the disciples' prayer' or 'our prayer', since it is not just for Jesus or even for just the first disciples, but for us. Early Christians called it the '*Abba* prayer'. Catholics refer to it as the 'Our Father' or '*Paternoster*'. It has profound missional implications, and so we could call it 'the Missional Prayer'. I like to refer to its results, so call it the Dangerous Prayer.

Willimon and Hauerwas write that Christianity is a journey, not just a set of beliefs or list of behaviours, and that the journey is dangerous. When Jesus calls us, we let go of what the world offers to make us secure and are enlisted to the cause of building his kingdom. We re-orientate our lives around opposing evil and promoting the life Jesus offers the world. They suggest, 'The prayer names the danger you will face as well as providing the help – the necessary skills – you will need for negotiating the dangers of the journey.'[33] This prayer is dangerous in its results, dangerous in calling us to be part of the answer to our prayers, and a prayer to equip us for the dangerous journey of radical discipleship.

A good biography does not merely describe a timeline narrative but identifies and expands on key important elements of a person's life. The disciples, in watching the life of Jesus about which some of them wrote biographies – the gospels – saw that what made Jesus 'tick' was prayer and the mission that flowed from that. This is what they wanted to learn. Jesus' entire approach to prayer and mission is distilled in this simple prayer.

Since its inception, the Dangerous Prayer has been used throughout all ages and across the globe. Churches recite it. Sunday school children memorize it. Students analyse it. Authors write books about it. But sadly it can be frozen and meaningless when recited by rote. Often it has been prayed word for word as a liturgical congregational prayer. Any religious form can lose its meaning if the form continues without its underlying meaning. Perhaps the Lord's Prayer lost its underlying missional purpose in the days of Christendom. After the Reformation, some radical Christians stopped using it.[34] But in the same radical tradition of discipleship, instead of doing away with it and forgetting it (or ignoring it), I want to dig deeply into its missional inspiration and dangerous nature.

One significant approach I adopt, however, is that I see the prayer as more a *pattern* for prayer than an incantation to say again and again. It tells us how to pray more than what exact words to pronounce. It is like a skeleton to flesh out, or a list of bullet points to cover, or a table of headings to expand on.[35]

Part of the missional genius of the prayer is its comprehensiveness. Martin Luther commented, 'Whatever needs are in the world, they are included in the Lord's Prayer. And all the prayers in the Psalms and all the prayers which could ever be devised are in the Lord's Prayer.'[36] The words and phrases of the Dangerous Prayer grab the imagination, but so too does its structure. The way Jesus outlined the different things to pray through is instructive about what to prioritize. The Dangerous Prayer begins with worship. God is not identified in vague terms but in language that articulates both God's personal nature (our Father) and God's superior but accessible place in the universe (in heaven). This leads confidently on to three prayer points towards God – praying beyond ourselves for God's holiness, kingdom and will in the world. In poetic parallel, the final three prayer points are more for us – for our provision, forgiveness and protection from temptation. The prayers to God are not just expressions of worshipful love, but requests for God's dream for the world. Even the prayers for us are not just for our sake but also for the world. Praying these elements with a missional mindset is prayer at its best. The Dangerous Prayer includes prayer to God, prayer for the world and prayer for us. It has the potential to enliven our prayer life but also give us a framework for praying for and cooperating with what God is doing in the world. The very structure of the prayer reminds us of God's missional passion.

In our book *Sentness*, Kim Hammond and I explained how the need for a shift in paradigm is the most significant challenge facing the church in the Western world today. There are two competing imaginations for the people of God – seeing church as consumers who expect religious goods and services, and understanding church as a tribe of missionaries.[37] To imagine a missional church, or a tribe of missionaries, we need the 'aha' moment of missional paradigm shift. This includes a shift in spirituality and prayer away from individualism and consumerism, and instead to embrace our neighbourhoods and world in prayer and missional action.

The chapters in this book invite readers to rediscover Jesus and his prayer as a radical pattern for life, prayer and mission. Each chapter will unpack one of the missional phrases of the prayer, but with common features and themes:

- Emphasizing the missional intent of the prayer and Jesus' interest in our neighbourhood, Western world and global needs
- Exploring foundational missional principles, e.g. kingdom of God theology, mission as restoring hope and justice, *missio Dei*, holistic mission, reconciliation, social inclusion and cultural discernment
- Examining pressures and ideologies that compete with missional spirituality, especially consumerism and violence
- Illustrating the discussion with stories from the gospels, contemporary movies and personal experience
- Presenting a grace-based and life-giving invitation to pray actively and act prayerfully; to explore prayerful reflection *and* active response; to help missionaries cultivate a sustaining spirituality *and* help contemplatives develop missional practices.

Taken together, the chapters constitute the genius of missional spirituality – whether we live in a city or the bush, slum or suburbia, Asia or Australia, Africa or Latin America, Europe or North America.

Dangerous Prayer forms a deeply personal memoir that explores the experience of prayer and when it is at its best in the midst of the action of mission.

Radical Signposts

To summarize, this is what this book is about: we join the early disciples in asking Jesus to lead us to engage freshly with God and the world through this prayer. It offers radical inspiration from Jesus to pray for local neighbourhoods and global needs – 'glocal' coverage. *Dangerous Prayer* frames each chapter around a pressing need and discusses how our prayers can address it locally and globally – five ways to change our world.

1. Radical inclusion of 'Our Father'

We live in a world that is diverse and often divides or excludes people along lines of ethnicity, gender, age, abilities, wealth, sexuality, education, and religious beliefs (or lack thereof). The paradigm-changing nature of the Dangerous Prayer starts when we address 'our' Father; the God who is interested not just in me and mine, but who cares for the whole world. We honour the name of God who is good and generous in hearing our prayers for a love-starved world. In response to cultural and other diversity and discrimination, this chapter will unpack the radical inclusive hospitality of God who wants to welcome all people now, as in heaven, and how we as God's people mirror that.

2. Subversive justice of 'Your kingdom come'

We live in a world that struggles with injustices, selfishness and individualism. When we plead for God's kingdom to come, we haggle with God for God's dream for the world to be outworked. In a world marred by sin, ploughed by terror, and suffering injustice greater than we can often imagine, we cry, 'God, work out your purposes!' We engage in 'rebellion against the status quo' and cry out on behalf of a hurting world for God to bring heaven on earth. Following the example of Jesus in Gethsemane, we offer our lives as sold out to God's purposes. In response to injustice and rampant selfishness, this chapter will unpack the profound implications of the kingdom of God and countercultural discipleship for our mission and our prayers advocating for justice.

3. Integral mission of 'our daily bread'

In a poor and hungry world, this prayer dangerously stands against any acceptance of a prosperity gospel or tolerance for excessive consumption. As Jesus fed the five thousand, God who is Father of all people invites us to pray and act so there will be food (and water and shelter) enough for all. We pray for daily bread, not just for ourselves, but for a hungry world. In response to poverty, this chapter underlines the importance of integral mission and our calling to work to restore our neighbourhoods and world as places of compassion and *shalom*.

4. Countercultural reconciliation of 'Forgive us'

We live in a violent world where people's safety cannot be guaranteed in our neighbourhoods, and wars have scarred the globe. The missional challenge and dangerous prayer is to work for peace, forgiveness and reconciliation. It is easier to be forgiven than to forgive, and easier to forgive friends than enemies, but Jesus calls us to pray and act with subversive grace and forgiveness. This chapter includes a focused response to violence in the world. It will challenge readers to pray for and live out what really is good news about the power of the gospel for reconciliation.

5. Discerning guidance of 'Deliver us'

We live in a consumerist world that distorts the value of things over people, and influences even our churches to look out for 'what's in it for me'. For a consumerist culture struggling with dysfunctionalism and addictions, we need the example and help of Jesus and our church tribe to live simply. Just as Jesus' temptation preceded his mission, we need to face what most tempts us, consumerism and other 'idols' of our culture, and the evil that detracts from God's dream in our neighbourhoods. In response to subtle or explicit temptations, this chapter teaches the kind of discernment that is necessary to deal with temptation and evil, especially consumerism and other addictions that subvert a missional life of sentness.

Conclusion: Confident celebration of the mission of God

We conclude with confidence in celebrating the purposes, ability and awesomeness of God who invites us to cooperate with God's mission wherever God sends us: 'Yours is the kingdom, the power and the glory, forever.' Thus the conclusion will underline the importance of discerning the *missio Dei*, to see what God is doing and how we cooperate with what God is doing in the world, and agree to be part of the answer to our prayer in working for a more just world.

In its parts and as a whole, this is a dangerous prayer. It is dangerous in addressing the discrimination, injustice, selfishness, poverty, violence and consumerism rampant in the world. It is dangerous in its countercultural and radical stance, and dangerous because it invites us to be, in part, the answer to our prayers. We look for God's help and cooperate with what God dreams to do in our world. But if we pray for God's name to be honoured, God's kingdom to come and God's will to be done, then we need to cooperate with that and work in those directions. When we pray for daily bread for the world, reconciliation, and deliverance from oppressive systems, it is our responsibility to pursue countercultural lives of generosity, forgiveness and holiness that foster

God's dream for the world. This is where the prayer is most dangerous – in embracing neighbourhoods and global interests beyond ourselves, and in inviting us to live our prayer and be an answer to it.

Journaling and Discussion

Be encouraged to journal your reflections from reading each chapter and discuss your responses with a small group. At the end of each chapter there are questions to help prompt your reflection and discussion.

1. Watch a video clip about 'Bruce Almighty' answering prayer, and share your response to the clip.
2. It is not usually helpful to suggest that you should pray exactly the way someone else does, or that they should pray like you. George Buttrick suggests, 'There is no rule of thumb, for the reason that every thumb-print is different and distinct.' What is your 'prayer thumb-print'? What prayer practices have been most helpful for you?
3. What has challenged and limited your prayer life? What do you find most difficult and challenging?
4. In what ways does preoccupation with appearance detract from your experience of prayer? What difference does seeing God as your 'audience of one' make?
5. What has been your experience of using the Lord's Prayer? In what ways would you like God to 'teach us to pray' using it as a missional prayer?
6. What would you like to stop doing, start doing, or do differently as a result of reading this chapter and reflecting on its implications?
7. In 2015, leading into Easter, the Bible Society and Common Grace in Australia invited Christians to join in praying the Lord's Prayer, 'that is deeper than the needs of every human heart and wider than the pressing problems of our world'. Watch the video of Jarrod McKenna introducing this call to prayer.[38]
8. Finish by meditating and praying through the words of the Dangerous Prayer in your favourite translation.

1

Radical Inclusion of 'Our Father'

Once we have said 'Our Father' in the morning, we can treat no one as stranger for the rest of the day.
(Mary Hughes, English Quaker)

Learning from a Father's Tears

Blood Diamond opened my eyes to an ongoing human rights tragedy – the plight of civil wars and 200,000 child soldiers in Africa. The 2006 movie is set in the Sierra Leone civil war in 1996–2001. It depicts families ripped apart, power abuses, gross injustices, the atrocities of war, and the complicity of Western multinational corporations. The 'blood diamonds' are mined by slaves and sold to finance rebel war efforts. Solomon Vandy (played by Djimon Hounsou), one of the slaves, wants to do whatever it takes to see his son Dia (Kagiso Kuypers) freed and educated. He teams up with soldier-turned-smuggler Danny Archer (Leonardo DiCaprio) and journalist Maddy Bowen (Jennifer Connelly) to track down a huge buried pink diamond that they can sell to realize their dreams. The movie shows the indifference of Western media when they are more interested in a famous politician being 'sorry' for what had happened in his office, rather than what most political leaders in office should be pleading sorry for ignoring. The underlying genocide and child slave trade brought me to tears. My wife Jenni says I do not cry enough, and she is right. But the scenes of *Blood Diamond*, especially Solomon doing what he could for his son Kagiso and weeping when Kagiso could not, touched me deeply.[1]

The movie scenes, though created by Hollywood, reflect a blatant evil that brings tears to the face of God. Slavery is no longer legal anywhere in the world, yet 35.8 million people live as slaves today. Modern slavery generates profits of US$32 billion for slaveholders. Many goods we take for granted – including clothing, sporting goods, flowers and chocolates – are slave labour products. Some countries do little to enforce laws against slavery, and local culture accepts it.[2] In Mauritania, Haiti, Pakistan and India it is estimated that more than 1% of the population live in slavery. Developed countries may have lower rates of slavery, but even in the USA there are 60,000 slaves, including some sex workers and illegal migrant workers forced into servitude.[3] Globally, 1 million children are trafficked each year for labour or sex. It is reported that 350,000 children are forced or tricked into being soldiers across forty countries, and the number is growing each year.[4] The child slavery statistics are just one sign of a world in a mess. What is going wrong? Surely, a big part of our prayer ought to address these kinds of issues and include concern and pleading for people affected.[5]

New Testament scholar John Dominic Crossan argues that addressing God as Father is broader than what we understand as father. He suggests the term is not exclusively masculine but can be understood as shorthand for addressing God as our parent – father and/or mother – in charge of children. Furthermore, it can be understood in an even broader sense as a householder in charge of the extended family. A father in the ancient Near Eastern context was responsible for a whole household. A good householder runs a home that protects and provides for everyone in it, equitably. Thus when we address God as our 'Father in heaven' we are addressing God as 'Householder of Earth'.[6] The intended focus is global.

I have learned a lot about God as Father from being a father to my children. My youngest daughter Emily and I were walking to her sports class one day, and she said 'Dad, do you know that I have two dads?' 'What do you mean by that?' I asked curiously. 'Well, you are my dad.

But also, God is our Father, so he is like my dad.' 'And what is our job?' I asked, meaning God and me as fathers. 'To look after us,' she replied. Emily is right. God her heavenly Father, and I who have the privilege of being her earthly father, want to look after her. But God, our Father in heaven, has that concern for *all* God's children on earth.

When we grasp that the fathering interest of God includes the world beyond ourselves, it transforms the way we pray and act. And I reckon it pleases the heart of God when our prayers reflect God's heart for the world. That is another thing that delights our hearts as fathers – when our children grow in love and concern for a hurting world. My son Benjamin has developed a strong sense of social justice and concern for equity in the world. As a 16-year-old teenager, he began volunteering for Baptist World Aid and practising self-imposed fasts from furniture – including sleeping on the floor – to identify with people in the world who live with less. Jenni and I are proud of Ben, as well as Emily and Jessie, as they dream and act for a better world.

Playing Small Does Not Serve the World

Nelson Mandela (1918–2013) was voted in as President of South Africa on 27 April 1994. South Africa had been operating under apartheid laws for forty-six years since 1948, dominated by the vision of Afrikaner racial dominance and purity. Sadly this was motivated by distorted racist theological convictions. The system segregated and oppressed black and coloured peoples by telling them where to live and restricting voting rights, educational access and interracial marriage. For his opposition to the system as part of the African National Congress (ANC), Mandela was imprisoned for twenty-seven years, from 1962 to 1989, mainly serving hard labour on Robben Island.

Speaking at a trial for sabotage, he gave his 'Speech from the Dock' on 20 April 1964, detailing the disparities between black and white life in South Africa and appealing for equal rights and non-racial democracy:

During my lifetime I have dedicated myself to this struggle for the African people. I have fought against white domination, and I have fought against black domination. I have cherished the ideal of a democratic and free society in which all persons live together in harmony and with equal opportunities. It is an ideal which I hope to live for and to achieve. But if needs be, it is an ideal for which I am prepared to die.[7]

Mandela's sentence was 'reduced' from execution to life imprisonment. From prison he wrote and advocated to end white minority rule. In February 1990 the ANC was 'unbanned'. Mandela was released and he worked with President F.W. de Klerk towards options for shared political power. In 1994 Mandela was voted in as the first fully democratically elected president and the first black president. He sought then to represent all South Africans and was insistent on not reversing racism against white people. His lifelong activism for social and political inclusion inspires me to advocate and pray for human rights and equality for all people today.

Mandela famously quoted from Marianne Williamson's *A Return to Love* at his inauguration:

Our deepest fear is not that we are inadequate. Our deepest fear is that we are powerful beyond measure. It is our light, not our darkness that most frightens us. We ask ourselves, who am I to be brilliant, gorgeous, talented, fabulous? Actually, who are you *not* to be? You are a child of God. Your playing small does not serve the world. There is nothing enlightened about shrinking so that other people won't feel insecure around you. We are all meant to shine, as children do. We were born to make manifest the glory of God that is within us. It's not just in some of us; it's in everyone. And as we let our own light shine, we unconsciously give other people permission to do the same. As we are liberated from our own fear, our presence automatically liberates others.[8]

'You are a child of God', Mandela reminded us, encouraging people to live up to that as people of the light, and to recognize the right of others to be all they are created for. Mandela became known as 'the father of the nation' because of his activism for equal rights – a whole nation looked to his leadership in birthing a whole new order. We pray to 'our Father in heaven' – the whole church looks to our Father's vision for a better world.

Parenting Experience

No human father – biological parent, religious leader or political figure – fully reflects the parenting heart of God. Unfortunately for some, 'father' is simply not a helpful image for God, especially if their own experience of a father is not positive.

I count myself fortunate that I have a great dad, John Cronshaw. When I was a child Dad took time to cheer on my academic and reading interests, my karate and horse riding, and guided me with an open mind in my faith and vocational explorations. When I launched my first book, *Credible Witness*, Dad flew from Sydney to Melbourne to celebrate with me. He is among the number-one cheerleaders for my brother Jason and me.

My mum, Lorraine Pratt, is terrific too. When I was a child, she prayed and offered us boys to serve God. When I was recovering from an operation recently, she rang me every day for a few days in a row to see how I was improving. She has always watched my back. One primary school afternoon, I was scared that Adam Meyrick was going to bash me up after school. We were usually good friends, but something happened to change that for a day. I waited inside the school gates, but he waited just outside. I told the teacher, but Adam slipped around the corner. I tried to escape out the school's back gate, but he chased me. As I ran around the corner to head down my street, I could see him quickly catching up. By this stage Mum wondered why I was late coming home, so headed out the front gate and towards school. As I came over the crest of the hill, just as Adam was about to tackle and pummel me, there was Mum. I turned around in front of her and proudly shouted, 'Get stuffed, Meyrick!' It's amazing how brave you can be when your mum is standing behind you.

Together my parents expressed loving parenting. God describes himself like a mother (Isaiah 66:13), and Jesus himself sometimes adopts a maternal posture (Matthew 23:37; Luke 13:34). When I think of God as Father or loving parent or nurturing mother, it is a helpful image that readily invites me to trust and rely on God.

Moreover, I find great enjoyment in fathering my son Benjamin and daughters Jessie and Emily. We live in a father-hungry genera-tion. Inspired by the literature of the Men's Movement, I am eager to cultivate close and attentive relationships with my children.[9] I have a long list of negatives that I have worked on as a dad – impatience, control and workaholism among them. But at my best I can display generosity, self-sacrifice, attentiveness and encouragement. A parent who loves, nurtures, encourages, guides and leads is a picture I find helpful (and biblical) for God. Though I have a long way to grow in my reflection of God's fathering style, I find it a wonderfully warm and inviting archetypal image.[10]

One evening when my children were smaller, I took them to the local shops to get football cards, which Ben was collecting, and takeaway fish and chips for dinner. As we got out of the car, 4-year-old Emily called up to me 'Daddy, Daddy' till I extended my hand. When she was a kindergarten kid growing in independ-ence, I let her walk alone sometimes. But I held her carefully when she needed it. I still do. I pulled her back from the traffic, and picked her up in my arms to walk back to the car after buying the food. Is that not what each of us needs? We all need a father, daddy or *Abba*, who will hear us when we call, hold our hand when we are weak, and guide us through the busy intersections of life. Each of us needs a Father who can lovingly sweep us into his arms to take us home.[11]

Divine Parenting

God as Father is a biblical picture of God in relation to Israel, who see their paternal relationship and care deriving from God (e.g.

Deuteronomy 14:1; Psalm 103:13; Isaiah 64:8). The psalmist declared: 'As a father has compassion for his children, so the LORD has compassion for those who fear him' (Psalm 103:13 NRSVA). Another psalm portrays God's interest particularly for those on the margins: 'Father to the fatherless, defender of widows – this is God, whose dwelling is holy' (Psalm 68:5). Referring to God as Father echoed for Israel their experience of God rescuing them from Egypt in the exodus. Through Moses God said to Pharaoh, 'Israel is my firstborn son . . . Let my son go . . . Let my people go' (Exodus 4:22–23; 5:1). Hosea wrote: 'When Israel was a child, I loved him, and I called my son out of Egypt' (Hosea 11:1). On the lips of Jesus, and when we pray with Jesus 'Our Father', it reminds us that Jesus came to rescue people with a New Exodus.[12] God has a whole new social order in mind. God is not just Father of a nation, but Father of all people and the whole created order.

In relationship with Jesus, and by extension to us as Jesus' adopted siblings, there is a particular picture of God as Father (John 1:10–14; Hebrews 2:10–18). Recall the picture of the prodigal son's father in Luke 15 who represents God. The boy stops acting like an obedient son, but the father is never willing to stop being father, but waits and hopes for his son to return home. Paul celebrates what really is good news that God is willing to adopt us as God's children: 'So you have not received a spirit that makes you fearful slaves. Instead, you received God's Spirit when he adopted you as his own children. Now we call him, "Abba, Father"' (Romans 8:15).

In biblical times, there was a profound difference in being a child in a household rather than a slave or servant. David Seamands expands on the difference, encouraging us to move beyond a performance mentality by seeing ourselves as children of God, accepted primarily for who we are rather than what we achieve:

> The servant is accepted and appreciated on the basis of what he does, the
> child on the basis of who she is. The servant starts the day anxious and

worried, wondering if his work will really please his master. The child rests in the secure love of her family.

The servant is accepted because of his workmanship, the son or daughter because of relationship. The servant is accepted because of his productivity and performance. The child belongs because of her position as a person.

At the end of the day, the servant has peace of mind only if he is sure he has proven his worth by his work. The next morning, his anxiety begins again. The child can be secure all day and know that tomorrow won't change her status.

When a servant fails, his whole position is at stake; he might lose his job. When a child fails, she will be grieved because she has hurt her parents, and she will be corrected and disciplined. But she is not afraid of being thrown out. Her basic confidence is in belonging and being loved, and her performance does not change the stability of her position.[13]

Can you see the different mentality of a servant and a child? Which do you identify with the most in your relationship with God? Is God 'Father' for you as a child of God?

How does God as 'Father' help us as we pray? Luke 11 follows the teaching of the Lord's Prayer with an invitation to ask and expect to receive because God is like a good father who gives God's children good things: 'Which of you fathers, if your son asks for a fish, will give him a snake instead? Or if he asks for an egg, will give him a scorpion? If you then, though you are evil, know how to give good gifts to your children, how much more will your Father in heaven give the Holy Spirit to those who ask him!' (Luke 11:11–13 NIV; cf. Matthew 7:9–11) This prayer begins with addressing God as Father, rather than having us in the foreground. When we begin our prayer with getting a fresh perspective on the character of *who* we pray to, it can make a difference to *what* and *how* we pray.

The God You Pray To

J.B. Philips wrote *Your God Is Too Small* to encourage people not to be bound by images of God that are less than who God really is.[14] Some people see God as an annoying nuisance who just wants to tell them what not to do. Psychotherapeutic types learn from Freud to see God as an overbearing parent created in the imaginations of insecure people who feel the need for a certain type of father figure.[15] Militants see God as justification for subduing their country's enemies, forgetting that those people are equally made in the image of God and ought to be recipients of our love rather than missiles. Secularists see God as an optional extra for people who feel the need for a personal religious hobby, but are not open to God or faith having any influence on public life. With those pictures of God, it is no wonder people have no interest in God. I don't believe in those sorts of God either.

Part of the problem for prayer, and the mission of the church overall, is that we have collected distorted images of God. The United States is not immune from this. My friend and *Sentness* co-writer Kim Hammond loves the USA and has been inspired by Americans' capacity for believing in the God of courageous vision and bold world-changing endeavours. But American perspectives can bring their own distortions about how God is understood. Voltaire suggested God made us in God's own image, and we have returned the favour. We have sought to imagine God in our image.

It is also the case for Australians. Australia has a different history from that of the USA. Europeans went to America with a sense of destiny under God and a vision for a new world. European settlers in Australia were mainly convicts, not pilgrims. Instead of wanting to build the church on the new soil, they burned the first church down in protest. The first religious leaders were government-appointed military chaplains who doubled as magistrates. They would preach on Sundays and hand out judgments of whippings on Mondays. The second chaplain, Samuel Marsden, became known as 'the flogging parson'. This is part of the woeful inheritance we have as the church in Australia.[16]

I want to reclaim a proud sense of a biblical picture of who God really is – for people of all cultures, but including Aussies. John Smith, who started 'God's Squad', the incarnational mission among the outlaw motorbike scene, reminds me of the importance of communicating a picture of who God really is:

> It's not that we haven't presented an Australian God, but that we haven't presented the biblical God – the God of the Bible is relevant to Australia simply because He is God. The key to evangelising Australians is to begin to rectify the shocking images of God we have developed – the God who is a standover merchant, the God who is not interested in wholeness, but who snoops around ready to wallop me when I mess up, the kind of God who says 'no' more than he says 'yes'. They're the images the Aussies have of God. Australians have had the wrong image of God bequeathed to them by a history of neglect and tragedy and a delinquent church.[17]

I don't believe in that God. But our poor history reminds me to ask, what God are we portraying? And what God are we praying to?

For me as a father, nothing delights me more than when my children share with me what is on their hearts. Richard Foster paints a word picture of prayer as coming before an attentive father:

> We bring ourselves before God as we are, warts and all. Like children before a loving father, we open our hearts and make our requests. We do not try to sort things out, the good from the bad. We simply and unpretentiously share our concerns and make our petitions. We tell God, for example, how frustrated we are with the co-worker at the office or the neighbour down the street. We ask for food, favourable weather, and good health.[18]

As we reflect on our experience with God, and ask for God's help, our Father listens in compassion and love, as good parents do for their kids. The invitation of the Dangerous Prayer, however, is that we can also share God's heart and pray for others. We pray with greater self-awareness for ourselves, including confession, provision and protection. But we also let God's parental concern for the world guide and focus our prayers.

This leads to what I believe is the most transformative word of the whole prayer. To start the missional prayer addressing God as Father is significant. It reminds us of God's attentive interest and commitment to us. But the most significant word of the whole prayer is an easily overlooked word, the possessive pronoun that identifies Father as 'our'.

'Our' Father

Luke goes straight to 'Father' in his usual more succinct way, but Matthew helpfully describes God as '*our* Father'. That little word 'our' reminds us that although this is a prayer we pray on our own sometimes, it is never a prayer we pray alone. I need that reminder. We pray this prayer in community with our local church and with the church globally.[19] Saint Cyprian spoke wisely in saying: 'You cannot have God for your Father unless you have the church for your Mother.' We pray the Dangerous Prayer well when we pray in solidarity with the broader church.

Praying 'our' Father reminds us that we are praying this Dangerous Prayer not just for Christians but for all people in the world. This is a big part of its radical inspiration. Young and old, rich and poor, people who are educated to greater or lesser degrees, people with different abilities, all nations and continents, across all differences and boundaries, God is *our* Father. It is true that God takes a particular adoptive interest in those who believe in Jesus – whatever their cultural background (Romans 4:16). Yet God is interested in all people as their creator. We are all, as Paul said to the Athenians, God's offspring (Acts 17:28–29). God is 'Father to the fatherless, defender of widows' (Psalm 68:5a) and Father of us all (Ephesians 4:6). Quaker Mary Hughes said, 'Once we have said "Our Father" in the morning, we can treat no one as stranger for the rest of the day.' The *our* in the missional prayer is not just about those whom God has adopted as

Father because of their belief in Jesus, but it is broader, encompassing God as Father and Creator of us all.

When my children, perhaps in the company of new friends, refer to me as 'my daddy', it gives me pride and joy. But when they refer to me as 'our daddy', encompassing the relationship that they share with their siblings, then I am even more proud. It is a reminder of our family solidarity. The form of address, 'Our Daddy', suggests a sense of community and mutual family interests.

Jesus teaches us to pray in the first-person plural: 'our Father'. Imagine if it was first-person singular and we limited ourselves to 'my Father'. It would be fine for private prayer and quiet times alone, but not be communal enough to pray in church. 'My Father' would not suggest praying with Christians who are not present with us around the world. It would not remind us to pray for others who are in need. Even when praying it on my own, the 'our' links me with humanity in humility before the Father of all.

Our Western context can influence us to pray with individualistic and consumerist tendencies. Prayer just for me and mine, and for things we need, is not how Jesus intended this model prayer. It is not how the church has prayed it through the centuries. Hundreds of years of Christendom and colonialist interpretations have distorted it. But early church writers taught the broad missional scope I am advocating.

One of my early church heroes is Martyr-Bishop of Carthage, St Cyprian. He wrote during persecution and was himself executed in AD 258. But in 252 he was the first to name the prayer as the Lord's Prayer, or in Latin *'De Dominica Oratione'*. He commented:

The Teacher of unity and peace did not wish us to pray separately and privately: that is, He did not wish each one to pray only for himself. We do not say, 'My father' or 'give me this day my daily bread.' Each one does not ask that only his trespasses be forgiven or that he only be preserved from temptation or freed from evil. We have a public and common prayer. When we pray, it is not for one person but for whole people – because we all are one.[20]

This prayer has always had the potential to help the church get a global perspective.

When we pray 'Our Father' we do not just pray for our own needs but for the needs of others – in the church, our neighbourhood and the world. We pray 'Our Father' not just for me and mine, or we and ours, but for all *our* people to whom we belong in the world – the poorest 20% who use less than 2% of the world's resources as well as those who live in the Western world, and those who are forgotten in our society – the homeless and aged, refugees and asylum seekers. We pray for rich and poor, young and old, educated and illiterate, able and differently abled, Australian, American and British but also Botswanian, Zimbabweans and Zululanders.

We live in a diverse world that too often divides or excludes people along ethnic, gender, age, ability, wealth, sexuality, education and religious lines (or lack thereof). For whom do you passionately want to pray '*Our* Father'?

When we pray 'Our Father' we pray with and for people of all cultures. Martin Luther King Jr challenged the church that 11 o'clock on Sunday morning was the most segregated hour of the week in 'Christian' America.[21] The prophetic critique can still apply for many of our churches. God is the Father of all cultures. Failure to celebrate this truth limits the inclusive embrace of the church. When Mahatma Gandhi was a student in South Africa he was deeply interested in the Bible and the Sermon on the Mount. He saw Christianity could be the answer to India's caste system and he considered converting to Christianity. He visited a church service to ask for religious instruction. Those at the door stopped him and explained that if he wanted to participate he was welcome in a church appropriately reserved for blacks. He never returned.[22] As we cry 'Our Father', let's stand in solidarity and include all cultures in our prayers, and in our churches.

When we pray 'Our Father' we pray as women and men together. If you are a man, you may not realize what it is like to live in a world where your gender limits your opportunities to be educated, to work, to be safe from harm, to make choices. For many women the greatest predictor of health is the age when you have your first and last child; consider what it is like for somebody else to make that decision on your behalf. Margaret Drabble commented: 'A man's greatest fear from a woman is that she will laugh at him; a woman's fear is that a man will kill her.' As we pray 'Our Father', let's recall God is Father for our sisters as well as our brothers.

When we pray 'Our Father' we pray with and for people of all abilities. Imagine wearing your vulnerabilities and dependence on the outside. Imagine everybody being able to see and focus on what you can't do. What would it be like to be defined by those weaknesses, so that everything else about who you are and what you have to offer is eclipsed? Imagine going to a church and instead of finding acceptance and love, you are told that you could be whole if you had enough faith, or going to a church building and finding that there are no facilities provided for differently abled people, or steps and no ramps. We are all different. We all have unique needs and have unique gifts to contribute. As we pray 'Our Father', let's pray for people of all abilities.

When we pray 'Our Father' we pray with and for people who have homes and those who are displaced. We pray for those who are educated and those who are desperately eager for a basic education. We pray for those who have water and those who need access to clean water. We pray for those who are heterosexual, and those who are gay, lesbian, bisexual, transsexual or still working out their sexuality. We pray for those of Christian faith and those of other faiths, those who have lost their faith, and those who have no faith or interest in having one. As we pray 'Our Father', let's pray for all different sorts of people, and pray our churches would be as loving and welcoming as God our Father. In response to cultural and other diversity, this prayer underlines and invites us towards the inclusive hospitality of God who loves and welcomes all people now, as in heaven.

Postcolonial biblical scholar Warren Carter contends that Matthew wrote the gospel to challenge Roman domination and to upstage the lordship of the empire with the lordship of Jesus.[23] Carter comments: 'The Gospel trains its readers to be suspicious of the people-subjugating, health-destroying, death-bringing, coercion-oriented

powers of empire.'[24] With the Lord's Prayer, Carter explains, Matthew
was appealing to readers to pray not as the Gentiles do with lots of
rhetoric and for their own good impression, but to pray concisely and
as an act of justice. In contrast to looking for help from the emperor,
known as *Pater Patriae*, 'father of the fatherland', the prayer is addressed to 'our Father in the heavens'. Carter comments on the significance of the communal nature of the prayer and the egalitarianism of
God's children with those with whom we pray: 'This pronoun [our]
. . . places all who pray on the same footing before God regardless of
social or gender roles and everyday status in a hierarchical world. It
draws them into an undifferentiated community in which relationship
with God, not cultural markers, provides their identity as children.'

Children in the ancient world symbolized not innocence and purity but marginality, vulnerability, threat to and exclusion from the
adult (male) world. This community of children, defined by the practices of Matthew 5:3 – 6:8, prays a prayer whose petitions subvert
dominant cultural commitments and practices, envisage the transformation of the current order, and anticipate the completion of God's
purposes and the establishment of God's empire. The prayer sustains
the identity and lifestyle of this community.[25] Carter underlines the
nature of the community of those praying, as children together before
their Father in heaven. But Carter's argument can be extended as we
pray 'Our Father' in solidarity with and intercession for all those who
are oppressed by unjust systems.

Community Solidarity

Muriel Lester (1884–1968) is an inspiring saint who knew the power
of praying this prayer to 'our' Father. She was a Baptist in Essex,
but not widely known even in Britain. Born into a wealthy family,
she travelled to London and became aware of the grinding poverty
and enormous gaps between rich and poor. At 19, she relocated and
started a ministry in London's East End by challenging men in a local pub to study the Sermon on the Mount in Matthew for thirty

minutes on Sundays for ten weeks. Her enticement was that if they found nothing in it relevant for local problems, she would campaign with them to close down churches, since it would be a wasted effort to keep churches open if Christianity had no answers for the world's troubles. This showed her conviction about the power of Jesus' words. The men studied Matthew with her, continuing beyond ten weeks, and together planted a revolutionary community with a positive and lasting influence on a needy urban area of London.

The Sermon on the Mount and especially the Lord's Prayer impressed Lester's group who studied the Bible. Inspired by Jesus' declaration of 'Blessed are the poor', they took vows of voluntary poverty, which freed up their finances to pioneer a school for children in need, several orphanages and free clinics, and to provide milk for all the borough's children. They adopted a stance of pacifism during the world wars, arguing that if Jesus' words offered a way of life in peacetime, they could not jettison them in wartime. Lester asserted, 'We should stop praying the Lord's Prayer until we can see that "our Father" means that we are tied to the same living tether not only with our fellow countrymen but with everybody on the planet.'[26]

Her Lord's Prayer-inspired global concern took Muriel to India. Gandhi challenged her to act on her beliefs, and so she campaigned for Home Rule for India and advocated against the drug trade that was profiting British companies yet spoiling thousands of lives.[27] Gandhi said he saw the value of the Christianity he longed for in her community: 'The value of Muriel's conversation lies in the fact that she endeavours every moment of her life to practise what she professes and preaches in her writings.'[28]

She lived out the power of prayer through action. Muriel Lester made a life-giving difference to her neighbourhood. In her borough, the infant mortality rate went from the highest to one of the lowest in London. Nationally, she campaigned for women's rights. Globally, she was a major factor in stopping the British opium trade in China and India. She led many people to Christ, and started and led a community that sought to both study and embody the Sermon on the Mount and the Lord's Prayer. Anne Wilkinson-Hayes, our Mission

Catalyst team leader at Baptist Union of Victoria, celebrates Muriel Lester's life and asks, 'Where are Sermon on the Mount communities today? Where are churches who not only pray the Dangerous Prayer but live it out?'[29]

Echoing Jesus

'Our' embraces the world, but also reminds us that we pray not alone but *with* Jesus. This is another aspect of radical inspiration from this phrase. We are children of God along with Jesus. When we voice 'Our Father' we echo Jesus praying to our Father. Jesus lets us share in his prayers.

Recall that in Jesus' last days, he took time to pray for us. John 17 tells of an imagination-grabbing scene of Jesus praying with and for us. In current times, ascended and present with the Father, Jesus is praying for us (Romans 8:34). When you struggle to have faith, or find it difficult to articulate the words to pray, or despair over whether God pays attention, be encouraged that Jesus is praying with and for you. Pray the Dangerous Prayer knowing that we echo Jesus' prayer. We need this prayer, especially when times are tough or when world needs seem overwhelming. Hebrews 2 teaches that Jesus is our brother and understands our challenges. When you have had a hard time, or face tragedy, or struggle with disappointment, or feel over-whelmed by global needs, have you ever had someone say, 'I know how you feel', but they really don't? Jesus, as our brother, does know the depth of what we feel. I can love a saviour and brother like that.

Jürgen Moltmann helps us understand that Jesus is the crucified God and the suffering God.[30] Moltmann explained that the fact that God in Jesus died on the cross questions the impassibility of God – the idea that God does not experience pain or pleasure. He elevates the human view of Jesus, not above the divine but alongside, helping us see that God *does* experience and understand suffering. Moltmann told the story of Elie Wiesel who witnessed a Jewish boy hanged by the Nazis, along with two men, at Buna (Auschwitz III) concentration camp. It took half an hour for the boy to die. A man in the camp asked, 'Where is God now?' Wiesel heard a voice answer from within, 'Where is he? He is here. He is hanging there on the gallows.' Wiesel took the voice as a voice of despair to express disbelief in a just and loving God.[31] But Moltmann used the story to argue for a God who suffers together with those who suffer – whether in the midst of the Holocaust or other horrendous suffering: 'Any other answer would be blasphemy. There cannot be any other Christian answer to the question of torment. To speak here of a God who could not suffer would be to make God a demon. To speak here of an absolute God would make God an annihilating nothingness. To speak here of an indifferent God would condemn [people] to indifference.'[32] Death, cancer and tsunamis are not God's plan, but in the face of them we can pray with the suffering God as our brother.

From the same era as Moltmann, Helmut Thielicke was a pastor who knew the reality of praying the Lord's Prayer in abysmal surroundings. He taught through this prayer in war-torn Germany. In the midst of the terror of screaming bombs, lonely war widows, homelessness and an uncertain future, he taught his congregation to pray 'Our Father'.[33] Thielicke taught his congregation to remember that Jesus was with them as they prayed: 'In every cellar that shakes with detonations he is a guest. In every troop of straggling refugees the Saviour trudges too – as he has for ages and will continue to do until the last day.'[34]

As CEO of World Vision Australia, Tim Costello has visited some of the most damaged and struggling communities around the world. Costello had been working with World Vision for less than a year when the terrible tsunami of Boxing Day 2004 devastated communities in Asia. While Costello flew to Sri Lanka to assess the damage and start to mobilize a compassionate response, another Australian Christian minister commented that the tsunami was God's judgment on Asian nations. It is a simplistic way of explaining how bad things can happen to people. But Costello quickly critiqued the statement as unbiblical and cruel, and published a response in *The Age*, a widely read Melbourne newspaper:

When I arrived in Galle, home to a once thriving tourist industry and a famed, but now destroyed, cricket ground, I was confronted by the stench of death from the many, many unidentifiable corpses, and by those left alive whose homes were destroyed, who had lost loved ones, and had barely escaped the waves.

As these Sri Lankans looked to the sea, which before the tragedy, along with tourism, made up 80 per cent of the town's economy, those that could find words asked me 'Why did this happen?' 'Why is God punishing us?' Others just stared blankly . . .

We live on a globe with a fragile ecological and geological balance. A few degrees change in the global temperature and millions will perish. The tsunami was a very natural disaster, not an Act of God punishing the world for its materialism, violence and selfishness; not a judgment on the sex trade in Thailand or the civil strife in Sri Lanka or the rebels in Aceh.

With all its terrible and catastrophic consequences, the tsunami was predictable and is explainable. Continental plates grind against each other, producing earthquakes and sometimes tidal waves. It is a disaster that has a history and such disasters will happen again.

In fact, if there were some relationship between morality and natural disasters, as was once thought, it would make God out to be an unconscionable bully to the coastal poor and a chief benefactor of cities such as Zurich, Palm Springs and Paris. And it would also make a mockery of Jesus' teachings about the special place for the poor in the heart of God.[35]

In praying to our Father, we plead with Jesus to God who is not sitting judgmentally afar off in heaven, but concerned for all in the world, especially those who are poor and suffering.

Dangerous Apprenticeship

The Dangerous Prayer challenges us not to close our eyes to the hunger and pain of the world around us. Christian faith is involved with the challenges of the world. Christian spirituality is engaged with the pain of people. Tom Wright teaches:

> When we call God 'Father', we are called to step out, as apprentice children, into a world of pain and darkness. We will find that darkness all around us; it will terrify us, precisely because it will remind us of the darkness inside our own selves. The temptation then is to switch off the news, to shut out the pain of the world, to create a painless world for ourselves.[36]

Modern entertainment and isolated living encourages this kind of disconnection from the world, as do some forms of contemporary spirituality. But the Dangerous Prayer recalibrates us back to feel the heartbeat of the missionary God and to get in step with God's missionary Son. Jesus understood the propensity of human nature to gravitate to our own needs, but his prayer will not let us retreat to an isolated world of personal spirituality. Living the prayer and being open to being the answer starts here with this phrase. When we pray 'Our Father' we are praying with Jesus and joining Jesus in the privileges and responsibilities of being children of God.

While addressing God as Father, Jesus was acting like God, who acted as Father in rescuing Israel from Egypt. In Jesus' life and ministry, he was following the Father's family business and also calling for a revolution. When we call God 'our Father' with Jesus, we are offering to join the Father's revolution. Like any good child in biblical times, we are offering to be apprenticed by our parent. Tom Wright teaches the surprisingly profound implications: 'Calling God "Father" is the great act of faith, of holy boldness, of risk. Saying "our Father" isn't just the boldness, the sheer cheek, of walking into the presence of the living and almighty God and saying "Hi Dad". It is the boldness, the sheer total risk, of saying quietly, "Please may I, too, be considered an apprentice."'[37] Praying the missional prayer means signing up for the cause of the kingdom of God. Coming alongside Jesus and praying together with Jesus to 'our Father' means we stand in solidarity and commitment with him for Jesus' purposes.

The other phrases of the missional prayer spell out in concise summary form what those purposes are – nothing short of God's kingdom or dream for the world, daily bread for all, forgiveness for our neighbours, liberation from evils. But before we are invited to imitate our older brother Jesus in pleading for those world-changing ends, there is an encouraging additional explanation about the accessibility of who we pray to.

Where is God?

What does praying to our Father 'in heaven' mean?

So much in the world makes it seem like God is up in heaven, conceived as some far-off place, like the imaginary home of the old Greek gods. Why are there wars, terrorism, disease and doubt? Do bad things happen, as this view of God in heaven implies, because God is so distant and not involved in or caring about life here on earth?

This is a question Thielicke asked. Remember that he prayed and taught this prayer in a warzone. From his viewpoint, the state of the world suggested God was like the rhyme, 'Twinkle, twinkle . . . up above the world so high'. It seemed as if God was up in heaven and not on earth, as if the world did not have a father and was orphaned and alone.[38] That may be your experience at times. God may be up in heaven, but what about lending a hand down here on earth in the midst of pain and struggle?

Tom Wright teaches there are three views of God in heaven.[39] One view separates heaven from earth, and conceptualizes God as far away 'out there' in a distant heaven. God or the gods may be enjoying themselves and we ought to respect them, but they are distant from life on earth and don't intervene (Deism). Prayer, for the Deist, is calling to a distant G/god, but being unsure of whether that lofty figure will hear or answer. This is the picture that the movie *Thor* portrays of the gods: off in a far-distant sphere in space, with little involvement or interest in human activity.

Another view is to slide heaven and earth together, and conceptualize God as 'right here' everywhere (pantheism). A variation on the theme is to see everything existing within God (panentheism). Prayer, for the pantheist, is discovering the truth of divinity within, in nature and everywhere. However, this view has minimal space to appeal to God against evil. It is a view portrayed in a movie like *Avatar*, where a mysterious divine force inhabits everything in nature, which people can connect into, but with minimal personal engagement.

The third option is that heaven and earth are neither separated nor identical, but overlap in intricate and mysterious ways. We see this in the history of Hebrew people seeing and hearing God: Abraham meeting God, Jacob's ladder between earth and heaven, Moses on holy ground where earth and heaven intersected with a burning bush, and Israel meeting God in 'the Tent of Meeting' and later Jerusalem's temple. Similarly, the God of the Bible was present to people on earth in the life and ministry of Jesus; the reign of God came and heaven overlapped with earth. The earth is not yet fully redeemed, but as we cooperate with Jesus and as God's Spirit groans with and through us in prayer (Romans 8:26–27), a new order comes to birth. As you might guess, this third option is Wright's preferred view. It is the biblical view that informs our prayer as we pray to God our Father 'in heaven'. God is neither far off and uninterested, nor existing in everything, but accessible and wanting to hear our prayers to bring heaven to earth.

Addressing God as 'Our Father who is in heaven' reminds us whom we pray to. In the face of evidence to the contrary, we remind ourselves that ultimately God is in heaven and is interested and committed to fostering the kingdom of God. We can have confidence and peace, even in the midst of bombshells dropping out of the sky, that God is a good father and that he is accessible and in control. If we pray without the confidence that God is in heaven, our prayers will be faint-hearted. If we can grasp that God is in heaven and let that empower our prayers, then those prayers can have a world-changing influence.[40]

God, You are Awesome

The prayer begins with identifying whom we pray to and then directs our worship in God's direction. A boy once thought God's name was Harold, thinking he heard, 'Our father in heaven, Harold be your name.' It is not that we pray to Harold, but that we hallow, or set apart as holy, God's name.

My family travelled through Europe in 2012. At one lookout in Austria, we stopped and enjoyed the view and it could not be described as anything other than breathtaking. It stopped us in our tracks and we praised God, expressing quietly our appreciation to God who made the world. We could have said words of praise, but actually it was more worshipful to stand silently and adore the view. When you do speak at such a time and place, the appropriate words are 'Hallowed be your name.'[41]

Cultural commentator Mark Sayers warns against practising faith as religious consumerism and viewing God as merely the facilitator of our personal dreams. In *The Road Trip That Changed the World*, Sayers analyses contemporary young adult culture and spirituality through the lens of the anti-materialistic road trip of Jack Kerouac's 1957 novel *On the Road*.[42] He suggests younger generations are interested in spiritual journeys and re-enchantment, as long as it does not restrict their individual life choices:

> They recognize that their culture is bereft of the transcendent. Yet they also revel in the personal freedom that the immanent frame brings. They want holy rantings, epiphanies, and divine revelations. They want the enchanted world back.

> Yet at the same time, they desire no authority, no external moral codes. They want Christ, but they also want the girls and the drugs. They want the solace of God and meaning, but also the freedom of godlessness.[43]

The Dangerous Prayer calibrates our spirits towards transcendence but without rejecting an authority framework. What is interesting in how we pray the Dangerous Prayer is that Sayers observes that our view of God is often influenced by how we were parented. Baby boomers grew up with a generation gap and wanted to distance themselves from authoritarian father figures. When baby boomers had children, they re-envisioned parenting in more permissive directions, described by Sayers as 'peerants'. Boundaries, responsibility and discipline became less dominant, and parents wanted to be (and children grew to expect them to be) more relational, having ethical flexibility and prioritizing self-esteem. This is not necessarily all bad, but it has implications for how we perceive God as parent:

> Unlike previous generations who had fallen into the trap of viewing God like their stern, distant fathers, today we are more likely to imagine God as something akin to a permissive mother. The Mom who would drop anything to come and give you a lift, who would pay for all of your breakages, write you sick notes when you took a day off school, and who let you eat chocolate just before bed because you threw a tantrum. When you view God as a permissive mother, it is natural that the universe becomes morally insignificant. Faith becomes a favour to God. Devotion and worship is transformed into an expectation of entertainment and a desire for reward.[44]

It is important to start with a correct view of God's awesomeness – not imagining God as our ideal permissive parent.

It is helpful to know the nature of the God whom we pray to because that can motivate us to pray and fill us with faith, knowing God is a caring parent who wants to hear our prayers. But as we come to our loving parent in prayer with a sense of family intimacy and easy access, it is also appropriate to come with a sense of respect and gravitas. Wright comments: 'This prayer starts by addressing God intimately and lovingly, as "Father" – *and* by bowing before his greatness and majesty. If you can hold those two together, you're already on the way to understanding what Christianity is all about.'[45]

Don Postema, in *Space for God*, acknowledges that in prayer we often come to God for requests, which we can do because of the intimacy we have with God; but we also pause to honour God for how great God is and how good it is to be with God:

> We come so often to God, if we come at all, as beggars. We ask and beg: give me; bless me; help me; guide me; grant me. And that's one necessary level of existence.

> But in thanksgiving and adoration we come to God not to ask but to give! We come not whimpering but shouting praise; not in guilt but in gratitude. We feel not distant from God but close to God. We are like a traveller who is home again at last, the prodigal at a banquet. Those moments may be seldom, but when they happen we know that we were created *for* God.[46]

By beginning the missional prayer with a plea for God our Father's name to be honoured, we make space for those moments of worship.

God's name is holy already, but this prayer asks for help that everyone will treat God's name with honour. In ancient times a name was much more connected with something than it is today.[47] This part of the prayer is thus not merely praying against people taking God's name in vain; like 'Please, God, let people around at work not swear "Oh Jesus Christ".' It is a cry that God's name be respected and God's character honoured. And since we bear God's name, we pray we would act and react to honour God's name. Nietzsche observed critically that Christians would have to look more redeemed before he would believe in their redeemer. A challenging saying, attributed to Gandhi, is, 'When I look at Jesus, I think I would like to be a Christian. But when I look at Christians, I decide no.'[48] Our lack of honouring God with our lives calls for repentance – in prayer and in action. I care less about my sports friends saying 'Oh God' in frustration, and am more concerned that my actions bring honour to God. God's reputation may be challenged in our neighbourhoods, but we look to God who wants to honour God's name through us.

As we pray for God's work in the world, let's start with reverence for God. But how do we honour God's name? This is a question of worship – both as we traditionally understand that term and also how we worship with our lives.

Worship

I have had many different experiences of prayer and worship. I grew up with the Anglican prayer-book liturgy. It was beautifully comprehensive but it could become ritualistic. As a teenager and young adult I worshipped at Pentecostal churches and felt I was experiencing God in the midst of worship. As a theological student, I appreciated being exposed to quiet and contemplative prayer, to enjoy solitude and silence. In Indonesia, I grew in being able to pray without the normal church supports I had known. After returning home to Melbourne from Indonesia, prematurely it seemed to me, my challenge was to pray when I did not feel like it. A valuable lesson I learned is to be able to experience and worship God in all sorts of ways. Sadly, some people feel they can only worship God in one way and it has to be their way – whether that is accompanied by old hymns, a contemporary music band, or candles and chanting.

Worship wars are unfortunate. In Western contexts they are limited to discussion and debate about the style of music songs. My friend James Petticrew, a Nazarene pastor in Edinburgh, explained to me that the Scots literally have been in worship wars at certain times in their history. When England tried to impose Church of England forms of worship and prayer liturgies on the Church of Scotland, one lady swung her prayer stool at the bishop and said 'No Popery here!' The bishop, having been forewarned there might be some trouble at church that morning, made a hasty exit as pistols were drawn. The bigger question is not about our worship style and a myopic devotion to certain forms, but how we express our love for God and 'hallow' God's name.

According to the Gospel of Luke, before Jesus taught his disciples to pray, he sent the seventy-two disciples out on mission, explaining that the most important commands are to love God and neighbour (and illustrating his teaching with the parable of the Good Samaritan). Then he visited Mary and Martha. Martha the activist is busy preparing and serving the dinner party while Mary sits contemplatively at Jesus' feet. Martha criticizes Mary for her bias, and Jesus – and history since – put Martha back in her place. Yet activism and contemplation are both important. Jesus values the contribution of both Mary and Martha, and does not want either downplayed. Jesus would have enjoyed the food Martha prepared, and it was Martha, in John's narration of the raising of Lazarus in John 11, who confesses that Jesus is Messiah, the Son of God. It is as important as Peter's confession in Matthew 16. We need Mary's contemplative spirit and Martha's activism. This is a message given by the biblical prophets, like Micah, who said: 'the Lord has told you what is good, and this is what he requires of you: to do what is right, to love mercy, and to walk humbly with your God' (Micah 6:8). Our call is to work *and* to pray – and to do both in order to alleviate the suffering on the streets of the world.

Whom do you identify with, Mary or Martha, or do you naturally have both tendencies through which to honour God? We can honour God's name through our worshipful living, but also with quiet worship from our hearts. Richard Foster writes, 'The contemplative life is the steady gaze of the soul upon the God who loves us.'[49] The Dangerous Prayer invites us to start in this place – coming before our Father God in heaven who loves and nurtures us, and honouring God's name. Praying 'Hallowed be your name' invites us into a contemplative worship space, but also challenges us to be the answer to our prayer and to honour God with how we act.

The Dangerous Prayer is not content with inner contemplation without active external engagement. It calls us outward to serve the world, as well as inward to quietly draw close to God. Any outward move of engagement needs a corresponding inner move of contemplation for sustainability. The danger is that outward engagement can be so exhausting that there is no energy for the inner work. But on the other hand, contemplation relies on missional engagement in order to be complete. N.T. Wright bemoans any separation: 'There is ultimately no justification for a private piety that doesn't work out in actual mission, just as there is no justification for people who use their activism in the social, cultural or political sphere as a screen to prevent them from facing the same challenges within their own lives.'[50] Simone Weil, a mystical writer and seeker of God around the time of World War II, urges total attention towards God in prayer and academic study, but furthermore suggests that such attention can also help us pray for and be present with people who suffer.[51] The Dangerous Prayer and 'hallowed be your name' invites us back into this rhythm, to both stand in the presence of the world's pain, and kneel on its behalf in the presence of the world's creator.[52]

The remainder of the Dangerous Prayer is in two halves – half for the world, and half for us. It is like the Ten Commandments – the first set of four are about God, and the second set of six are about our relationships and us. It is beautiful literature but also life-giving spirituality. The 'elegant poetry becomes profound theology', as Crossan says.[53] However, even the prayers that may seem at first for us can also be prayed for the world.

Journaling and Discussion

1. Watch a video clip about prayer and worship, such as 'Tim Hawkins Comedy – Worship & Prayer' and just share your response to the clip.[54]
2. What names are used to refer to you and where do they come from? What do your names mean, including any names that you have changed or have had changed for you by marriage, nicknames or changing culture?
3. Churches of different styles around the world worship in lots of different ways. What are some different forms of prayer and worship that you have experienced and appreciated?
4. What aspects of God as Father help inspire and shape your prayer life? In what ways would you like to grow to understand the character of God more? Who is the God you pray to? Do you hold any 'misinformed' images of God?

5. Do you consider yourself to be a Mary or a Martha in focusing on contemplation or action? Or in what ways do you combine both?
6. What would you like to stop doing, start doing, or do differently as a result of reading this chapter and reflecting on its implications?
7. View together the video of Jacqueline Grey discussing the radical message of praying 'Our Father', and discuss it with your group and/or journal your response.[55]
8. Finish by meditating and praying this prayer of blessing:
   May you experience the peace of God in your trouble,
   Hope when you are tempted to despair,
   Joy through your pain,
   Faith and courage when the heavens seem silent,
   And the sure knowledge that the Lord has been through it all too.
   He understands, he cares, and he loves you, very much.[56]

2

Subversive Justice of 'Your kingdom come'

We do well not to pray the prayer lightly. It takes guts
to pray it at all . . . 'Thy kingdom come . . . on earth'
is what we are saying. And if that were suddenly to
happen, what then? What would stand and what
would fall? Who would be welcomed and who would be
thrown the Hell out? Which if any of our most precious
visions of what God is and of what human beings are
would prove to be more or less on the mark and which
would turn out to be phony as three-dollar bills? . . .
To speak these words is to invite the tiger out of the
cage, to unleash a power that makes atomic power look
like a warm breeze.

(Frederick Buechner)[1]

Citizenship Benefits

In 2154, in the imagined future earth of the 2013 dystopian science
fiction movie *Elysium*, most of humanity lives on an overpopulated
and polluted earth. In the orbit of space, however, there is a protected
and luxurious existence possible, for those who can afford it (the rich
1%), in a newly created habitat, called Elysium. The class of people
on earth struggle with crime-controlled neighbourhoods, an oppressive justice system, under-resourced healthcare, unfulfilling industri-
alized jobs and monitoring by robots. Citizens of Elysium live idyllic

lives and are well provided for. Each house has a 'Med-Bay' that can repair any injury or cure any disease. Naturally, people stuck on earth long to get to Elysium, either by making lots of money or by travelling there as illegal immigrants (on hijacked rocket ships).

Elysium is a caricature of the world and its rich Western nations that have the resources to help solve global poverty, but keep it to themselves for their own security and enjoyment. Moreover, there is poverty in the Western world too – our neighbourhoods do not perfectly reflect the idyllic scenes of Elysium. This global system needs a reboot. What is questionable is whether that can come, as the stereotypical Hollywood movie suggests, from the violent overthrow (led by Matt Damon) of a few bad guys who are preventing resource distribution. But the movie showed a powerful image for me that every home in Elysium has the means for healing people who are sick. And my home has resources that can make a real difference in the lives of my neighbours – in my street and across the world.

The Elysium global system, rebooted, sent aid to help everyone who was sick. The heroes helped bring Elysium's resources to earth, where those resources were most needed. People on earth were treated as people who belonged in Elysium. The cry 'On earth as in heaven' was answered. Can things be that stark and simple? Is a reboot of our global system, to a greater or lesser extent, possible? When we cry 'Your kingdom come', and when we follow that up with 'Your will be done on earth as in heaven', we are pleading on behalf of everyone in need – and that everyone would be treated as citizens of heaven.

What would you like to recalibrate in the world? What do you see that you know breaks the heart of God? What breaks your heart?

It breaks my heart that children are enslaved for people's profit and/ or pleasure. It breaks my heart that not all the world's children have access to primary school education, or primary healthcare, or simple sanitation and clean water. I am devastated that the global system locks up so many resources for the rich and leaves too many in poverty. I hate that people with disabilities not only have unequal access to meaningful work, but are respected less and treated less well. Our global system is sick. Our neighbourhoods are in pain. In desperation it leads me to pray, 'God, please help us do better – let your kingdom come.' Let the benefits of heavenly citizenship spread.

Feel Their Pain?

What does it mean to pray 'Your kingdom come'? A kingdom or reign is a place where the ruler's will is done. When I pray for God's kingdom on earth, I am praying that our world would reflect God's reign. I am not a monarchist and the idea of a kingdom is not attractive to me. So I more often conceptualize what the Bible talks about as God's kingdom with other metaphors. One helpful image, carrying a similar overlapping meaning to that of the kingdom of God, is 'the family of God'. In God's family, we can be confident God will provide for its members. Some writers remove the 'g' and conceptualize what Jesus had in mind as the kin*dom – we are the kin or children of God, and kin with one another.[2] My favourite idea is to think of God's dream. 'Let what you dream and long for in our world and our neighbourhoods come to pass, please God.' That's what 'Your kingdom come' means for me, or 'Set the world aright' in the *Message* translation.

I was drawn to cry 'Set the world aright' as I heard stories of faith under pressure when I visited Chile and Peru in 2012. Some say the church should not be involved in politics. But in South America many of the heroes of political advocacy for human rights, defending liberty, advocating against the mistreatment of workers and the abuse of women, have been evangelical Christians. They were some of the first to speak up when struggle and persecution got most difficult. For example, one hero of mine is Dr Roberto Lagos-Schuffenegger, a well-known Baptist in Chile. He 'stood in the gap' for many victims, who now stop him in the street and express their thanks. He says love for your neighbour is not just a feeling but expresses itself in concrete ways, as the Good Samaritan showed. In Chile after 1973 and its contentious political period, 250,000 people were exiled and left the country to save their lives; 120,000 people lost their jobs; 40,000 people were jailed; 3,000 people were killed; and 1,363 people 'disappeared', including 54 children.[3] These are numbers to us, but it is also very real personal and family pain and suffering. I can only barely begin to feel their pain. But I know this does not reflect God's dream for our world.

One day in Chile soldiers came to a village with a list of people to collect. The soldiers asked a 6-year-old boy where his father was. He said he was not there. As the soldiers turned to leave, he said, 'My daddy's over the hill in the other paddock.' They detained his father, put him in the back of a truck with many others on their list, and the son said, 'I want to go with you.' His dad said, 'No, son. Take care of your mum, and if I am to die it is OK if God wills.' On that day in October 1973 there were eighteen Baptist farmers detained and killed. I am inspired by the faith of those who face such persecution, and those who stand in the gap and advocate against it as something that is *not* God's dream for the world.

I can only barely begin to feel their pain, and the pain of how that kind of tragic incident might affect a 6-year-old boy.

Another of the highlights of that 2012 trip to Chile was hearing from Baptist sisters and brothers from around the world. One thing we were acutely aware of that year was that suicide bombers were threatening churches in Nigeria.[4] The levels of violence caused by Muslim extremists and their acts of inhumanity meant Christians were hesitant to freely assemble and worship. In July 2012, one church of a thousand people had only 150 attending for fear of attacks. Boko Haram is a jihadist group wanting sharia law, and its members initiated bombings against churches and government buildings, especially police stations, the UN headquarters in the capital, and media outlets. The group also attacked mosques and Muslim leaders whom they accused of colluding with the authorities. The Nigerian Baptist Convention has more than 2.5 million members in more than 9,300 churches; it is one of the largest Baptist unions in the world. How do the churches respond to such inhumane violence? How do they function and relate as neighbours to those who are out to get them, literally? In a context that is far from God's dream for the world, how do God's people live lives that reflect the kingdom of God? I can only barely begin to feel their pain and their desperation for a better world.

These stories urge me to ask, how do we live as neighbours, to these sisters and brothers of ours who face such persecution? How do we pray and work for a world that is worth living in and restored to something more like God's dream? Hebrews 13:2–4 urges: 'Don't forget to show hospitality to strangers, for some who have done this have entertained angels without realizing it! Remember those in prison, as if you were there yourself. Remember also those being mistreated, as if you felt their pain in your own bodies [NIV: as if you yourself were suffering].'

Around the world and in our own neighbourhoods, we do not have to look too far to see the suffering of things messed up and in need of restoration. It is estimated that 200 million Christians face the persecution of jail, torture and death for professing their faith. Upwards of 34 million people are enslaved in one form or another, including more than a million children trafficked each year for sex or labour. Wars are started and fought on religious grounds (or ethnic grounds presented in religious guise). About 21,000 children die of starvation daily (a silent tsunami every fortnight). Over 80% of modern war casualties are civilians. More than 40 million people are living with HIV in the world; 800 million children live without easy access to clean water; 2.5 billion people do not have adequate toilets. The Bible is still to be translated into 2,000+ languages for those who need it but do not yet have a Bible. Of the world's 7 billion people, 3 billion are in unreached people-groups with minimal opportunity to hear the gospel explained in their own language and cultural context.[5] What is going on in this world that Jesus came to restore? Do you feel that pain? I confess I sometimes look around the world and ask, 'What is happening and where is God?'

We live in a world that is dark and strained. After Christmas most years, I preach 'Keep Herod in Christmas'. Our church recognizes that for all the good news of the Advent of Jesus, there is still a dark side to our existence on earth – even now Jesus has come. Max Lucado penned this prayer in response to violence:

Dear Jesus,

It's a good thing you were born at night. This world sure seems dark. I have a good eye for silver linings. But they seem dimmer lately.

The whole world seems on edge. Trigger-happy. Ticked off. We hear threats of chemical weapons and nuclear bombs. Are we one button-push away from annihilation?

Your world seems a bit darker these days. But you were born in the dark, right? You came at night. The shepherds were nightshift workers. The Wise Men followed a star. Your first cries were heard in the shadows. To see your face, Mary and Joseph needed a candle flame. It was dark. Dark with Herod's jealousy. Dark with Roman oppression. Dark with poverty. Dark with violence.

Herod went on a rampage, killing babies. Joseph took you and your mom into Egypt. You were an immigrant before you were a Nazarene.

Oh, Lord Jesus, you entered the dark world of your day. Won't you enter ours? We are weary of bloodshed. We, like the wise men, are looking for a star. We, like the shepherds, are kneeling at a manger.

We ask you, heal us, help us, be born anew in us.

Hopefully,
Your Children[6]

Part of the dangerous stories Jesus calls us to live is to join with Jesus in restoring the world from the situations that bring tears to our eyes and that break the heart of God. My passion for our churches and missional tribes is to equip others, and my passion in prayer is to help bring the world more into line with God's dream for it; in other words, to advance the kingdom of God.

More Than Life Forever

The kingdom of God, as Jesus' central message, is bigger than we might have imagined. It is helpful to frame ministry, including evangelism, around a kingdom-of-God vision – inviting people to join a cause to remake the world rather than just getting a ticket for heaven.

Dallas Willard celebrates the character and calling of God, and critiques what he labels a 'gospel of sin management' that suggests faith is *either* only a private matter of forgiveness *or* merely inspiration for social action, without relating Jesus to the whole of life.[7] It is important not to hold too narrow a view of the kingdom. Sometimes the gospel message has been packaged as, 'Say sorry to God and go to heaven when you die', as if that is all there is to it. But just as importantly as where we go when we die is what we live for before we die. It is not just about what happens when we die, but what happens when we live. Let's not squeeze the life and relevance out of the gospel and make it just about eternal life insurance and sin management. The kingdom is more than that. It relates to public and domestic, friendship and sex, leisure and business, war and economics, clothing and community, transport and holidays.

Vineyard church planter Steve Gee was inspired by Willard and questioned whether the role of churches is to 'just help us warehouse Christians till they die?' Rather than narrowly seeing the gospel as Jesus dying for our sins and guaranteeing a place in heaven, Gee asks:

But what if heaven isn't the goal of God's story, what if it is just our destination? What if the goal of the gospel (salvation, Christ dying for our sin, etc) was something else? What if the goal was more about life than death . . . about the start of a whole new life? A kingdom kind of life? . . .

Perhaps our evangelistic question should change from 'If you were going to die tonight, do you know where you would go?' to 'If you were going to live tomorrow (and live for a very long time), whom would you live for? What would you do? What is the basic and fundamental story around which you would live your life?'[8]

Michael Moynagh argues that the gospel message of the kingdom is more than 'Say sorry to God and go to heaven' (being 'saved') and more than even 'God has a wonderful plan for your life.' The gospel message is that 'God has a wonderful plan for the world (the Kingdom of God or the reign or the network or the family of God) and he invites you to come on board and join in. God accepts you – come and acknowledge that. God calls you to change your life and serve the world (and not just live for yourself) – grasp the enormity of that.'[9]

More Than Sunday

The kingdom of God is something we pray for, and what we live and work for, and not just in church. The church is a context to foster the kingdom. Lesslie Newbigin taught that the church is the 'sign, instrument, and foretaste' of God's reign.[10] Yet we do not see the best answer to this prayer in our church gatherings on Sundays. The real rubber meets the road through the week – Mondays to Fridays in our work, and Saturdays at play, and Sundays at worship. Of course most people's work and play and worship does not divide up that neatly, but my point is that the kingdom of God is not limited to church gatherings. Emerging church leader Brian McLaren suggests the kingdom breaks out through the mission of the whole people of God: 'What if the real difference is made in the world not by us preachers but by those who endure our preaching, those who quietly live out the secret message of the kingdom of God in their daily, workaday lives in the laboratory, classroom, office, cockpit, parliament, kitchen, market, factory, and neighborhood?'[11] We pray and live this prayer for God's kingdom, not primarily in our sacred gatherings but in our everyday worlds.

John the Baptist preached, 'Jesus is on the way, the kingdom is near, put your garbage out and start afresh' (paraphrasing Matthew 3:2). John knew that Jesus was bringing in a whole new approach to life and community, politics and economics, with specific and global-reaching claims. This is not just about what happens in church on Sundays. It's a far broader-reaching vision.

If you want a picture of what the kingdom of God is like, in person, look at Jesus and what he said and did. The kingdom of God is Jesus' dynamic and dangerous dream that life 'on earth' would be 'as it is in heaven'. As Jesus *lives* this dream – as he teaches and heals and casts out demons – heaven is breaking in and this earth is being transformed. We can see something of the kingdom of God with Jesus' miracles. Jesus set people free, cured the sick, raised the dead, and drove demons away. These were all signs that the kingdom was here. The miracles showed things were back in line with God's purpose for creation and people (cf. Matthew 11:2–6). Jesus' teaching also pointed to the kingdom of God and opposed injustice and hypocrisy. As the new King starts having his way in this broken world, this kingdom dream can also take root and grow wings among us. Do we dare to join Jesus in seeking this 'heaven-on-earth' dream in all its fullness? Are we bold enough to live into such a *big* prayer that asks God to move heaven and earth?

Here and Now

Andrew Knight, writer of a popular Australian television series, *Seachange*, spoke at a World Vision event saying he loved supporting World Vision but did not understand the Christian bit. Tim Costello, a Baptist pastor currently serving as World Vision's CEO, asked him what bit, and he replied 'Heaven'. Floating on clouds, playing a harp, and daily Bible study did not offer significant doses of hope. He suggested, cheekily, 'You really need to do better than that – at least the Muslims seem to offer virgins in the afterlife.'[12]

Knight is actually in sync with one of the most significant theological rediscoveries of recent time. The church is realizing that salvation is not just about saving souls for eternity but restoring hope and God's dream for our current world. This realignment comes when we understand the nature of the kingdom of God. When Jesus came and ministered on earth, he set people free and healed them. His ministry was about restoring people to the ideal of what God had created them for. When Jesus did this for people he said, 'The kingdom of God has come' (Matthew 12:28 NRSVA). The kingdom of God is where God is in control, where God reigns or where God's dream for the world is brought to reality. Mission, then, is fostering the kingdom of God or the dream of God. It is not just about getting as many souls as possible across the line into heaven and rescuing them from a bad world, but redeeming and restoring the world and inviting people to work with God towards that dream.

N.T. Wright develops a theology of hope that is not just about heaven but about remaking our world, for now and afterwards. He challenges Christians to proudly own their citizenship in heaven (Philippians 3:20–21) but also colonize and transform earth. He reminds us that Jesus was crucified not just so our personal sin could be forgiven, but also to overcome the evil that enslaves the world and to restore the world to God's ideal. The kingdom of God is *not* something we have to wait for heaven to see realized, but it has begun here on earth. It is manifest in the life, death and resurrection of Jesus and through the Spirit-led work of the church.[13]

Thielicke prayed 'Your kingdom come' fervently when he saw how transitory the world was. He looked at the façades of buildings that had been bombed. He preached this just after the attempted revolution of 20 July 1944, which was put down, to the despair of those hoping for an end to Hitler's lunacy. 'One can never draw God too deep into the flesh', Thielicke quoted Luther, then adding: 'and one can never draw the Kingdom of God too deep into the misery of the world.'[14]

World War I was supposed to be the war to end all wars, but World War II came with new horrors, not least of which was civilian bombing. Dreams for the twentieth century to be the Western world's golden century were dashed. In the seventy years since World War II the world has hardly improved – Cambodia and other multiple genocides, Iraq and other multiple invasions of sovereign countries. In the midst of escalating violence in our neighbourhoods and between nations, how do we pray? We need Jesus to teach us to pray. In a world struck by disasters and afflictions like AIDS, how do we pray? We need Jesus to teach us.

In a world marred by pain, ploughed deep with terror, and suffering injustices often greater than we can imagine; in a nation where children suffer too young, where families break up too early, where neighbours live close but lonely and distant lives; in neighbourhoods where people make less than fulfilling choices, where workers pursue less than upright practices, where even Christians engage less than godly priorities, we cry, 'May your kingdom come' and 'May it come soon.'

We don't bring the kingdom – we invite, welcome and long for it. We don't build it ourselves – we merely proclaim what God is building. Let's avoid activism as if it depends on us, and celebrate instead the agency of God. We don't pray 'Our kingdom come' nor 'Your kingdom take us away.'[15] The prayer we plead is for God's kingdom and will to come, here and now. At our church we pray, 'Bring heaven to Hawthorn. May your will be done in Melbourne as in heaven.' Be encouraged to pray that for your city and neighbourhood.

Rebellion Against the Status Quo

This is a subversive prayer. For the first century it was clearly dangerous. In the ancient world, citizens worshipped emperors, and the empire exploited the early church, and the poor were oppressed. But Christians prayed and looked for another kingdom (Acts 17:7).[16] In the Middle Ages the church thought the Crusades were a way to bring in the kingdom of God. They were mistaken. St Francis was antimilitaristic and crossed the lines to talk to the sultan. He went in the face of the Crusader kingdom policies and ethos of his time.[17] Similarly in our world there are competing kingdoms. For instance, consumerism is the dominant religious alternative to Christianity.[18] Violence is the preferred tool for changing systems. To plead for God's kingdom is to supplant competing alternatives in any form. Karl Barth said, 'To clasp the hands in prayer is the beginning of an uprising against the disorder of the world.' Prayer is 'rebellion against the status quo', as David Wells describes, 'the absolute and undying refusal to accept as normal what is pervasively abnormal . . . the refusal of every agenda, every scheme, every interpretation that is at odds with the norm as originally established by God'.[19]

Hadassah is a hero of mine for her subversive and countercultural appeal for a different world. She changed the destiny of 127 nations. She lived in the fifth century BC and you may know her under a different name, Esther. She was queen to powerful King Xerxes. One day she went from obscurity to royalty through success in a Miss Persia contest.[20]

There are two other main characters in Esther's story. Haman is second-in-charge to the king but a real jerk. The book *Don't Let Jerks Get the Best of You* divides the world into three categories of jerks.[21] First-degree jerks, like most of us, sometimes display jerkish behaviour. Second-degree jerks habitually demonstrate jerkish behaviour, and need careful management and maintenance of boundaries if they are in your family or workplace. Nth-degree jerks are systemically jerkish and difficult to relate to – normally you are better just resigning than trying to get on with an Nth-degree jerkish boss. Haman was an Nth-degree jerk. Some people are evil and seemingly unredeemable.

Haman's jerkishness was played out on a global scale when he plotted to kill the Jews. He was not the first to plan genocide for the Jews, and tragically not the last, but his egotistical plotting meant the Jews of Esther's day were under threat. So Esther, as a Jew herself, wanted to go to the king and appeal for her people.

In ancient times, however, you did not presume to go into the throne room. Anyone who went uninvited into the throne room was automatically killed. The death sentence was prearranged, unless the king held out his sceptre and granted you access.

Esther figured she had a reasonable chance of access, but was nervous. Mordecai, Esther's cousin who had been looking out for her, counselled:

> Don't think for a moment that you will escape there in the palace when all other Jews are killed. If you keep quiet at a time like this, deliverance for the Jews will arise from some other place, but you and your relatives will die. What's more, who can say but that you have been elevated to the palace *for just such a time as this?*
>
> Esther 4:13–14, emphasis mine and probably Mordecai's too

Mordecai's words to Esther capture my imagination. Why does God place us where we find ourselves? Who knows whether God has placed you in your family, street, school, vocation or community group for just such a time as this? The *missio Dei* or mission of God is active in the world, and God seeks people to cooperate with God's purpose and kingdom. Our challenge is to be open and available.

Esther rose to the occasion. To Mordecai she responded, 'OK, you pray and I will go.' To her beauty advisors and hairdresser I imagine she said, 'OK, you had better do a special job today.' She beautied herself up. She added a prayer to Mordecai's. She rehearsed her speech. She went into the throne room with a tinge of nervousness. When the king saw her in her beauty he said, 'Hubahuba – what can I do for you today? You can have whatever you want.'

Thus Esther had the opportunity to plead for her people.

Haman got the rope. Mordecai, Esther's cousin, got the second-in-charge job. And the Jews avoided genocide and lived another day.[22] Why? Because Esther went into the throne room and asked.

God's presence is not scary, and God is not influenced by the way we look or the gifts we bring. But just as Esther approached the king with her request, we go to God's throne and plead, 'May your name be honoured. May your purposes be fulfilled. May your kingdom come soon. May your will be done. May your dreams for our world

come to fruition – in our communities and workplaces and relationships, and in the biggest and most complex challenges of the world.'

This is no longer the Lord's Prayer. They were Jesus' words, but he
handed them over to his disciples, and the prayer became 'the disciples' prayer'. But it has become 'your prayer' as Jesus' body and the
church prays it. It is also 'the missional prayer' to pray in radical ways
that change our world.

Shopping List?

I have emphasized that one of the problems with modern society,
including our approach to faith and church, is consumerism. Even
prayer can become just a 'shopping list' of what we desire. Seeing
prayer as a shopping list can be questioned. It includes listening and
being attentive to God. Someone asked Mother Teresa about her
prayer and what she says to God. She replied, 'I tend to just listen.'
When asked what God says, she replied, 'God tends to just listen.'
A growing edge of prayer is sitting in silence and solitude with God.
Nevertheless, there is also a place for asking God to intervene in the
world. Part of prayer is asking God for things and interceding for people. Jesus implied our problem is sometimes we do not ask enough.
James said, 'You do not have because you do not ask . . . When you
ask . . . you ask with wrong motives' (James 4:2–3 NIV). Australian Anglican preacher Michael Raiter, in his survey of contemporary
spiritualities, commented:

> It is often said that we should not bring our shopping list of requests to
> God. This is poor advice. The average Christian's problem is that their
> shopping list is far too short! Of course, our requests are to conform
> to God's will, but petition, along with thanksgiving, ought to be the
> hallmark of our prayer life. We can feel sometimes so full of a sense of
> our own adequacy and strength, we don't need divine aid. The point of
> prayer is that it is a continual acknowledgement of our childlike depend-
> ence on the Giver for everything.[23]

Raiter says our prayer shopping lists are too short. But are they also often too narrow? The missional prayer reminds us to pray for the needs of the world around us as well as our needs. We pray to 'our Father' on behalf of all people, whom God cares for. We pray that injustice would not be tolerated, families would not break up, suffering would cease, young people would not lose hope, old people would not feel forgotten, and our cities would not be places of ethnic violence. Please God, bring heaven to earth. We need it here. Let the benefits of citizenship broaden. And may your will be done.

It Pays to Haggle

Another biblical character from whom I learn 'pushy prayer' is Abraham.[24] God had visited and called Abraham, promised him children, and invited him towards a greater destiny than he thought possible. Then he shared with Abraham his plans for Sodom and Gomorrah (Genesis 18:16–33). These cities were wicked places whose inhabitants did not care about justice (see Isaiah 1:9–23). It was not just about immoral behaviour or distortions of sexuality common in the nightlife of any city but accentuated in Sodom and Gomorrah, but the fact that these cities allowed bloodshed of innocent people and senseless violence that grieved God.

It seems that God has left heaven and does not want to act, refusing to listen to the appeals of God's people. As the people of the nearby neighbourhood bring destruction on themselves, God fills Abraham in. The encounter in Genesis 18 is the first extended account of prayer in the Bible. After God explains what has been happening and what will happen to the cities, Abraham responds with his plea. Abraham gathers his arguments and states his case: 'Will you indeed sweep [them] away? Suppose there are fifty righteous people within the city; won't you forgive it for the fifty righteous there?'

That is a bold thing to say to God. Abraham and Sarah had already laughed at God's promise of children. If God were any lesser

God or prone to push his weight around, we might expect God's patience to be overstretched. But God listens to Abraham spelling out his concerns.

Abraham continued with his pleading: 'Would you really do it if there were fifty righteous people? [Think, God, about the impact they could have after receiving your mercy. And surely you would not destroy them along with the wicked.] Far be that from you. Shall not the judge of the earth do what is right?' This is not a feeble, quiet request. It is not mumbled piety. There is no 'If perhaps it be your will, then maybe, please God . . .' The request is strong, clear and challenging.

God accepted Abraham's impassioned plea and replied, 'OK, I would spare it for fifty.' You can almost hear the wheels turning inside Abraham's head: *Do I dare keep going?* He dares: 'Let me take it on myself to speak to the Lord. I who am dust and ashes. Could I negotiate you down to forty-five?' Who does he think he's talking to? It sounded like he was on the street in Asia bartering for a cheaper price for a pair of jeans. Abraham did know whom he was addressing, and God agreed. It seemed God encouraged such forwardness in prayer on behalf of others.

Abraham continued to whittle the number down. Forty? Thirty? I don't like presuming, but twenty? Then one last shot. 'Oh, don't let the Lord be angry if I speak just once more. Suppose ten are found?' God nodded his head once more: 'Yes, for ten I won't destroy the city.'

What does this account of prayer suggest? Abraham bargains with God. God not only stoops to listen but also agrees. They had been face to face and they see eye to eye. Abraham was learning to see things as God sees. Abraham was even challenging God to see things as Abraham sees them. The result is that Abraham sees God's mercy is generous.

Why did Abraham stop at ten? Maybe he had done some mental arithmetic: Lot, his wife, two sons, two daughters, their husbands, two unmarried daughters or two others. But there were not ten. Tragically Sodom and Gomorrah were destroyed as God's last and sorrowful resort for dealing with their wickedness and rebellion. In the end God spares Lot and his family even though they were only four.

But what is the moral to this story? Don't stop at ten? According to progressive biblical scholar and activist Walter Wink, the moral is that *it pays to haggle with God.* Prayer in this view is persistent and impertinent, not polite and hesitant. Says Wink:

> We are required by God to haggle with God for the sake of the sick, the obsessed, the weak, and to conform our lives to our intercessions. This is a God who invents history in interaction with those 'who hunger and thirst to see right prevail' (Matt. 5:6) . . .
>
> Prayer is rattling God's cage and waking God up and . . . cutting the ropes off God's hands and the manacles off God's feet and washing the caked sweat from God's eyes and then watching God swell with life and vitality and energy and following God wherever God goes.[25]

That was a new thought to me of prayer as releasing God to work. God does work independently of our prayers, but thinking of God initiating action after we pray – something God may otherwise not have done, and seeing prayer as co-creating with God, is motivation to persevere in prayer.

I posted Wink's quote on Facebook and appreciated one comment in particular: 'No doubt we change ourselves as we pray and open up to God. And no doubt as we pray we think about how we can be the answer. But, biblically, prayer is more than that. It changes the world and changes what is "possible" for God to do. The field of possibilities change. Space opens for God to act.' Prayer visualizes an alternative future to the one apparently fated by current forces. It is a force of hope. It is a powerful vision for a better world. The good news about Christianity is that God did not just make the world and let it spin, but stayed involved. The God we pray to is not the God of the celestial White House where we send letters to be sorted among piles of others. The Lord does not treat our prayers as unwanted spam.[26]

Pushy Prayer

Although the world works against what we pray for and although answers seem sporadic, nevertheless through prayer we create new possibilities. We negotiate with God for a new deal, rebel against the status quo, and change people's destinies. Let's not stop praying for heaven on earth because prayers seem unanswered. Hang on for what God has put on your heart. Feel free to vent the full range of your feelings – frustration to outrage to joy and everything in-between. But storm God's throne for what you know God wants to see happen in the lives of people around you; and the city around you; and the countries around you.

Praying 'Your kingdom come' is a pushy prayer. Jesus' story of the persistent widow teaches that she is granted justice because she kept coming back with her plea (Luke 18:1–8). 'Your kingdom come' is not a feeble request but a bold invitation for God to come into every corner of our lives and world (Romans 12:1–2).

I think having some 'pushyness' in prayer is what Jesus was inviting when he said, 'Ask . . . seek . . . knock' (Matthew 7:7). Persistence is a virtue when it comes to pleading for God's kingdom and will. God invites (even commands) us to 'haggle' with God for the sick and the obsessed, the weak and the marginalized. Prayers for God's kingdom are based not on wishful thinking but a reminder of the purposes of God. The writer of Hebrews urges us, 'Now that we know what we have – Jesus, this great High Priest with ready access to God – let's not let it slip through our fingers. We don't have a priest who is out of touch with our reality . . . So let's walk right up to him and get what he is so ready to give. Take the mercy, accept the help' (Hebrews 4:14–16 *The Message*). This is not your average quiet time.

I am ready to haggle with God for Hawthorn. I want to see God's kingdom flourish in my city of Melbourne. I long for God's will to be outworked in my life and my family, and my church and my neighbours.

I learned this from my dad. One day Mum told me about a sad and difficult situation in a friend's family. And I thought, *That's sad and difficult.* Mum said she was not going to tell Dad. But that night I heard a cry of anguish followed by tears come from my parents' bedroom. My first thought, in a teenager's moment of insight, was that Mum must have told Dad after all. My second thought was the real learning curve. I thought Dad had responded to the situation with an appropriate amount of empathy. I thought, *That's sad and difficult.* Dad felt the sadness and difficulty, deeply. After listening to Dad quieten down, I went outside and walked and prayed. First I prayed that God would break my heart with the things that break God's heart. I prayed, 'Help me to feel for people's pain like Dad and God do – my earthly and heavenly fathers.' And then I prayed for our friends and their struggle. I prayed, 'No, God, don't let evil have its way.' That was a night I learned to pray deeply into people's pain.

Prayer is not just quiet self-reflection with no effect on the world. Karl Barth said, 'To clasp the hands in prayer is the beginning of an uprising against the disorder of the world.' Prayer boldly exercises faith to change circumstances.

Dreaming Big

C.S. Lewis suggested our lives are full of dreams that are too dreary, wishes that are too weak, longings that are too lame. He believes that our problem in prayer is not that we come with desires that are too strong for God to handle, but that we settle for second best:

> It would seem Our Lord finds our desires, not too strong, but too weak. We are half-hearted creatures, fooling about with drink and sex and ambition when infinite joy is offered us, like an ignorant child who wants to go on making mud pies in a slum because he cannot imagine what is meant by the offer of a holiday at the sea. We are far too easily pleased.[27]

Often we are there in the mud, ignorant and caught up in our own busyness and importance, while Jesus is inviting us to lift our eyes up towards a bigger dream than we had imagined. We get a glimpse of that when we pray 'Your kingdom come. Your will be done. Bring heaven to earth.'

The adventure, challenge and invitation of the kingdom of God is that God would be in control, and that God's dream would become reality. We pray that God's ecosystem, counterculture and purposes would burst forth in our lives and neighbourhoods; that they would take root and flourish around us. Let's be passionate, but about what most matters.

Another way of picturing the kingdom of God is revisiting the parables or stories Jesus told to illustrate what it meant. One of our resident biblical scholars, Julia Rhyder, introduced 'the Mustard Tree' to AuburnLife.[28] We were asking what we aspired to as a church. If we might grow in particular directions, where would we most love to branch out? What would the kingdom look like if God answered our prayer: 'Bring heaven to Hawthorn. Let your dream for our neighbourhood happen'?

What captured our imagination most about the mustard seed was not the small seed growing into a whole bigger tree, but the nature of the tree that gives a safe nesting place and shelter to many birds: 'What is the kingdom of God like? And to what should I compare it? It is like a mustard seed that someone took and sowed in the garden; it grew and became a tree, and the birds of the air made nests in its branches' (Luke 13:18–19 NRSVA). A mustard tree, or more accurately bush or shrub, is not impressive in size. But what makes it a significant image of the kingdom of God is that it becomes a safe place for many. It is what the structure can serve and the hospitality it fosters. Dreaming big, therefore, when it comes to Mustard Tree aspirations, is not to grow big, but to be big and generous with our hospitality. The context of the parable suggests this too, as immediately before Jesus tells this story, he heals a marginalized crippled woman, and the synagogue leader criticizes him for healing on the Sabbath (Luke 13:10–17). Jesus provides an object lesson in what faith and worship is supposed to be about – not big programmes or buildings, or keeping ceremonies or laws, but offering healing to people who are vulnerable.

God is a God of hospitality, and invites the people of God to reflect that hospitality. We are learning to move beyond our idolatry of size (whether aspiring to be large or comfortable with being small), and reframe our aspirations primarily around hospitality and inclusion. Jesus' picture of the kingdom of God inspires me to place our little seed into the place where God wants to plant us, and let God organically grow us into places of hospitality for our neighbourhood. These are 'Mustard Tree Aspirations' we are growing, as we pray 'Your kingdom come, your will be done.' We at AuburnLife want to be a church where the stranded have a nest; where healing happens; where the lonely find community.

Jean Vanier is a hero of ours who wrote beautifully about his vision for church hospitality:

> In the midst of all the violence and corruption of the world God invites us today to create new places of belonging, places of sharing, of peace and of kindness, places where no-one needs to defend himself or herself; places where each one is loved and accepted with one's own fragility, abilities and disabilities. This is my vision for our churches: that they become places of belonging, places of sharing.[29]

Hospitality, especially to others who are different from us, is a central way of offering new life and fostering the kingdom of God. Many churches are discovering in fresh ways who Jesus is through hospitality. That is the experience at AuburnLife in the hospitality hub we host for international students. In our English classes and Bible studies, and community meals and coffee times, we see glimpses of what God is doing in people's lives. It is true also for 'Slow Church' advocates, who urge us to avoid the temptation of modern so-called hospitality that keeps people at arm's length, and instead sit with people patiently, celebrating opportunities to share life and seemingly 'waste time' together.[30] That might not seem like 'dreaming big', but it can be a countercultural display of hospitality in a hyper-mobile and driven society.

Countercultural Discipleship

Welcoming God's kingdom and inviting God's will is part of the journey of churches and followers of Jesus. As a young Christian I more often adapted 'Your will be done' into another prayer, 'What is your will for me, God?' In high school, while my friends were exploring career choices, I wanted to know what God wanted me to do. One day in my graduating year I saw a church sign which captured my imagination and spoke to my heart. I had been grappling with what to do with life as my friends and I considered university or work preferences. But this sign reframed my decision-making process. It said, 'Give God your life. God can do more with it than you can.' That called me to hand over my life to God and ask God to do God's will rather than mine. I did not need convincing and I took that as a sign from God, literally, and offered to God my life to influence the world as God wanted.

Seeking personal guidance from God has an important place. But praying 'Your will be done' invites us to pray in broader directions – not only for me and my life, but the life of our neighbourhoods and the world around us. I want to see God's will for me happen, and God's will for the world fulfilled. We could also say 'Give God your world. God can do more with it than you can.' Praying 'Your will be done' for me and for the world, albeit also through me, takes this prayer to a whole new level.

Old Testament scholar Christopher Wright encourages us to see the purpose of our lives wrapped up with the mission of God: 'We want to be driven by a purpose that has been tailored just right for our own individual lives . . . when we should be seeing the purpose of all life, including our own, wrapped up in the great mission of God for the whole of creation.'[31] Praying for God's will to be done in the world is what best helps me seek God's will for my life. My vocation is to cooperate with God to see God's will fulfilled in the world around me. Self-awareness is knowing where our strengths lie and where God is calling us, and pursuing that with passion. Oscar Wilde suggested: 'Be yourself. Everybody else is taken.'[32] Let's not be driven by the demands of others or the expectations we put on ourselves, or strive to be something or someone we are not. Parker Palmer, a master-teacher by vocation and Quaker by faith, often quotes Frederick Buechner to describe vocation as 'where your deep gladness meets the world's deep need'.[33] It suggests that God's will for us is to address the most challenging needs of the world through how God has made and gifted us.

What is it that most captures your imagination? What brings you life? Where do you feel most glad about contributing to the world around you? Your answer to those questions may be vocational clues about what God's will is for you.

I was struggling recently with a dilemma of whether to apply for a job in an area I had always wanted (teaching theology and ministry in a college where I had studied). If successful, it would have meant leaving a current ministry role that allocates time to research and writing. The decision was about whether I wanted to focus on teaching or writing. Was my teaching or my writing where my deep gladness would meet the world's deep need? I was praying, 'Your will be done, God', but I was not clear about God's will. I could leave it to the process and see if I was invited to fill the job. Over dinner with friends, Tim and Julia Rhyder, Julia asked me, 'Darren, what gets you up in the morning?' When I realized in this season of ministry it was writing, and the opportunities and challenges of my current main role, the answer was clarified for me. I withdrew my application.

Career planning and vocational discernment is a first-world dilemma. Even in Western countries, meaningful work is elusive. A principle for me is to pray for God's will for what best suits me, and what best heals the world. It is good to be encouraged, 'Give God your life. God can do more with it than you can.' But it is equally or more significant to be encouraged, 'Give God your world. God can do more with it than you can.' What will spread the benefits of citizenship of heaven?

Bringing Heaven to Earth

Where do you pray for God's will to be done? What is it that breaks your heart that you can see is not God's will in the world or in your neighbourhood?

The homeless figures in my home city of Melbourne are appalling. There was a poster a few years back that called us to pray. It said 'Homeless – I said No!!!' It was a play on words suggesting how we all too often deny or turn away from a problem: 'No, there is no problem' or 'No, I won't get involved.' But at another, better level it also suggested what we ought to say: 'No, homelessness and the conditions that cause it should not be tolerated for those who want a better option.'

My daughter Jessie and I were driving to church one morning when I was serving as interim pastor at West Preston Baptist. Jessie saw a homeless person waking up from his sleeping place in a shopfront alcove. She cried and said, 'What is happening that he has to sleep on the street? Charities are supposed to help people like that. Aren't the Red Cross supposed to help them? There's hundreds of charities and there are still homeless people.' She was touched by the person's isolation from housing and other resources. It was not the 'homelessness figures' that broke her heart; it was seeing a person sleeping out in the street, on Sunday morning at 9:30. I was touched that she had eyes to see and tears to cry on their behalf. She challenged me to pray and to cry for those whom society all too often forgets.

Oscar Romero said, 'There are many things that can only be seen through eyes that have cried.' My friend Kim Hammond says people can be actively involved in mission but have dry eyes. We desperately need to learn from the heart of God and let what brings tears to God bring tears to our eyes, motivating us to pray beyond ourselves.

This is not easy to pray when God's will is not done. In a world where millions starve, women are sold, children are enslaved, minorities are denied freedom, young people are homeless, the environment is being destroyed, where some Western countries are ruthlessly restricting the numbers of refugees, where the income and education gap between rich and poor is exponentially widening, this prayer stretches our faith. Yet the state of the world calls me to pray this prayer on its behalf. My eyes are wet and my prayers are full – with pleading – as I look at the world's needs. It challenges my faith. But my spirit is also full of hope as I look to the generosity of God.

It takes a bold step of faith to pray this prayer confidently, in the face of dark circumstances. Let's pray it boldly for the sake of the world. Let's dream up a storm for how God's will can be done. U2 singer Bono said, 'Here's to the future. The only limits are the limits of our imagination. Dream up the kind of world you want to live in. Dream out loud and at high volume. That's what we do for a living.'[34] What's your dream for our world? What is God's dream for the world? Let's dream with God and pray and work in those directions.

African theologian Musa Dube Shomanah writes, 'Christian communities and their institutions should be active ambassadors of God's reign, constantly scrutinizing local, national and international policies and structures to assess whether they allow God's rule to be realized on earth as in heaven.'[35] What would God's reign look like in your country if it was held under that scrutiny? I imagine for my neighbourhood how people would be treated differently. Our indigenous people would not need to beg to have education and health gaps narrowed. Our political leaders would not be saying with pride, 'We turned back the boats.' Our approach to the environment would not be to exploit it before its sustainability is completely undermined. This is the vision I want to pray and work for.

Reflecting on God's will for the world – a world in need of salvation – challenges me to lift my prayers beyond 'What is your will for me, God?' to 'Please God, may your will be done in the world.' This was emphasized at Auburn as we prayed through the missional prayer. Beth Barnett encouraged us to look at the whole of Isaiah 53, focusing on the phrase: 'yet it was the will of the LORD to crush him' (v. 10 NRSVA). Interestingly, this is one of the few times in the Bible that the Lord's will is specifically mentioned and defined. Our fears were that if God crushed Jesus then it might be the will of the Lord to crush us. We noted it was the will of the Lord to crush God's self in Jesus, not the will of the Lord to crush us or anyone else. The reason it was the will of the Lord to crush Jesus was to bring salvation to the world. When Jesus prayed in Gethsemane, 'Not my will but yours be done' (Luke 22:42 NRSVA), he was echoing this element of the will of the Lord – that Jesus was to be crushed in his death. It was a cruel time in the Godhead. But the reason for and result of that dilemma was that God wanted to bring healing and wholeness to the world. When we pray 'Your will be done', remember all that Jesus went through to bring wholeness to the world and pray that his costly offering would bring healing to the places of the world where most suffer. We need both an expanded vision for the world and an expanded vision of what Christ has done for the world.

Tom Wright urges us in our prayers to embrace both the love God feels and the grief God experiences for the world:

> To pray this prayer means seeing the world in binocular vision. See it with the love of the creator for his spectacularly beautiful creation; and see it with the deep grief of the creator for the battered and battle-scarred state in which the world now finds itself. Put those two together, and bring the binocular picture into focus: the love and the grief join into the Jesus-shape, the kingdom-shape, the shape of the cross . . . for heaven and earth to be married at last. And if we pray this way, we must of course be prepared to live this way.[36]

Wright invites us to pray in a way that foreshadows what God dreams to foster in the world. To adopt a music metaphor, he urges the church to reflect 'a returned orchestra to play the kingdom-music until the world takes up the song',[37] in order that 'the medicine and the music of the gospel might make fresh inroads into the sick and cacophonous world all around us'.[38]

Dangerous Harmony

In writing this book, inspired by classical Lord's Prayer writers, I wanted 'to make prayer and living harmonious'.[39] The missional prayer is not merely a prayer to pray but a life to live prayerfully. Robert Fryling refers to this theme in discussing Carmen de Gasztold's poem 'The Peacock'. A peacock is a colourful-feathered and beautiful bird, but the sound it produces is wailing and woeful.

De Gasztold praises the peacock's beauty but bemoans the discordant note, and concludes with a plea for integrity. The challenge of the missional prayer is to ask Jesus to teach me to pray in ways that have integrity with how I live, and to live a radical life that has integrity with the words of this prayer. Writes De Gasztold, 'Lord, let a day come, a heavenly day, when my inner and outer selves will be reconciled in perfect harmony.'[40] That is the dangerous missional prayer: to integrate character and behaviour with beliefs and teaching, and to synergize inner contemplation with engagement with the world.

Be encouraged to pray dangerously and live dangerously – let your prayers and life embrace the world. Since we bear God's name, we need to act in ways that honour God. An inconsistent life is a poor witness to Christ. Peterson commented, 'People can think correctly and behave rightly and worship politely and still live badly – live anemically, live individualistically self-enclosed lives, live bored and insipid and trivial lives.'[41] It is not primarily about what we say we believe or what we say to God, but how we live our lives. This is why James said, 'Faith by itself, if it is not accompanied by action, is dead' and then repeated himself to underline the point: 'Faith without deeds is dead' (James 2:17, 26 NIV). Sheryl Haw, Director of Micah Network, said, 'We judge others by their actions, but ourselves by our good intentions.' It is not about good intentions. Too many prayers are said with good intentions that are not backed up by action. Better yet, let's both pray and act in ways that embrace the world.

This is a dangerous prayer. It is no use praying, 'God, may your will be done to help victims of the tsunami', if we have money in our pocket that can help. It is no use crying out, 'God, change me', if we are not willing to act and live differently. It is no use pleading, 'God, help my friend know you', if we are not prepared to ask a question or open up a conversation about faith. It is useless articulating, 'Your kingdom come here on earth in our country and bring heaven to our city', if we are not prepared to have our eyes opened, our arms stretched out and our hearts broken with what bothers God. 'Your will be done' is a dangerous prayer because God invites us to be willing to be part of the answer to our prayer. Sometimes the answer to our prayer is completely beyond us, and we need to rely on God completely. Often, part of the answer to our prayer is within our own resources, and we can then be part of the answer to our prayers, in cooperation with God.

Wilkinson-Hayes suggests that God is unlikely to intervene in the world if we have the resources available to be the answer to our prayer, yet drawing close to God in prayer helps us align our will with God's:

> Now I am in no way saying that prayer is not important. Prayer is vital if we are to live as disciples. Prayer draws us towards the heart of God. Prayer reminds us of the source of our life and being. Gazing on the face of God helps us to let go of the unimportant and the irrelevant in life. Prayer helps us remember where we really belong, and stops us getting too preoccupied with things that have no eternal value. But our prayer has to be lived in order for it to be completed and to make a real difference.[42]

Prayer and action are linked. Crosby comments that there is no dichotomy between action and prayer, 'no dichotomy between our prayers, wherein we cry to the Lord to be heard, and our ministry, wherein we respond to the cries of people in need.'[43]

Crossan develops the valuable missional lesson that prayer is not divorced from action. He frames prayer as 'empowerment by participation in and collaboration with God'.[44] It is about request and gratitude, saying 'please' and 'thanks', and about participating and collaborating with God in action for justice. Moving through prayers of request and thanksgiving to prayers of empowerment is a healthy sign of maturity. Although not using the explicit term, Crossan encourages participating and collaborating in *missio Dei*, the mission of God. This includes taking care of all of creation and treating our earthly home as consecrated. Says Crossan:

> We owe it to God to run God's world responsibly. . . . We owe God adequate care of all God's creation. We owe God collaboration in hallowing

God's name, in establishing God's kingdom, and in doing God's will 'as in heaven so also on earth'. We owe it to God to cease focusing on heaven, especially in order to avoid focusing on earth. We owe it to God to ensure that there is enough food and not too much debt in God's well-run Household.[45]

Our neighbourhoods and our world need this kind of scrutiny. The missional prayer is a framework for interceding for the world but also a challenge to action and a measuring stick for the value of applied faith.

Living Our Prayer

Jesus did not have a 'prayer life' as much as he lived a 'life of prayer'. It might be more helpful to speak of the 'Life Prayer of Jesus' (especially when referring to the 'Lord's Prayer') rather than the 'prayer life of Jesus'. Jesus lived his one life well, and prayer was at the heart of this life. When we look closely at the way the gospels present the person of Jesus, we discover an authentic and fully integrated relationship between life and prayer. Jesus lived what he prayed and prayed what he lived. It seems that Jesus lived prayer and prayed life in all its dimensions.

When Jesus responded to the disciples' plea for a lesson on prayer (Luke 11:2–4), what he gave them was not a checklist or formula for a new and improved 'prayer life' (although this is precisely how the Lord's Prayer is often treated). Instead, Jesus provided a window into the 'Life Prayer' that so shaped and empowered his daily existence.

When we ask Jesus, 'Teach us to pray', we will pray this dangerous prayer but also live it in being sold out to God's will. This is a big prayer to pray – that God would bring heaven to earth. It is a big prayer to live – as if our life-purpose is to bring heaven to earth. If we live this prayer we seek to outwork God's purposes and initiate God's counterculture. As in all things, Jesus is our example in praying 'Your will be done.' The phrase was on Jesus' lips in the Garden of Gethse-mane (Matthew 26:36–46). But he prayed it and then lived it – being taken from the garden to his trial and then the cross. Following Jesus' example, we offer our lives as sold out to God's purposes. In an in-dividualist society of self-determination, the life of a Jesus follower is radically countercultural, inviting God's will to be outworked in our lives and world.

Praying the Dangerous Prayer is not a 'stained-glass' approach to prayer that separates us from the world. It is not a mere challenge about the importance of a half-hour prayer each morning, as if that is the ultimate test of spirituality. God invites us into a love relationship that is far broader than merely prayer during quiet times or in church. Authentic prayer does not come from gritting teeth and determining 'I should pray more', but from realizing we are loved, wanting to love God in return, and wanting to love the world and what God wants to do beyond our walls. Thus we pray, 'Your will be done – like it is in heaven, God, where things reflect your purposes and what you have created us for.'

Jon Owen, a Christian urban mission worker, moved to Sydney with his family a few years ago. He found two families, neighbours, who had been arguing and facing each other off. The police were regularly called. Fighting was escalating and violence was expected. When the fight literally broke out, there was actually a police car in the street, which had been stationed there for a week. But the two police officers decided caution was better than valour as the fight spread to include a hundred people. It was an awful situation of a neighbourhood descending into violence.

The fight made headlines in the media. Questions were asked. People wanted to blame someone. Jon Owen commented that the most striking commentary was made by a Community Police Officer. Matter-of-factly he said, 'As the tension was bubbling away before the riot, all it would have taken was for one respected, non-partisan mem-ber of the local community to stand up and say "Enough is enough, let's talk" and it would have been enough to have gotten both sides to communicate, and yet, there was no one, no one willing to take a stand for the local neighbourhood. All it needed was one person, and that person did not step forward.'[46]

Who of us is willing to count the cost and *stand in the gap* when the world around us is most distant from God's dream and needing restoration?

Journaling and Discussion

1. Watch one or more World Vision video clips about prayer and justice and 'wrapping children in prayer' (from http://now. worldvision.org/prayer) and share your responses to the clip(s).
2. Watch the video of Chrishan Jeyaratnam from Hillsong Sydney discuss what it means to pray for God's will to be done.[47]
3. How do you view prayer? How might the view of prayer from this chapter, including Abraham's prayer-haggling, affect how you pray?
4. What situations of injustice and issues in the world do you feel most passionately about and are most likely to bring you to tears? How can you and your church pray and act to make a difference about them, using the missional prayer?
5. What does it mean to pray 'Your kingdom come in Melbourne [or your city], your will be done, in Hawthorn [or your suburb] as in heaven'? Where could you stand in the gap for your community?
6. What would you like to stop doing, start doing, or do differently as a result of reading this chapter and reflecting on its implications?
7. Watch the Common Grace and Bible Society video of Arch-bishop Mark Coleridge from the Brisbane Catholic Archdiocese reflect on 'Your kingdom come', and discuss or journal your response.[48]
8. Finish by meditating and praying this prayer, and expanding on it in praying also for the global issues that bring tears to your eyes and God's:

> Christ Jesus, our Lord, we refuse to let our hearts be troubled because we believe in God and believe also in you.

Yet we pray, with tears, for those who are troubled:
    the cancer patient facing pain and struggle,
    the pregnant girl fearing family condemnation,
    the businessperson with crippling debts,
    the social worker swamped by need,
    the unemployed youth.
May our hearts never accept a superficial peace
that exults in our own peace with God
while other hearts are troubled.
(Tony Cupit)[49]

3

Integral Mission of 'our daily bread'

Lord let me hear, hear more and more:
Hear the sounds of great rejoicing, hear a person barely sigh,
Hear the ring of truth, and hollowness of those who live a lie,
Hear the wail of starving people who will die,
Hear the voice of our Lord in the cry.
Lord let me hear.
            (Ross Langmead, 'Lord Let Me See' [song], from On the
                                      Road, *used with permission)*

Reframing Communion

It was the same routine almost every day after primary school in
Year 5 and 6. David, Owen, Mark, Eddie and I would ride together
to Eddie's place, bounce on his trampoline and listen to music. In-
between somersaults and listening to U2 or Rose Tattoo, we went
into the kitchen and cooked slice after slice of toast. We would liber-
ally smother the white bread with butter and Vegemite – good Aussie
boys that we were – and devour loaves of bread over the afternoon.

Our experience partly reflected the camaraderie Jesus shared with
his disciples over meals. When Jesus said, 'I am the bread of life' (John
6:35), he was referring to white bread and Vegemite. But Jesus' approach to meals meant more than consuming food. My mates and
I used to say, 'Let's go to Eddie's for the trampoline and toast', but we
were mainly looking forward to the chance to hang out. Today I often

say to friends, 'Let's do coffee', not for the caffeine but out of a desire for social connection (but it is good when the coffee is good too). In Jesus' day, people would say, 'Let's break bread.' The agenda was not mainly to consume that element of a staple diet but to celebrate their culture's rich expression of hospitality. Sharing bread together implied a deep relational connection and commitment to one another's wellbeing.

Jesus' eating patterns embodied inclusive hospitality at its best. He celebrated parties, some would say with all the wrong people. One of the harshest criticisms his opponents could cobble together was after Jesus ate with 'tax collectors and other disreputable sinners' and they asked, 'Why does your teacher eat with such scum?' (Matthew 9:10–11). After teaching one day, Jesus' disciples told him to send people home because they needed to eat, and Jesus said, 'You give them something to eat', and distributed a feast of bread and fish (Luke 9:13–17 NRSVA). There was a miracle of multiplied food to fill the stomachs of the hungry crowd, but also a social miracle as people from diverse backgrounds ate together. Then on his last night with his disciples, he hosted the Last Supper and told his followers to keep eating like that to remember him. He was not urging them, predominantly, to have a regular ritual to eat a minuscule piece of bread and a mouthful of grape juice. I am convinced that the main point of Jesus initiating the Lord's Supper or communion was that Jesus wanted his disciples to continue his patterns of eating; with inclusive hospitality. Jesus was saying, 'I'm going, but let the party continue.'[1]

Community and mission can happen at their best in the context of eating our daily bread. I agree with Michael Frost that a simple and natural approach to sharing life together starts with sharing meals, which can lead in surprising and eye-opening directions: 'Serve up something delicious, and then just watch the conversation flow and trust God to stick his nose in somewhere.'[2] When we are too busy to have meals with one another in our church community, and with neighbours and friends (and strangers) in our broader community, then we are too busy. As we pray, 'Give us today our daily bread', let's pray and make time for eating our daily bread in the same ways Jesus did – as a context for sharing life and fostering relationships. A danger of a materialistic society is to restrict food to a utilitarian commodity, rather than view its sharing as a context for relationships.

One of the best things our church AuburnLife has done over recent years is host a community meal as part of our community ministry 'AuburnHub'. It started as a lunch and moved to dinner, with English conversation classes for international students, migrants and visitors. We've shared weekly meals and hospitality with hundreds of new friends from dozens of countries. Sometimes people from church cook. Other times our new friends cook a meal from their cultural background. The food has been tasty. But the conversation has been nourishing too. For those of us with a church background, we've learned about other people's cultural and faith (or no faith) backgrounds. For visitors curious about Christianity and the church where we eat, it has been an opportunity to ask questions about faith.

We have stained-glass windows in our church, including a beautiful picture of Jesus at the end of our building, which is unusual for a Baptist church, but they were there when we inherited the building from another church denomination. When one student asked, 'Who is that?', Rob Hand, our AuburnHub coordinator, had to explain who Jesus was. Before we started the Hub, not many of us realized that people from some parts of the world have no exposure to Christianity or Jesus. We don't make listening to an evangelistic message a part of our programme or a condition of learning English. But informally, breaking bread over a meal has been our best opportunity to share about Jesus and the life he offers. As a Baptist church we share communion on Sundays once per month, but there is something about Wednesday night community meals that feels more authentically eucharistic, a time of sharing the life of Jesus.

The image of Jesus as the bread of life, and using bread to symbolize his body, is especially powerful remembering that Jesus used this image in a Middle Eastern context. A group of recent Hub visitors were Iraqi engineering students. I love their preferred menu. If you have ever been to a Middle Eastern meal with friends, you would know that the drink, meat and salad come in generous and bountiful supply with rich tastes and textures. There is more bread than any other food item – thick, freshly baked loaves of bread which sit in the middle of the table. After the dishes are emptied, the beautiful thing about the bread is that it can be used as a mopping-up tool. Similarly, Jesus wants to be at the centre of our tables and lives; and as we enjoy Jesus, he helps us experience and bring out the tastes and fullness of life.[3]

When I pray, 'Give us today our daily bread', my prayer includes a longing to reconnect with Jesus as the bread of life. There is a spiritual element to this prayer. It also reminds me to pray for and give priority to sharing daily bread with neighbours and friends, and strangers who can become friends. There have been periods in the church's interpretation of the Lord's Prayer that suggested 'daily bread' was all about spiritual nourishment. Although we might pray for 'daily bread' and include in our request the desire to reconnect with Jesus spiritually and with friends over meals, the main application is more literal – for God to provide us with our daily bread and needs.

A God Who Provides

Teaching about God as provider is a wonderful yet abused belief. Viewing God as a divine butler who serves up whatever we ask feeds right into the consumeristic and greedy lifestyles of Western society. Prosperity theology, or the health and wealth gospel, is heretical teaching that says God wants all of his children to be rich and prosperous, usually conditional on whether we have faith and donate to Christian ministries.[4] It promises wellbeing, health and wholeness that we can enjoy as gifts of God, and we should not expect that we need to suffer as Christians. My main objection to prosperity theology for Western Christians is that it feeds into our consumeristic desires and transfers materialism into our faith. For non-Western Christians, tragically it simply does not always work and in situations of outright poverty the effects can be drastically worse. Christians still get sick and go hungry, and it is not because they lack faith. To suggest suffering is a result of lack of faith is to heap spiritual abuse on top of the unjust treatment that the world dishes out to the world's poor.

A God who grants us every wish is an attractive idea.

My wife Jenni remembers her primary school religious education teacher explaining how she prayed to God for $20, went home and found $20 in her letterbox. It is terrific when God provides in surprising ways. When Jenni heard that God answered prayers for exactly what was asked for, in $20 notes, she went home and asked God for $20, and went and looked for a note in her letterbox. To her disappointment, there was no financial provision posted by God that day. A number of Jenni's classmates found similarly empty letterboxes.

God does sometimes provide in serendipitous ways. But it is destructive to link faith to an assumption that God will always provide miraculously when we ask. It also distorts our view of who God is and how God shows love for us.

The adult cartoon *Family Guy* has an episode where Jesus comes to dinner. After Jesus tells his Easter weekend story, Brian, the talking dog, asks Jesus to prove he is really who he says he is. 'OK, I'll be the one to say it. How do we know you're really Jesus? Can you perform miracles?' 'Sure. How about this?' Jesus turned their baked dinners into ice-cream sundaes. The daughter Meg says, 'I love you, Jesus.'

It is natural to express love for a God who provides us with nice things that our hearts desire.

Despite the dangers of prosperity theology, one of the characteristics of God is generous provision and hospitality. It is the nature of God to care for people. God put Adam and Eve in a garden with everything they needed. God made a world with all the food and sustenance we need, and beauty and fun that adds goodness to life. When God rescued Israel out of Egypt he provided for them (and was known as *'Jehovah Jireh'* or 'God our provider'). Jehovah provided for Israel every day. Jesus, the new Moses, noticed the lack of lunch at a teaching seminar and provided bread in a remote place (Matthew 14:13–21). He provided for the lack of wine at a wedding (John 2:1–11). As one of his last acts, he offered bread and wine to his followers and invited them to remember him through eating and drinking together (Luke 22:7–30).

Revolutionary Prayer

The missional prayer has a beautiful pattern. It balances prayers to God with prayers for us. It sends our life to God and invites God's life to us. The prayer moves from bringing heaven to earth, to prayers for meals, relationships and temptations. It honours God – 'Our Father, hallowed be your name' – with an amazing and radical picture of God as loving Father, who cares for and loves and is committed to his children. It invites God to create a revolution in our world – 'Your kingdom come, your will be done' – and the associated rebellion against the status quo. And it leads on to prayers for us – for provision, forgiveness and protection – but with revolutionary implications.

The good news of the gospel is that God is a generous provider, gracious forgiver and reliable protector. God is committed to us and committed to act in these ways. Sometimes we do not feel like it. But these are prayers we can build our lives on.

Let's note, however, what we are not asking for with our daily bread. Firstly, we are not asking for delicacies we want but basics we need; it is bread, not cake, that is the object of request. The quality and sustainability of what we are asking for is important. Secondly, we are not asking for provision for each and every day into the future, but for needs for today. This prayer invites us to a revolutionary place of contentment. Thirdly, most significantly, we are not asking for ourselves individually ('give me what I need') but for us communally ('give us'). The 'us' for whom we invite life and provision is all of us, all the world. The missional prayer brings these revolutionary ideas that refocus our prayers.

Slow-Food Revolution

In telling us to pray for bread, Jesus reminds us to look to God for basic good food. In a day and age of fast food, fatty cooking and over-indulgent delicacies, good-quality sustainable food is invaluable. We pray for bread, not cake.

Over the last few years I have developed a keen interest in endurance running and triathlons. Preparing for events takes consistent training and exercise. But the biggest thing I have learned is that success and sustainability is not only about working hard at physical training, but also staying healthy in other ways, especially good nutrition. As I prepared for my first Ironman triathlon, friends from my club told me that race day is difficult, but it's even more difficult to arrive at race day without injury or sickness – with all the training and preparation that leads up to an event. So I have developed more discipline about going to bed early, getting sufficient sleep and eating well. Isabella De Castella, my sports nutritionist, advised me on eating well for training and events. I have cut down on sugar and processed foods, and been careful about combining food types – good combinations of protein, fats and carbohydrates, with 3 litres of water a day to stay hydrated. I have become more aware than ever about what I put into my mouth. As well as setting me up for better success in sporting events, it has made a huge difference to my overall health and wellbeing.

I am also learning a lot from the 'slow-food' movement. In response to the mushrooming of 'fast-food' practices, slow food advocates want their eating to be different. Fast food encourages people to eat quickly, not necessarily enjoying the food or the relationships that go with a communal meal. The food that fast-food providers sell is usually imported from a distance and not very healthy. Slow food, in contrast, is meant to be enjoyed slowly and in relationship with others. The ideal is that it is good wholesome food, grown locally and organically, and cooked healthily.

Slow food might be more expensive, but only in the short term. It is a long-term investment for our own health. Buying organically and locally is also a long-term investment in our future. Buying organic food encourages growers and retailers to give more priority to organically grown food. Buying locally encourages and rewards local farmers. This cuts down on the environmental costs of transporting food too far. I am not an advocate for buying from one's own country for nationalistic reasons. Workers in China and Peru deserve a job (and a fair wage) as much as workers in the West. When we buy food that is grown locally, there are fewer environmental costs related to transport. I am also challenged by slow food to eat what is in season, and look forward to different fruits and vegetables as their seasons come around rather than after they have been frozen for six months or more. There is also something about denying oneself – it is good to learn to live with less volume and variety of food rather than being relatively greedy and gluttonous as a consumer.

Not everyone in the world can afford good organic food. But our household prefers it, and are voting economically (with our purchases) for its development. I hope and pray the agricultural sector will develop in more organic directions, for the sake of the whole world. When I pray for *bread*, I want to pray and plan to eat healthily. Let's pray ourselves into a slow-food revolution.

Contentment Revolution

Another big lesson is trust and contentment. When we look to God as provider, we pray for bread (not cake) and for today (not tomorrow as well). I tend to be preoccupied with planning, scheming and working out various eventualities. Having food not merely for tomorrow but for the next fortnight, and means of security for the next year or even decade, is what I prefer. But this dangerous prayer invites me to recalibrate towards contentment for today.

Two movies drove home for me the gift of contentment.

The Aviator was a 2004 film about Howard Hughes (played by Leonardo DiCaprio), at one time the richest man in the world. All he ever wanted in life was to *get* more. He lived for more of everything. He wanted more money, so he turned his inherited wealth into a billion dollars of assets. To get more pleasure, he paid richly to indulge his sexual fantasies. To seek more fame, he broke into Hollywood to make and star in his own movies. For more thrills, he built and piloted the fastest jet plane of his time. He wanted more power, so he dealt political favours and manipulated government. All he wanted was more, convinced it would lead to true satisfaction. History tells a different story. Hughes finished life colourless, addicted and driven insane by fears. He finished with enough money for years, decades, even centuries.[5]

There is a warning here. It is also an implied caution in Jesus' teaching. It is the call of 'danger danger danger' related to provision. When investing, financial advisors have to watch out for insider trading and be careful not to use confidential information to get a financial advantage. Jesus offers appropriate insider-trading advice. He counsels selling out on losses. The toys of this world do not last. We come naked into the world and, in effect, leave it naked. Billy Graham says no one leaves earth with a furniture removal truck following their hearse. They who die with the most toys still die. Edmund Burke reminds us, 'All you own at the end of your life will belong to someone else.' The secret is: life is not about accumulating and grabbing for security, as much as that message is widespread.

Australian social analyst Clive Hamilton describes the rampant disease of our society as 'affluenza'.[6] The term suggests our drive for success without contentment. It applies when we are unwilling to settle for less than the best of everything. But affluenza's effects are not satisfying, even for people as rich as Howard Hughes.

The 2003 film *Mother Teresa*, starring Olivia Hussey, is another film featuring contentment. All Mother Teresa ever wanted in life was to *give* more to the poorest of the poor. She gave her time, committed to a life of service. She gave her resources, committed to a life of simplicity. She gave her heart, committed to a life of compassion. The movie showed that she lived what she preached. As well as leading a large, growing organization, she cleaned bandages and swept floors. She used to go through the boxes of donated shoes and pick out the shoes that were most ill-fitting for herself, so no one else had to wear them. That seems dysfunctional and self-abusive, or at least unnecessary. But she epitomized storing treasures in heaven. Although managing huge budgets and speaking to presidents, she was not swayed by money and power, and lived with contentment from day to day.

The aviator – Howard Hughes, and the Catholic nun – Mother Teresa, are in stark contrast. Who reflected the ethos of the missional prayer? Who had the most positive influence on the world and those around them? One demonstrated the epitome of business success and political influence, but at the expense of manic drivenness and mental ill-health. The other displayed the epitome of sacrificial service, helping so many and inspiring millions to live for others.

The positive example of Mother Teresa which I aspire to emulate in some small ways (and the negative example of Howard Hughes which I want to avoid) leads me to pray this dangerous prayer and ask God for the contentment of 'bread for today'. This is the prayer I ask Jesus to 'teach me to pray' and 'teach me to live'. Remember, Jesus did not have a prayer life as much as he lived a life of prayer. He lived the basic trust and contentment suggested by this prayer for provision of needs. I need Jesus to teach me to trust more, rather than strive for more.

Praying for enough for today offers a promise of provision, but also this challenge towards contentment. Brazilian theologian and activist Leonardo Boff suggests, 'As we settle into deep listening for God's word, how ludicrous the grasping ways of daily life become!'[7] The dangerous prayer helps us with this transformation from drivenness and grasping towards contentment and generosity.

The Mazatec Indians of Mexico have a culture where they do not give information or share faith because of their concept of 'limited good'. They believe there is only so much good, and so much knowledge, and so much love, friendship and land to go around. If you love a second friend, you love the first friend less. When you say, 'Have a nice day', that decreases your own pleasure. If you teach something, you drain your own knowledge. If you admit learning something from someone, you are admitting stealing it from them.[8] Of course, that sounds ludicrous. But how different am I with material possessions or living generously? How much of our culture influences us to want to *get* more rather than *give* more?

Greedy consumerism is rampant throughout the Western world and has infiltrated our approach to church.

Twentieth-century theologian Reinhold Niebuhr criticized Karl Barth for not speaking against communism in Hungary, implying the West needed to intervene and free that country's citizens to better serve God. Barth remained silent, albeit saying quietly to friends and students that people in the West had better watch themselves – they were in *just as much* danger from affluence as Eastern Europe was from persecution.[9] What evidence is there that consumerism is a primary religion in the Western world?

Religion determines values, guides behaviour, and is something we look to for meaningful life in the here and now – isn't that consumerism for many of us? We get identity from possessions, and increasingly from experiences. Even in relation to church, we 'church shop', for a place that meets our needs. We consider what we got out of a worship service (as if it is there to 'serve' us), and go home feeling well fed or not. Thus church turns into a mall for consuming religious goods and services, rather than an equipping station to send us into our world.

Russian novelist and philosopher Leo Tolstoy tells the instructive story, 'How Much Land Does One Man Need?'[10] A peasant, who becomes a landowner, is given the opportunity to run as far as he can in one day to accumulate more land, as much land as he can pace out in one day. However, in the physical exercise of striving to run further to get more land, he dies. Instead of hundreds of hectares of land, he gets a small plot of land to be buried in, and the story concludes: 'This is how much land a man needs.' The story illustrates the tension of goals common to many of us. The man goes from peasant poverty to rich capitalist, but in the process loses his life and soul.

I have learned more about contentment from sisters and brothers in the Majority World or global South. Wong Young Soon, Director of Malaysian Care, inspired me about what God's people are doing to alleviate poverty and build neighbourhood resilience in Malaysia. He told Tolstoy's story, and then observed that indigenous people have traditionally owned land communally, with a different concept of ownership. Everything can be shared. Communal rights to land are only for those who can use it. Land ultimately belongs to the Creator. *Owning the Earth* explains this history, and that communal ownership is also tied to social obligations, including sharing resources, taking care of the sick and working communally.[11] Some parts of this still exist in slums. Unfortunately, traditional concepts of communality are in decline. In Soon's context, for example, Malaysian indigenous people are now more likely to sell game (wild animals they have killed for food) to their neighbours rather than share and give it. This increases productivity, as the promise of profit increases output, but social obligations and equality are lost.[12]

The challenge to contentment and the need to consider basic needs for all is imperative given that 20% of the world's population use 80% of the world's resources, and 80% have to get by on 20%.[13] If all lived like we in the Western world do, the earth would not survive. In fact, we are already at unsustainable levels of consumption and pollution from many angles.

Contentment is not limited to a personal spiritual virtue but is a global imperative. When emerging church leader Brian McLaren left pastoral ministry, he decided to explore two important questions: (1) What are the biggest problems in our world today? And (2) how do the life and teachings of Jesus address these problems? His resulting appeal, *Everything Must Change*, analyses the environmental, poverty, security and spirituality crises that the world faces. The ways we consume resources (the prosperity system), protect our resources and borders (the security system) and share resources (the equity system) is a 'suicide machine'. We demand more resources and produce more waste than the environment can cope with. The military machine sells more weapons than anyone needs, a fraction of which would care for the world's poor and their basic needs. Developing countries pay more in debt repayment than what they receive in aid. Six million children under 5 years of age starve each year, equivalent to an annual twenty-first-century holocaust. This adds up to a dysfunctional and psychopathic system.

McLaren passionately calls for a new kind of Christianity that engages with these global issues. He asks, why have Christians debated the origin of species but given minimal attention to the conservation of the species? Why is there widespread commitment to the protection of the unborn but less conviction about not killing *enemies* who are already born? Why do churches allocate time to brainstorm dreams for our churches but give less space to dreaming about transforming the world? He suggests that rather than eschatologically guessing the date for the end of the world, let's consider what world we are leaving for our children.

Moving from a suicidal global system demands a contentment revolution. McLaren calls for a new global love economy and other societal systems that facilitate us living with our creaturely limits to help avert self-destruction. We need a living faith that offers us fresh imagination, and a framing story that is not focused on accumulating, defending and competing:

> If our framing story tells us that we are free and responsible creatures in a creation made by a good, wise, and loving God, and that our Creator wants us to pursue virtue, collaboration, peace, and mutual care for one another and all living creatures, and that our lives can have profound meaning if we align ourselves with God's wisdom, character, and dreams for us . . . then our society will take a radically different direction, and our world will become a very different place.[14]

A contentment revolution is not limited to personal spirituality, but a globally minded spirituality embracing Dangerous Prayer can help transform our global systems.

Parker Palmer counsels not saying our prayers with special pleading for a scarce resource before someone else gets it, which is playing by the world's rules, but instead aiming for 'a life that returns constantly to that silent, solitary place within us where we encounter God and life's abundance becomes manifest'.[15] Crossan continues his metaphor of the Lord's Prayer, praying to God as a good householder and pleading for him to care for the household. The prayer for daily bread reflects the biblical prophets' appeal to distribute the goodness of the world fairly, like a well-run household with God as householder. This is something we can learn from the philosophical ideals of communion: 'Equality in Christ meant equality in menu.' 'Enoughism' for all of us is the virtue we need, which requires advocacy, especially for those who are socially and systemically vulnerable, and contentment, for those of us who are well fed and abundantly resourced.[16] This calls for a contentment revolution; related also to another revolution that is woven throughout this dangerous prayer.

First-Person Plural Revolution

As interesting as what we pray for (our food or bread), and when (for today), is what precedes the request (give *us*). The whole prayer is addressed not to *my* father who is in heaven but *our* father who is in heaven. When we pray the missional prayer, the radical revolution is that we pray in community with the church (not only as individual believers) and in solidarity with the world (not just thinking of Christian community). We are praying for all who are inside and beyond the walls of the church. Our prayers are focused towards young and old, rich and poor, people educated to greater or lesser degrees, and all nations and continents. We embrace Australia and Alaska, Chicago and Croatia, Melbourne and Mauritius. Across all differences, for all children and for all people of the world, we pray, '*Our* Father, give *us* our food for today.' There is a special adopted relationship of God as Father that those who accept Jesus are invited into. But there is a truth that God has parental interest in all people of the world.

How can we pray for provision for ourselves without consciously praying for others who lack basic needs? The inclusive and world-embracing nature of the missional prayer means we cannot pray just for ourselves without thinking of the needs of others.

This is especially significant when we come to praying for bread or food, when so many people in the world go hungry at night. I have never prayed this prayer for 'daily bread' with consciousness that the next meal might be a problem for me and my family. That has not been our experience. At times we are more likely to need to pray for self-control – keep too much food, and the wrong kind of food, away from us. As the writer of Proverbs says:

Give me neither poverty nor riches,
but give me only my daily bread.
Otherwise, I may have too much and disown you
and say, 'Who is the LORD?'
Or I may become poor and steal,
and so dishonour the name of my God.

Proverbs 30:8b–9 NIV

We need to be content with what we already have, rather than focusing on the provision of what we don't have. But every single day the lack of having enough is a problem for too many people in this world.

Daily bread is especially significant for people who live on a subsistence income. In Jesus' day, many day labourers worked and prayed for daily bread. It brings a fresh urgency to the prayer for food when your family may go hungry at night. Ulrich Luz says the phrase 'daily bread' is for day labourers and their need for food for today – being able to survive with basic nourishment, not all material desires.[17] He urges us to pray especially for those whose subsistence is a daily concern.

The Dangerous Prayer, as Crosby says, is a daily summons for those of us in the First World to be aware of the reality and causes of poverty and hunger in the rest of the global family.[18] Postcolonial feminist theologian Musa W. Dube Shomanah writes from the context of her impoverished nation:

> To pray for daily bread is thus a simple but clear reminder to all Christians that it is God's will that there be food for all but that food is *not* readily available to all on a daily basis. Praying for daily bread confronts those with refrigerators, storerooms and supermarkets stuffed with food with a question: Why do I not feel urgency to pray for daily bread while some homeless, some jobless and even some hard-working persons have nothing to put on their plates and that of their children? The Lord's Prayer gives Christian communities and institutions the task of being responsible sons and daughters of God who need to remember those members of the family who do not have any daily bread, but who cannot go on

without it. It challenges all who eat, store or throw away food to be producers and givers of daily bread.[19]

Are you aware of how many people starve daily? The world is coming through, hopefully, a hunger crisis unlike anything it has seen in more than fifty years. An estimated 1.4 billion people lived in extreme poverty in 2005, living on less than $1.25 a day. Thankfully this was down from 1.9 billion in 1981. However, a spike in global food prices in 2008, followed by the Global Financial Crisis in 2009 and 2010, pushed 100–150 million more people into poverty.[20] Bread for the World reports that today 805 million people struggle with hunger and 1.2 billion live in extreme poverty on less than $1.25 a day. Moreover, 2.6 million children die each year from hunger-related causes and 100 million children under 5 are undernourished and underweight.[21]

These figures are almost unbelievable – that there are people who do not have enough to eat while we live in a world of excess food and so much technology and infrastructure. The global context is reminiscent of Marie Antoinette – surrounded by luxury and opulence – saying of the peasants, 'What – they don't have bread to eat? If they don't have bread . . . tell them to eat cake!' She couldn't comprehend, in her life of excess, that others simply did not have enough to eat.

When we pray, 'Give us our daily bread', in the face of such a global lack of daily food, let's plead with God to set the world aright. Let's be part of the answer to our prayer by giving generously and living simply, so others can simply live.

The good news of the Bible is that God provides and cares for us. The challenge for much of the church in the West, including the missional church, is to lift our prayer and concern towards global issues. When I was travelling in the United States, the bus driver who picked up our group took us into the city and could not find a parking spot. Our local guide prayed, 'God, please help us find a parking spot and help the driver not to crash.' What a ridiculous prayer. Maybe it shows that God is interested in our daily lives. But what we needed was simple patience and another circle around the block, and to trust the skill of the driver. Is God really more interested in my parking spot than 20,000 people dying of starvation today? And if not, then why are we praying for parking spots more than for daily food for those who are starving?

Kim Hammond and I told the story in *Sentness* about a mum cooking breakfast for her sons.[22] Eddie and Murray fought over who would get the first pancake to eat. The mother, always ready for a teaching moment, said, 'Boys, boys, don't argue – if Jesus was here he'd say, "Let my brother have the first pancake."' Mum was pleased to see Murray's eyes grow large with apparent revelation. Murray turned to his younger brother and generously offered, 'Eddie . . . you be Jesus.'

The danger Kim and I identified is that our Christianity can become consumerist. Left to my natural tendencies, I admit that I choose religious paths that will comfortably suit *me*, and ways of following Jesus that offer *me* fulfilment. But this falls far short of radical discipleship. It is not the essence of missional spirituality. It fails to foster an outward-looking, world-engaging missional church. It looks to Jesus as a cosmic butler there to serve me, or a therapist to make me feel better, or a life coach to help me get ahead, or an image consultant who makes me look successful, or a lucky charm that gives me an unfair advantage over others. That is a distorted way of following Jesus that desperately needs recalibration. But it is not easy. For my spirituality, I need the recalibration tool of the missional prayer. It reminds me and forms me to follow Jesus in Jesus' way.

Jesus challenges me to see the dignity of humanity and the truth of Christ in everyone. We respond (or not) to people in need, as if we respond to Christ. Jesus sees it like that. In Matthew 25:31–46, Jesus told his disciples that in the final judgment he would reward those who provided him with food and drink, clothing and hospitality, and who cared for and visited him. Jesus said they will reply curiously,

'Lord, when did we ever see you hungry and feed you? Or thirsty and give you something to drink? Or a stranger and show you hospitality? Or naked and give you clothing? When did we ever see you sick or in prison and visit you?' They did not realize they had shown compassion to Jesus or done these acts. But Jesus as King will explain how he sees their acts of service done to others: 'I tell you the truth, when you did it to one of the least of these my brothers and sisters, you were doing it to me!'

Likewise, Jesus explains, those who refused to help the least of these were in effect refusing to help Jesus. Ray Anderson warns: 'If the church cannot see Christ in the eyes of those who suffer in this world, it will fail to discern the face of Christ when it kneels to receive communion . . . [It is an] injustice of serving themselves while ignoring the lack of bread in the hands of others.'[23]

Enjoying Food

In seeking to provide – through our prayers and action – food for others, it does not mean we cannot enjoy good food ourselves. Food is a gift to be enjoyed for ourselves, as well as a gift and resource to share beyond ourselves. Walter Benjamin commented, 'For it is only in company that eating is done justice; food must be divided and distributed if it is to be well received.'[24] Frost encourages us in a world of hunger to be like Joseph who saved food so he could distribute it generously; and in a world of poor food-choices in the West, to be like Daniel who didn't eat everything offered to him.[25] Let's be both generous and discerning about food.

I have learned a fresh appreciation for food, alongside a conscience about global inequality in food distribution, from chef-turned-pastor Simon Holt. His book *Eating Heaven* prompted me to think about where I most appreciate food, and the tables that help me live life to the fullest. I love eggs and coffee as a treat to start the day. Carrot, celery, apple and ginger juice is my afternoon drink of choice. Our family dinners are admittedly a mixed bag, but at their best help us reconnect and laugh together. Our church AuburnLife is at its best circled around the communion table praying for one another, lunching together after Sunday Stuff down the road at Hotel Hawthorn, or sharing hospitality with international students at AuburnHub. When I think about the places that are most life-giving for me, and where I most fruitfully cooperate with God in mission, our home dining table, church communion and dining tables, work lunch table, and café and pub tables are among my favourite places. Whether in the company of friends or family, or reading and writing alone in a café, heaven comes close for me at meal tables.

Like a seasoned travel writer, Holt guides his readers from the backyard barbeque to five-star dining, from the family kitchen to the multicultural table, and from city cafés to festive gatherings. Along the way, his love of food and friendship with diverse people is contagious. My favourite chapter was 'The Five-star Table'. Holt dines with his wife for a delightful and expensive nine-course culinary adventure (for the second time in his life), and then discusses how he balances being committed to justice as well as beauty. This a tension when 1.1 billion people in the world consume too few calories, and another 1.1 billion consume too many. How we eat, what we eat, where the food comes from, who we share food with – these are hugely challenging issues. Holt invites us to reflect on bigger issues, not by offering simplistic answers but by balancing the challenge for food security and justice for all with the delightful invitation to enjoy our food and relationships.

It is a timely message that we can live out our deepest values and celebrate the best of life – and invite others to do the same – sitting at different tables. Concludes Holt:

> It is through the daily practice of the table that we live a life worth living. Through the table we know who we are, where we come from, what we value and believe. At the table we learn what it means to be family and how to live in responsible, loving relationships. Through the table we live our neighbourliness and citizenship, express our allegiance to particular places and communities, and claim our sense of home and belonging. At the table we celebrate beauty and express solidarity with those who are broken and hungry.[26]

Who is at your table, I wonder?

We need a first-person plural revolution to pray for and provide food for all of us in the world. Some radicals pray this grace before their meals:

Some have food,
Some have none,
God bless the revolution!

Adrian Greenwood, from Uniting Church of Australia's 'morepraxis' movement, wrote a similar expanded grace: 'Jesus, as we eat we remember those who will not and covenant to be part of a solution. Grant all who are fed a hunger for justice and you. Amen.'[27] Those of us who don't need to pray for our literal need of daily bread ought to expend our breath praying for those for whom it is a desperate need.

The New Monasticism is a movement helping Protestants rediscover the richness of contemplative spirituality that is engaged with the world. One of its marks is 'sharing economic resources with community members and the needy among us'. Shane Claiborne suggests redistributing resources is a natural practice in a community or family that loves each other. As a church sees the nature and extent of local and global needs, sharing is the only fitting response. Catholic social worker Dorothy Day underlined this gospel ethic when she maintained, 'If you have two coats, one belongs to the poor' (cf. Luke 3:11; Acts 2:44–45).[28]

Youth for Christ New Zealand has reinvented itself as Incedo. Their reinvention revolves around common spiritual practices to form a new 'missional order'. One of their practices is to bring valuable goods to team events and make them available for other teams to take and use. This is collective and communal Christianity at its best.

At AuburnLife, one of our leaders, Julia Rhyder, suggested we start a list of goods and tools we own that we can lend (or give) to one another. At another time, a Papua New Guinean student, Elsie, had a relative die back in Papua New Guinea. Church friends pitched in and gave her money for the plane ticket.

When we are prepared to pay the price for community at the expense of our hip-pocket nerve, often the most sensitive nerve for

Westerners, we know we are doing something different. But what does it mean to really grasp *our* sense of community in our world? How can we pray to 'our Father' for 'our daily bread' and embrace the truth that God takes an interest in the whole world? That is the profound challenge of praying 'our'.

Basic Needs

The Dangerous Prayer pleads that our world would have daily food provided for everyone. There is enough food supply – our problem is the distribution and delivery system. But we also pray this for clean water, education, access to Scriptures in people's own language, and a church that speaks every culture's language. Let's keep the basic elements of provision in mind when we pray.

Pope John Paul II commented on our need for global compassion – considering all basic needs:

> In our own time, there are so many needs which demand a compassionate response from Christians. Our world is entering the new millennium burdened by the contradictions of an economic, cultural and technological progress which offers immense possibilities to a fortunate few, while leaving millions of others not only on the margins of progress but in living conditions far below the minimum demanded by human dignity. How can it be that even today there are still people dying of hunger? Condemned to illiteracy? Lacking the most basic medical care? Without a roof over their heads?[29]

Surely God's purpose for the world includes basic provision for all – it is how God designed the world, and where God is leading history. J.R. Woodward urges us to grasp a vision of God's preferred future – our hope in where God's story is leading – and let that shape our calling. We can join God in writing a new future:

> If God's future is the elimination of hunger and thirst, how are our economic practices at this moment anticipating the reality of abundance?

If God's future is the elimination of weapons of war and having people live peacefully with each other, how should we treat our enemies at this moment? If God's future is renewed creation with clean air, fresh air and natural beauty, are we living sustainable lives in the present? Future-oriented living forces us to answer these questions in concrete ways.[30]

Grasping a vision for God's preferred future for the world helps inform our praying and our action.

Sarah Thomson helped open my eyes to the simple unmet need for clean water for one in eight people in the world. Sarah did her first Ironman triathlon the year before me and encouraged me to give it a go. As we trained together she explained she works with Water Aid, an organization focused on helping the world's poorest communities access safe water, hygiene and sanitation.[31] Those of us who live in Australia, America or Europe do not usually have to pray or pay for clean water. We go to our tap, turn it on and have a fresh supply of clean water to wash in or even drink. We use our toilet and push a button to flush. These are luxuries that many people in the world do not enjoy. Actually it is not a luxury but a basic need and a foundational human right, but many people in the world would see it as a comparative luxury. It is estimated that 748 million people do not have clean water accessible in their home or even in their village and have to walk up to several hours to fill water containers. About 2.5 billion people do not have access to toilets and have to use outside areas.

Apart from the inconvenience, this brings huge health challenges. Children end up missing school because of sickness, apart from the time needed for collecting water. Mothers find it difficult to keep their babies clean. Young girls miss school for days when they menstruate. Farmers cannot irrigate their crops. Clean water is foundational for aid and community development. Without this first step in development it is difficult to develop community hygiene, health and education. Water Aid's advocacy reminds us to pray not just, 'Give us today our daily bread', but 'Please God, give our world access to daily clean water' and 'Give *us* this day our daily dunny.' I don't think that is irreverent. What is irreverent is if it is only a prayer and not something that leads us to do what it takes to see this dream lead to action and change.

I live in a prosperous suburb. I say that by way of confession, or at least transparency. I am not embarrassed about where I live. It is where God has placed me. But relative to 99% or at least 80% of the world, I am well off and well provided for. Our family is surrounded by people who make a decent living. Some of our neighbours live in apartments or flats. Many live in big houses, with a nice car (or three or four) in their driveway. Many of our neighbours have pools (an interesting lifestyle choice given Melbourne is cool for most of the year). There are pockets of poverty in our suburb that God is opening my eyes to see, but generally most of my neighbours are not worried about the next meal on their table. This breeds a certain outlook on the world.[32] It challenges me not to forget the poverty globally beyond my neighbourhood, and also the poverty that I know is there, albeit hidden, in my own suburb. For both contexts I plead, 'Give us today our daily bread.'

Dangerous Dreaming

Remember, this is a dangerous prayer. It is no use asking for daily food for our neighbours and for the world, if we hold back the resources which we have to be part of the answer to our prayer. It is no use praying for food handouts if we are not prepared to help give people a hand up. It is fruitless asking God to help the world arrange safe water for everyone, if we are not prepared to do our part for advocating and giving for the sake of this basic human right.

I have quoted Bono saying, 'Dream up the world you want to live in. Dream at high volume!' What's your dream for our world? Or what are you convinced is God's dream for the world? Let's dream with God and pray and work in those directions. Bono was dismissed as a hopeless romantic in his advocacy for Making Poverty History.

But here is a good-news story. Twenty-five years ago 60,000 children under 5 years old died daily from malnutrition and preventable disease. In 2010 it had halved to 30,000. By 2012 it was down to 'only' 21,000 each day. That is an obscene number still. That figure is the equivalent of the number of deaths in four September 11s or a silent tsunami every fortnight! But it also shows a remarkable difference that has been made for 39,000 children's lives daily, because of simple things like access to adequate food and clean water.[33]

A Fair Go for All

I have learned the ethos of this prayer from my own Australian culture. Giving a 'fair go' to everyone is an Aussie value. We value helping out a mate or a 'battler' (someone in need). We value lifesavers who patrol our beaches or the heroes who jump in to help a drowning person in a flood or a difficult river. Journalist Muriel Porter comments:

> There are signs that the wider Australian community will listen seriously to the churches once certain conditions are met. In the land of the 'fair go', where deeds speak louder than words, high-flown ideals are viewed with suspicion and authoritarianism is despised, the churches and leaders have to demonstrate, first and foremost, that they care. Once they do, they gain real respect.[34]

When this concern and action is lacking in the church, people notice. Worse, the church is not living up to its calling.

One of Australia's most famous prime ministers was Bob Hawke (PM from 1983 to 1991). In his upbringing he is more famous for being a big drinker while at Oxford University than for being a pastor's kid. As he grew up he was involved in church. As a young adult in his university years he went to India as a delegate to the World Conference of Christian Youth. Whatever Hawke may have heard in inspirational talks and heartfelt prayers at the conference was undermined by what he saw as a faith that was irrelevant to global suffering.[35]

Hawke was attracted by the Communist Party's interest in local human needs, and repelled by how Christianity seemed removed from people's basic daily suffering. His perception was that comfortable Christians were content to merely sing and pray about taking Christ to the world, but were irrelevant and not of any practical service in their neighbourhood: 'Firstly, a great feast was held in the Bishop's residence where, under the eyes of hundreds of poor villagers staring in through the fence, delegates gorged themselves on food. Secondly, on Christmas Eve they sang, "The World to Christ We Bring, Christ to The World We Bring". And it all seemed so bloody unreal and hypocritical.'

He wandered down the street, saw children who looked miserable, and: 'It all suddenly jarred in my mind. There were those comfortable Christians up the road singing about bringing Christ to the world, and the world to Christ, and here *was* the world. And to the Christians they seemed to be totally irrelevant as the Christians were irrelevant to them.'[36] People notice when faith is removed from its social implications. It is not enough for our churches to pray for daily bread for the world around us, although that is a great start; our churches also need to be actively involved in advocacy and humanitarian efforts to provide daily bread and water, and meet basic needs and human rights.

In the past, people committed to evangelism would often carefully explain the gospel message, so that people would understand what they need to believe. These days, people are as likely to come to a place of belief after they belong to a community and see belief lived out. At other times the opportunity to be involved in compassionate behaviour is an entry point to belief and belonging. Churches are often preoccupied with moral behaviour, and can tend to exclude people who do not match up to their behavioural expectations. But it is exciting to see what happens when churches invite people to behave and minister in Jesus-like ways, in fostering God's dream for the world, even if they do not yet fully believe or belong.

In 2006 'Peter' found a church that was seeking to make a difference against poverty and invited him to be involved. The church was Foothills Neighbourhood Communities in Melbourne. Steve Barrington, an inspiring urban missionary and member of God's Squad Motor-cycle Gang, was the church leader. Steve encouraged the church to host a Make Poverty History event in the local park, together with other churches and community groups. They had a guest speaker, John Smith the president of God's Squad, to talk about global needs, and invited the broader community to consider action against poverty. The members of Foothills do not know the extent of who they influenced that day, but they do know the significance it had for Peter.

At the time Peter was homeless, estranged from his family and sleeping in a car near the park. When he saw the action start, he walked over and asked what was happening. The idea of people working together to make a difference captured his imagination, and he offered his help. Through the day he supported the effort and in the afternoon he helped pack up. The group told him about Foothills church, and he said he was not really interested in church. But a new kind of church that hosted this sort of event was perhaps worth checking out. Their active faith impressed him. As he got involved he came to understand what Christianity is about, and encountered Jesus. His family and friends were amazed at the change in his life. What is impressive is that the church being active in advocacy invited Peter to work alongside them for justice, and as he was made welcome and participated in God's mission he came to believe and belong. He had his imagination captured and his life turned around by being invited to join a church that was seeking to make a global difference.[37] Peter came to faith through the witness of a community who pointed to God's fatherly interest in all the world, who were committed to working for the kingdom in all spheres of life and not limited to Sunday spirituality, and who were acting to facilitate bread for today for the world (and not just cake for some).

Let's keep crying out to God for more of that kind of transformation.

Experimental Farms

We need ways of feeding a hungry world. In 1788 the first convicts arrived from England to Sydney Harbour, but they found the immediate environment was not ideal for food production. It is a beautiful bay and its sandstone clay shelf is ideal for building a city, but it was not suitable for farming land. The early settlement nearly starved and had to rely on supply ships travelling halfway across the world. It did not help that they took a few years to work out the southern hemisphere's seasons – and planted as if they were still in the northern hemisphere. In 1791 the freed convict James Ruse asked for a grant of land on the westernmost part of the colony. He hacked out virgin scrubland and made the first viable crop-producing farm. He called it Experiment Farm. The whole colony held its collective breath. The farm produced a bumper harvest, and it was then renamed Model Farm. Ruse's farm became a model for others to follow. His original cottage stands as a national monument. Frost tells this story and suggests the church needs to be like an experiment farm and function as an example to others of the hope of the power of the gospel.[38] That is true in a spiritual sense. But today we also need whole new approaches to model farms for a world that is starving.

I don't know what new farming systems might look like, or what is needed to feed the world. I know it's not just about farms, nor the political and economic systems of the world that conspire against food for all. But we need innovative approaches to agricultural development. Praying 'Give us today our daily bread' includes a plea that God would raise up the best of minds and the most creative thinkers who can tackle these issues. If you are looking for a vocational challenge to make a difference, consider the ministry of tackling global poverty – not only through aid or advocacy, as important as those are; but through inventing new approaches to maximizing sustainable agriculture.

My Humanity Is Bound with Yours

As well as the Aussie value of a fair go for all, the world could learn new approaches to food distribution if we adopted the African concept of *ubuntu*. Ubuntu is the concept of communal identity: 'I am because we are.' Desmond Tutu drew on the cultural value of ubuntu in his appeal for forgiveness and reconciliation in South Africa: 'You can't be human all by yourself, and when you have this quality – ubuntu – you are known for your generosity. We think of ourselves far too frequently as just individuals, separated from one another, whereas you are connected and what you do affects the whole world.'

Ubuntu is an indigenous African concept, embracing a communal approach to life that is distinct from Western individualism. Tutu commented further:

> Ubuntu is very difficult to render into a Western language. It speaks of the very essence of being human. When we want to give high praise to someone we say . . . 'Hey, so-and-so has ubuntu.' Then you are generous, you are hospitable, you are friendly and caring and compassionate. You share what you have. It is to say, 'My humanity is caught up, is inextricably bound up, in yours.' We belong in a bundle of life. We say, 'A person is a person through other persons.' It is not, 'I think therefore I am.' It says rather: 'I am human because I belong. I participate, I share.' A person with ubuntu is open and available to others, affirming of others, does not feel threatened that others are able and good, for he or she has a proper self-assurance that comes from knowing that he or she belongs in a greater whole and is diminished when others are humiliated or diminished, when others are tortured or oppressed, or treated as if they were less than who they are.[39]

There is a story about a game which an anthropologist suggested to children in an African tribe. He placed a basket of fruit next to a tree and said the first kid to reach the fruit would win it all. After he told them to run, they grabbed each other's hands and ran together, then sat down together and enjoyed the fruits. Asked why they cooperated and ran together when one could have won it all for themselves, they replied, '*Ubuntu!* How can one of us be happy if all the others are sad?' The world needs more of that ubuntu connectivity.

Hunger for a Better World

Suzanne Collins captures my imagination about the fight for a more just world – with food for all – in *The Hunger Games*, and sequels *Catching Fire* and *Mockingjay*.[40] Part of the popularity of these dystopian young adult works of fiction is the struggle against an obviously unjust political and economic system. The post-apocalyptic country in what was North America but is now ravaged by environmental crises and war is called *Panem*, which is 'bread' in Latin. The name is ironic since most people in the twelve 'districts' struggle in slum-like conditions of poverty, working tirelessly for the benefit of the luxurious Capitol. The plot is based on a lottery-based fight to the death between twenty-four teenagers enforced by the imperial Capitol forces. The resulting 'Hunger Games' are presented as entertainment in a televised *Survivor*-like show, but are ultimately designed to punish the districts for a previous rebellion and keep them under control. It echoes the ancient Roman approach of 'peacekeeping' with 'bread and circuses' in return for subservience.[41]

Sixteen-year-old Katniss Everdeen is selected to represent her district, and along with Peeta the baker's son from her district and twenty-two other 'tributes', she is given weapons training and beauty treatments to prepare for the macabre gladiatorial contest. Part of the tension of the books is a romantic love triangle – as Katniss acts out a romance with Peeta, but also loves Gale her childhood buddy. The books strike a deeper chord with readers – not just around political intrigue and romantic passion, but with a hunger for a better world and what part each of us may play in that. Katniss and her collaborators rebel against the status quo, albeit at great personal cost. My favourite scene is after Katniss meets those wounded in a field hospital, and televises her cry for rebellion: 'We must fight back . . .

Fire is catching.'[42] St Augustine of Hippo reportedly said, 'Hope has two beautiful daughters: Anger, at the way things are, and Courage, to work for change.' Katniss embodies anger at the system's evils and a resolve to fight for transformation. She catalyses a movement and hope for a different future.

In our world, when we open our eyes to the pain and struggle, we see distortions. We all should hunger for a better world, given that many hunger for sufficient bread each day, while others enjoy abundance. The 99% in the world who are poorer do not exist to enrich the 1%. This is why Katniss and compatriots resist the Capitol's plans; and why youth today have their imaginations captured by a hunger for a better world.

Panem is set in a different world from ours and a distant future. Yet it's easy to imagine that our world *could* suffer the same military and environmental disasters that made Panem, and it has clear parallels to how our society functions. Panem's ancestors destroyed the world's environment. The rich became obsessed with fashion and appearance. The powerful used their power not to serve but to oppress, and the media not to inform but to manipulate. The Capitol hoards its riches in stark contrast to the poverty of the districts. Yet gross inequity exists in our cities in the Western world, let alone when we compare ourselves with the Majority World.

Hunger Games is 'dystopian' literature, as a cautionary tale of what the world can become.[43] It is also 'self-directed satire' that makes us look at how the world currently functions with our consumerism; our tendency to violence and acceptance of war; our acceptance of children in slave labour (making clothing and chocolate we like cheap); and our perverse view of entertainment.[44] *Hunger Games* is not merely dystopian about a potential future, but is a challenge to our current reality; it is a prophetic mirror that challenges how our world is dysfunctionally structured, and how we accept the status quo because it suits and comforts us, despite bringing harm to our souls.

Why are the *Hunger Games* stories so popular? We love Katniss and her co-conspirators for their stand for social justice. Their example is an antidote to feelings of powerlessness to change global systems that perpetuate injustice. Perhaps they spark hope and courage in readers to change the systems; not merely being aware of the needs around us, but doing something about them. Reading *Hunger Games* prompts me to ask what kind of society we want and how we can resist corrupting influences and forge a better world.

The Dangerous Prayer is a prayer for that sort of world. When we pray 'Our Father in heaven', we pray to God as a heavenly parent interested in justice and peace for all people in the world – including those who are equivalent to people living in poverty in the districts of Panem. When we pray 'Your kingdom come' we are praying for a rebellion against the status quo that opposes God's dream for the world. And when we pray 'Give us this day our daily bread' we ask not just for you and me, but for those for whom daily bread is a constant concern and lack. You and I do not live in Panem. But we have our own hunger problems in the world – and a whole host of other issues in which the world falls short of God's dream. As you work and *hunger* for a better world, 'may the odds be ever in your favour'. Even better, may God answer your prayer for our daily bread.

Journaling and Discussion

1. Watch a video clip about praying with your neighbour by *Thou Shalt Laugh* stand-up comedian Michael Jr: 'Pray with Your Neighbor' and share your response to the clip.[45]
2. What does it mean to pray, 'Give us today our daily bread'?
3. What is your experience of God providing for you?
4. As you pray this prayer for the world, what does it mean for you to be part of the answer to your prayer?
5. What would you like to stop doing, start doing, or do differently as a result of reading this chapter and reflecting on its implications?
6. Watch the Common Grace and Bible Society video of John Dickson inviting us to meaningfully pray, 'Give us today our daily bread', and discuss or journal your response.[46]

7. Finish by meditating and praying this prayer, and expanding on it in praying also for the global issues that bring tears to your eyes and God's:

> May your real needs be met, and
> Your imagined needs be seen for what they are.
> May your desires be holy and healthy.
> May you glorify God in your spirit, soul, and body,
> Until you meet him (hopefully after a good life 'full of years').
> Amen.[47]

4

Countercultural Reconciliation of 'Forgive us'

The injunction to forgive may seem like just one 'nugget'
of Christian wisdom. It is that but also much more. It is
the defining stance of Jesus Christ, wisdom personified,
and a central pillar of the Christian way of life.

(Miroslav Volf)[1]

A Bishop's Gift (*Les Misérables*)

The convict Jean Valjean, main character in Victor Hugo's *Les Misérables*, arrives one evening on the doorstep of the Bishop of Digne, Bienvenu Myriel, looking for a bed and a meal. The bishop invites him in and offers hospitality, but overnight Valjean takes the silver and escapes, only to be dragged back by the police. To Valjean's amazement the bishop lies and says he *gave* the silver to Valjean and meant him to take more. The bishop holds loosely to his belongings, and generously gives to Valjean two silver candlesticks. The musical brings out the emotion of the moment as Bienvenu sings to Valjean, appealing for him to use the silver to become honest, redeemed out of darkness for God's purposes. He encourages Valjean to see it as God's provision to change his whole life direction. Surprised by the bishop's display of unmerited favour, Valjean breaks parole and sets out to start life with a new identity. He becomes a respected businessperson and mayor of a town and cares for the beautiful Cosette, illegitimate daughter of Fantine. Empowered by the grace he was shown, he lives with grace towards others – especially Cosette and ironically Inspector Javert. But he must flee, at different times, from Javert who feels driven by the law to identify and imprison him again.

It inspires me whenever I watch that scene that the affirming words of forgiveness and call to repentance spoken by the bishop had such a revolutionary impact on Valjean's life. *Les Misérables* is fiction, and as an unfortunate reflection of how religious leaders were seen, sadly Hugo's positive picture of the bishop was satirical.[2] Nevertheless, it is a powerful illustration of grace and conversion. It reminds us to seize the day in speaking and demonstrating good news into people's lives.

We live in a violent and often bitter world where people's safety cannot be guaranteed in our neighbourhoods, and wars have scarred the globe over the last century. The missional challenge and dangerous prayer is to work for peace, forgiveness and reconciliation. It is easier to be forgiven than to forgive, and easier to forgive our friends than our enemies, but Jesus calls us to pray and act with countercultural grace and forgiveness (Luke 5:19–25; 6:27–42). This chapter is thus a response to violence in the world – at a global level of militarism, and at a local level of abuse and lack of respect for people's humanity. It challenges readers to pray for and live out what really is good news about the power of the gospel for reconciliation – among friends and families, in neighbourhoods and community groups, and on broader intercultural and global levels.

Life Beyond Regret

In 2009 I attended the funeral for Nana Dot Humphreys, my last surviving grandparent. Nana lived a full and vibrant life. She was a country girl, who married her wartime sweetheart, had four children, including twins for her last two, my mum Lorraine and Lynette. The four kids used to ride their horses to school. Lynette died when she was 20, a few weeks before her planned wedding. After

Nana's funeral, Mum showed me where the road accident occurred that killed Lynette. Nan and Pop farmed, till they moved into town for their health. Pop died back in 1983, when I was 12, the same age as my son Benjamin was at the time of Nana's funeral. Funerals have a way of getting you to think about the important things in life; what you want to do with life, and what you do not want to leave undone.

Erma Bombeck, after she found out she had a fatal disease, wrote this reflection before she died:

If I Had My Life to Live Over

If I had my life to live over, I would have talked less and listened more.

I would have invited friends over to dinner even if the carpet was stained and the sofa faded . . .

I would have taken the time to listen to my grandfather ramble about his youth . . .

I would have burned the pink candle sculpted like a rose before it melted in storage . . .

I would have sat on the lawn with my children and not worried about grass stains . . .

I would have cried and laughed less while watching television – and more while watching life . . .

I would have gone to bed when I was sick instead of pretending the earth would go into a holding pattern if I weren't there for the day . . .

Instead of wishing away nine months of pregnancy, I'd have cherished every moment and realized that the wonderment growing inside me was the only chance in life to assist God in a miracle.

When my kids kissed me impetuously, I would never have said, 'Later. Now go get washed up for dinner.'

There would have been more 'I love you's'. More 'I'm sorrys' . . .

But mostly, given another shot at life, I would seize every minute . . . look at it and really see it . . . live it . . . and never give it back.[3]

What is your response to that? As well as a desire for more 'I'm sorrys', life also needs more 'I forgive yous'. Many people go through life not acknowledging their own garbage nor being gracious to others with forgiveness. Pastorally, some of the saddest visits or pastoral conversations are with older people who refuse to acknowledge their own complicity with relationship breakdowns (I'm sorry) or refuse to let go of hurts or perceived injustices (I forgive you).

Complexity and Simplicity of Confession

When confession and forgiveness are abstract concepts which we accept intellectually, they are very easy. But when the issues are personal and complex, they get very difficult.

As a pastor, in some unhealthy conflict situations, I have been expected to say sorry but not had that reciprocated. It sometimes felt like the congregation thought they had hired a pastor as a punching bag. Sometimes I may have been quicker to confess than others, even too quick to say 'sorry' as a pastor. Sometimes in ministry I have said sorry more often than anyone has said sorry to me, which may be a reflection of my tendency to make mistakes, but it may also reflect a lack of mutuality. No longer do I automatically say sorry when someone feels offended or aggrieved. If I have been part of the problem, or have made a mistake, apology can be part of the appropriate solution and response. But being the 'hired holy person' does not put more responsibility on me to apologize – that is a responsibility on all of us in a faith community when the situation calls for it.

I have always been ready to confess and apologize, but recently I realize I have a lot to learn about confession.

Do you recall a time you got into trouble and had to 'fess up'?

I used to travel with my family on sightseeing trips around the Blue Mountains where we grew up. Dad and Mum were coach drivers and tour guides. My brother Jason was the apprentice tour guide – he went for the work experience. I went for the scones and cake at the afternoon tea stop in Megalong Valley. One day Jason and I found the train set of the café operator, Keith Duncan. This man's train set was not the normal arrangement for a spare room. He had built a 3-foot wide gauge train line and had an engine and several rail cars. We thought it would be fun to push one of the carriages, which gathered momentum. We were proud of our train-driving capabilities. But then we saw that he had not finished the rail tracks. Despite our efforts to slow the carriage, it went off the end of the tracks and got bogged in the dirt. We gathered up the courage and confessed to Dad, who was not impressed. Dad told us we had to apologize to Mr Duncan. So we apologized. We were graciously forgiven. It was one the hardest things we had to face. But it was also one of the most useful lessons I learned. When you do wrong, you confess. It was made easier when Mr Duncan smiled graciously.

Apologizing for childhood pranks when you are little and cute is relatively straightforward. Confession becomes more complicated as we grow older.

I warm to the sentiment of the title of a book on my shelf, *Yes Lord, I Have Sinned, but I Have Several Good Excuses.*[4] It reminds me of my own self-justifying behaviour when it comes to prayer. It urges me to examine myself and ask what sins I need to ask forgiveness for, without excuses. Perhaps excuses are a helpful pointer to sins which I hide from God and myself. Confession and forgiveness are sometimes complex and difficult.

Public Confession

There are times when corporate confession is necessary. Political leaders can confess the sin of a nation against minority people. Australian Prime Minister Kevin Rudd gave an apology in 2008 to Australia's indigenous peoples for the removal of Indigenous children from their families in the 'Stolen Generations'.[5] Church leaders can confess the abuse and negligence of leaders in the past, as has been necessary over abysmal treatment of sexual abuse victims.[6] Corporate confession is a potentially healing process. It is negligent when leaders cannot accept the responsibility of sins that their groups have instigated in the past.

University years are commonly filled with a mix of campus sport, part-time work, fears about the future, wild parties, anxious planning, tentative relationships and occasional career planning. This flurry of activity is interspersed with occasional tutorials and lectures. Donald Miller and his university friends had an unusual idea for expressing their Christian witness in the midst of a campus party. They constructed a confessional booth with a sign advertising that they were open for confessions. They were not sure whether there would be any interest or whether they would be burned down, in opposition to their bold witness.

But while other students were getting drunk, stoned, naked or all three, Miller and his friends constructed the confession booth, dressed like monks, smoked pipes and opened the confessional curtain. The catch was that instead of accepting confessions, they asked forgiveness. When the first curious students came through, the Christians confessed that, as followers of Jesus, they had not been very loving. They apologized for the Crusades, for televangelists, for neglecting the poor, for genocides conducted in the name of God, and they apologized that in their selfishness they had misrepresented Christ on campus. Rather than seeking to defend Christianity as a belief system, they acknowledged wrongs done in the name of religion and reasserted what Jesus really stood for.

Students responded with appreciation, hugged the Christian 'confessors', and some asked what Christianity was really about. Many students were followed up with invitations to participate in advocacy for the poor around the world, be involved in a local soup kitchen and attend evangelistic Bible studies.[7]

I suspect Miller's group was on to something timely in humbly creating space for honest faith conversations. Let's not underestimate the power of appropriate confession and making space for forgiveness.

Enjoying God's 'Enough'

My wife Jenni has a habit, at the beginning of each year, of asking her colleagues and fellow church members to select a 'word for the year'. One year I chose 'enough' and painted the word on a small canvas to remind me to sit with the message of that word. It invites me to a place of contentment and satisfaction without feeling the need for more things. It also invites me to a posture of grace, realizing I do not need to do or perform more in order for God to love and forgive me.

When Jenni and I have an argument, it comes between us. It is difficult to enjoy our relationship, or life in general, or focus on other things, until we sort it out, say sorry and forgive if necessary. It is the same with God. When things come between us and God, we need to sort it out.

When we confess to God and seek reconciliation by getting on friendly terms with God again, the good news is that the God of the Bible is a forgiving God. Our Father is one who is eager to answer our prayers for forgiveness.

I usually jog three times per week. In Western culture many people run for fitness. But in Jesus' day, senior people hardly ever even walked briskly because that would have reflected a lack of dignity or 'gravitas'. Today, it would be like a member of government wearing skimpy swimwear for the television cameras to see; or turning up late to a job interview wearing shorts; or a minister wearing a T-shirt to conduct a wedding. Those things are not dignified given the situation. Jesus told an imagination-grabbing story of an old bloke who saw his son coming home. This was the son who had snubbed his nose at him, manipulated him to get his inheritance and wasted his money. But when the father saw his son, he ran to meet him, the son who had acted like a jerk and cursed him. The inspiration I get from that story is about the forgiving and welcoming heart of God.[8]

Confession helps us accept the reality of forgiveness which is already offered. We do not earn forgiveness. Forgiveness lies in the nature of God, which is more than something we earn or deserve. It is a gift of grace. God described God's self to Moses in this way: 'The LORD, the LORD God, compassionate and gracious, slow to anger, and abounding in lovingkindness and truth; who keeps lovingkindness for thousands, who forgives iniquity, transgression and sin' (Exodus 34:6–7a NASB). When the psalmist described the praiseworthy virtues of God, he began with the forgiving character of God: 'Praise the LORD, my soul; all my inmost being, praise his holy name. Praise the LORD, my soul, and forget not all his benefits – who forgives all your sins' (Psalm 103:1–3a NIV). One of the earliest passages of the Bible that I read when I first became a Christian was about the confidence we can have in God answering our prayers for forgiveness: 'If we claim we have no sin, we are only fooling ourselves and not living in the truth. But if we confess our sins to him, he is faithful and just to forgive us our sins and to cleanse us from all wickedness' (1 John 1:8–9).

The beauty of enjoying God's forgiveness and grace means that we are then better equipped to show grace and forgiveness to others. Tom Wright explains that as we breathe forgiveness in, we have the freshness to breathe forgiveness out to others:

> It is our birthright, as the followers of Jesus, to breathe in true divine forgiveness day by day, as the cool clean air which our spiritual lungs need instead of the grimy, germ-laden air that is pumped at us from all sides. And, once we start inhaling God's fresh air, there is a good chance that we will start to breathe it out, too. As we learn what it is like to be forgiven, we begin to discover that it is possible, and indeed joyful, to forgive others.[9]

Life and Prayer Works Better When We Forgive

There are strong verses in the Bible on the importance of echoing the forgiveness we receive by generously forgiving others, as in this episode when Peter asked Jesus specifically:

> 'Lord, how often should I forgive someone who sins against me? Seven times?'

> 'No, not seven times,' Jesus replied, 'but seventy times seven!'
>
> Matthew 18:21–22

Jesus teaches us to pray, live and receive forgiveness, 'as we forgive those who sin against us'. We are forgiven *as* we forgive. The forgiving are forgiven. Forgiveness is at the heart of the message of the gospel, so let's not undermine it by neglecting forgiveness.

This is one point in the missional prayer where our prayer is linked directly with our behaviour. We ask God to 'forgive us' even as we behave in forgiveness towards our sisters and brothers – 'as we forgive those who sin against us'. Experiencing God's forgiveness helps us forgive others. If we refuse to forgive others, then that may be a sign that we do not really believe God's forgiveness. The father running towards his son shows the willingness of God to forgive us. The sulking brother shows the miserly approach of a sibling who thinks his brother should not be forgiven. There is 'no such thing as a free calf', according to the unforgiving sibling.[10]

A friend showed me a better response once. He said instead of shunning a friend who sins, we should reach out to them and – he showed me this with actions – grab and hold our friend.

If we refuse to be generous with grace and forgiveness to others, forgiveness will not flow to us from God. Expositor Douglas Hare explains it is not that God's forgiveness is in proportion to ours, but we have to repent of our hardness of heart before God will forgive us.[11] When Peter asked Jesus how often we should forgive, Jesus said seventy times seven; that is, an infinite number of times. To illustrate this, Jesus told the story of the unforgiving debtor. The king forgave him the equivalent of millions of dollars instead of foreclosing and selling off his family. But ironically that man went to another servant and demanded repayment of a debt worth thousands of dollars, and had him imprisoned. Understandably, the king was furious when he heard: 'You evil servant! I forgave you that tremendous debt because you pleaded with me. Shouldn't you have mercy on your fellow servant, just as I had mercy on you?' So the king threw him in prison. And Jesus warned, 'That's what my heavenly Father will do to you if you refuse to forgive your brothers and sisters from your heart' (Matthew 18:21–35).

There is a reason earlier English translations of the Lord's Prayer said 'Forgive us our debts'. We are in debt to God when we fall short of our obligations to obey God. But there are also literal financial debts to forgive. Financial obligations can be a challenge to forgive, at least to the extent that money is so important to us. I learned this when I had to let go of a number of 'debts' I was holding in my heart. I ordered a bookcase and paid extra for an additional shelf, but when delivered the additional shelf had not been added. The builder had spent more time on it than expected so thought he deserved the extra money without the extra shelf. I was convinced my cause was right, but negotiations did not work out to my advantage. On another occasion, a mortgage broker did not follow through on their commitment to donate part of their commission to charity. A tree-lopping contractor chopped a tree down but did not take the wood away, yet still expected full payment. I carried these financial debts in my heart. Then I realized it was going to be cheaper – emotionally – to let them go and forgive them. I don't believe that whenever we are ripped off we should roll over and pay. Sometimes justice demands we stand up for ourselves or advocate for someone else. But for the sake of my own heart, those debts were not worth fighting for – it was better to forgive and forget (although I remembered the details enough to write about them). When money is such an idol in Western society, it stretches our forgiveness muscles when we have to include financial debts.

Like confession, forgiveness as an abstract concept is easy. But when the offending party has really hurt us, it is not so easy. When we have been hurt by those closest to us, or by people who have not acknowledged their wrong and asked forgiveness, or by someone who continues to hurt us, then a forgiving approach is not easy to practise. Is it easier to rehearse retaliation in our minds? Have you ever, like me, gone over in your mind what you would say or do to get back at someone? What do we do about that? The issue at the heart of this part of the missional prayer is not whether we have been sinned against, but what our response will be.

Sometimes forgiveness might seem to be easy. Each one of us might react to different sins. It can make a difference who does the offending too. I have higher expectations for certain people, so that if a friend or colleague inconveniences me, I sometimes find it easier to let it slip than if it were a close family member from whom I expect more. It may not even be a 'sin' but a misunderstanding or miscommunication; however, it becomes a challenge to be gracious, even when formal forgiveness is not called for.

It costs to be unforgiving. Resentment is like a prison; when we put someone in the jail cell of hatred, we are left stuck guarding the door. It is emotionally, physically and spiritually taxing. How can we experience forgiveness, if we are holding off on giving forgiveness to others? Giving and receiving forgiveness are intimately connected.

Don't Forgive Too Soon

It costs to forgive too. There are plenty of distorted interpretations of 'You must forgive' which seem to support the view that victims must passively suffer abuse. We do not have to think and act like doormats. That is not what Jesus is encouraging here. 'Turn the other cheek' is not about accepting whatever slaps people send your way (Matthew 5:39). The act in those days was more a demand to be treated as an equal, rather than accepting a backhand insult.[12] Forgiving others is not about letting people roll us over and treat us less than we deserve. Even the contemporary cliché 'Forgive and forget' is unhelpful and sometimes a potentially dangerous combination. Moreover, forgiveness does not necessarily mean we have to be friends again with the perpetrator. We do not have to hold back from being assertive for fear of being rejected or abandoned, or because we want to avoid hurting others' feelings.

Don't Forgive Too Soon develops this idea. With a subtitle of *Extending the Two Hands That Heal*, it suggests forgiveness is about extending one hand to say, 'No, you can't do that any more', and the other hand calms the oppressor and urges them towards good. Forgiveness is not a passive exercise. The writers suggest it can be helpful to think of forgiveness as a process. Forgiveness, especially complex forgiveness, is like grief or any emotional wound that takes five stages to work through. It is outdated to think of these stages as a linear progression. But people might experience these responses in any order, and often cyclically, and sometimes without all of the responses. But consider which of these responses you have gone through when or if you need to forgive someone who has hurt you, or who owes you a debt:

1. *Denial.* I don't admit I was hurt, so I minimize it. 'It is not so bad – I can handle this.'
2. *Anger.* It is their fault that I am hurt. To work out who 'they' are, it is the person whom you least want to talk to when the phone rings, or about which we comment, 'They always do [such and such].'
3. *Bargaining.* At this stage we set up conditions to be fulfilled before we are ready to forgive; for example, I will only forgive when they treat me better or promise something.
4. *Depression.* At this stage we say to ourselves, 'It's my fault that I'm hurt. No one understands. I should have tried harder.'
5. *Acceptance.* Finally and hopefully, in this final stage we look forward to growth from the hurt, and are ready to face new things.

These steps offer a process to non-violent responses rather than striking back when we are hurt.[13]

Another helpful framework for forgiveness is considering our conflict style. New Zealand urban mission activist Michael Duncan suggests there are five styles:[14]

- First there are the avoiders, who walk away from conflict whenever it arises.
- Second are yielders, who respond by acknowledging the other person is right and they are wrong.
- Third are compromisers, who seek to give and take. They might give 50% of the ground to keep 50%.
- Fourth are resolvers, who seek to fix the issue.
- Fifth are competitors, who say 'I am going to win.'

Which style can you identify with? And which style would you like to adopt? Which do you feel is ideal?

You might think resolving the issue is always ideal. But actually it depends on the situation. Not all issues can be resolved or are worth the effort. Sometimes other approaches to conflict are appropriate:

- When is it appropriate to avoid? When you are in danger of losing the relationship.
- When is it appropriate to yield? Definitely when you are wrong.
- When is it best to compromise? When it is a secondary issue.
- When is it appropriate to compete and aim to win? When it is a life-and-death issue.
- And when is it appropriate to resolve? Only when you can.

Which is the most appropriate response? It all depends. Duncan's approach to conflict styles helps me understand when to forgive directly, when to be prepared to compromise, and when to discipline myself to move beyond avoidance to really resolving an issue.

Forgiveness is most challenging when people think the worst of me. For a season, I experienced people in my life who thought the worst of me, questioned my motives, belittled me, and held grudges for years. They seemed to be continually critical. These are people whom I loved and wanted to reach out to, and tried to believe the best of. But from my perspective they did not reflect respect and graciousness. At times I wondered if I would ever trust them, or count them as friends, or look forward to time with them. That grieves me. But what do you do with that sort of relationship? Where does confession and forgiveness fit there?

One important ingredient of healthy relationships is to maintain boundaries that do not accept manipulation and emotional abuse. Henry Cloud and John Townsend's book *Boundaries* popularized the idea that boundaries distinguish us from other people and help clarify what is mine and what is someone else's. Boundaries show what I am responsible for and what I am not. They show we do not have to meet every need and answer every complaint, as if my role in life is to be a people-pleaser.[15] Therapy and conversation helped me set boundaries with people who sometimes think the worst of me. It can be extremely challenging to live this out.

The 1994 romantic comedy movie *Forrest Gump* narrates the story of Forrest Gump (played by Tom Hanks) and his experience of North American history in the latter half of the twentieth century. He grew up with Jenny as his best friend. Yet Jenny has her own demons from her abusive family. She pursues a lifestyle of sex and drugs, but later returns to Forrest. They go on a long walk one day and return to her family home, a shack with horrible memories for Jenny. She grows angry, picks up a rock and throws it at the shack. It chips the paint, and she throws another – smashing a window. With reckless abandon she throws more, then collapses exhausted to the ground. Forrest looks down to her and philosophically sums up the situation that sometimes there are just not enough rocks.[16] Throwing hundreds more stones would not destroy the shack, but neither would they take away the abuse and remove the resulting misery. It was typically wise of Forrest not to say, 'What you really need to do is to forgive.' Forgiveness is a life-giving and burden-removing practice, but we can be too quick to expect it of people.

The 1989 movie *Field of Dreams* is a beautiful story of reconciliation. It alludes to the incongruity of much of our church culture – the farmer builds a baseball field in the hope people will come and fill it, just like churches can assume we build our buildings and that will be enough to attract people to come. But as can happen in the movies, it works for him. He turns his cornfield into a baseball diamond. Miraculously the old dead players turn up to play. The real miracle happens when the field that had turned into a baseball diamond then turns into a place of remembering and reconciliation between the middle-aged man and his dead father. The son's rebellion had led to the two of them not speaking. The father died. But their relationship is set right through a game of catch between this prodigal son and his ghost father. There is no apology spoken or screened. But a game of 'catch' without words better reflects the relationship reforged. The scene brings me to tears. It's a vision of the future to long for.[17]

When Forgiveness Stretches Us to the Limit

Some believers in history and around the world have stretched forgiveness to an extent that I can barely begin to imagine.

Bagina Selina was a Methodist and a 6 foot 4 inch champion boxer. In boxing he aimed for a knockout early so his opponent would not suffer; a very sweet objective for a boxer. He was socialist in politics. But he resigned months before a political coup in his country and returned to his home village. When the military came to pick him up he knew where it was heading. His wife and family heard nothing. They suspected he had been killed, but did not know for sure and knew not where his body was. One day a military man came to the widow's home and said that Bagina had been known in jail as 'a giant of the black book' because he was reading the Bible and sharing his testimony all the time and the military authorities decided to kill him. The man told the widow, 'I was one of the executioners. As we prepared to kill him, he said, "I know why I am dying but you don't know why you are killing me." He said, "Shoot me because if not they will kill you."' I cannot imagine what it would be like for Bagina's widow to forgive that man.

This story reminds me of Corrie ten Boom (a Dutch Christian Holocaust survivor) when she met a former Nazi guard who sought her forgiveness, and she instinctively prayed, 'Jesus, I cannot forgive this man. Give me your forgiveness.'[18]

Forgiveness is at its essence an exercise of letting go of a wrong. It actually helps us to move on and leave the issue in the past. Forgiveness doesn't change what happened in the past – it changes how we respond in the future. Howard Zehr comments:

> Forgiveness is letting go of the power the offence and the offender have over a person. It means no longer letting that offence and offender dominate. Without this experience of forgiveness, without this closure, the wound festers; the violation takes over our consciousness, our lives. It, and the offender, are in control. Real forgiveness, then, is an act of empowerment and healing. It allows one to move from victim to survivor.[19]

This leads me to ask, who am I struggling to forgive today? How is God wanting to be part of this process? How can the power to forgive (which comes from God alone) flow more readily through me?

Gladys Staines is someone who inspires me in forgiveness. Her husband was killed and martyred by the youth wing of a Hindu nationalist mob in Larisa, India, in January 1999. He was burned in his vehicle with their two young boys, Philip and Timothy. Graham and Gladys were in India operating a home and rehabilitation centre for lepers. Their evangelism and Bible teaching was often met with antagonism, rock pelting and death threats. And Graham and their two boys paid the ultimate price, leaving his wife Gladys and daughter Esther.

The tragic circumstances led to a groundswell movement of people protesting against the killings and pleading for tolerance. The Staines touched more people in death than in life. Gladys had a powerful testimony of forgiveness. Our family saw a television documentary where she explained, 'Jesus said, "Father forgive them, for they know not what they do." God has given me the strength to say, "Father, forgive them, for they know not what they do. I call you brother and sister and I forgive you.'" Hindu militants still have not asked for forgiveness, and still hate all Gladys stands for. Gladys's grace reflects God and the realization that people sometimes 'know not what they do'.

Gladys's forgiveness was empowered by her insight into God's forgiveness. Lack of forgiveness on our part hinders God's work of forgiveness, but vice versa an awareness of God's forgiveness helps us live lives of forgiveness. Writing in *Christianity Today*, David Seamands summarized his career and ministry with these words:

> Many years ago I was driven to the conclusion that the two major causes of most emotional problems among evangelical Christians are these: the failure to understand, receive and live out God's unconditional grace and forgiveness, and the failure to give out that unconditional love, forgiveness and grace to other people . . . We read, we hear, we believe a good theology of grace. But that's not the way we live. The good news of the Gospel of grace has not penetrated the level of our emotions.[20]

Forgiveness is a litmus test for the reality of our faith.

Thielicke preached this prayer of forgiveness in the Lord's Prayer before the occupation and fall of the Third Reich. It was a context in which something was obviously wrong with the world, then and since. In a context where evil was so evident, as Thielicke's congregation saw when they looked at Hitler's sadistic ethnic cleansing, or to the Allies' bombing of civilians. But Thielicke challenged his congregation to also look for the guilt in themselves. Like the prophet pointing to David, this prayer points its finger at us and says, 'You are the person.' This is not just the Lord's Prayer or the disciples' prayer. We are the people who need this prayer. We pray it, as the Anglican prayer book says, 'for the sins we have done and for what we have left undone that we should have done'; for sins of commission and sins of omission. Thielicke challenged his church to respond along these lines, in the context of ethnic cleansing and mass graves: 'as our armour grows thicker our debt of sympathy for our tormented world grows greater'.[21]

In the context of human rights abuses, there is a place for forgiveness, but there is also a place for bold objection and advocacy against injustice. We need liberation too, in order to denounce injustice and announce God's justice.

A church planter went to Moldova in Romania to plant a church. Local leaders did not want him in the town. They told him if he came and built anything, they would tear it down. Yet the young man went, and started by building a house for his family. The day after they moved in, they heard a knock at the door and eight men were waiting. They told him, as warned, that they were there to tear down the house. He stepped back and said, 'Do what you need to do.'

The men climbed on the roof, removing pieces one at a time. In the middle of the morning, the pastor said, 'Honey, we need to fix some lunch – please make it for twelve people.' 'What for?' she asked. 'They're our enemies. They hate us. They're tearing down our house.' The pastor replied, 'But Jesus said we are to love our enemies and to do good to those who hate us. They have been working hard. I'm sure they're hungry.' So the family invited the demolishers to lunch. The weary men came down and ate, and – no surprise – asked, 'Why are you doing this?' The pastor explained, 'Because we are followers of Jesus . . . We don't know why you're doing this, but you think you're doing something that is good and right. We don't understand that, but we love you anyway and we forgive you for doing this.'

After lunch the men climbed back on the roof, and put the roof back on piece by piece. When the church-planting couple opened a church in the village, those eight men were the first to attend.[22]

Forgiveness is intrinsic to the gospel, but is also a powerful communicator of the power and influence of the gospel.

First-Person Plural Revolutionary Forgiveness

The first-person plural revolution applies to this part of the prayer as well. We don't pray, 'Forgive me my sins', but 'Forgive us our sins.'

It is a prayer we pray for ourselves – for our need individually to be forgiven as well as our need to forgive. It is a prayer we pray collectively as a church, and on behalf of others. It is radical that we can pray this not just for ourselves, but for people in our neighbourhoods and cities, and in Athens and Amsterdam, Buton and Bangladesh. We cry to God, 'Forgive us, in this world, we your children, the garbage we go on with, the way we ignore you, the way the world is messed up.' There is a need, if someone is to be forgiven, that they cry out to God themselves. 'But God, those people in my street, people in Greece and the Netherlands, Tahiti and Thailand . . . God, help them to come to a place where they can ask for your forgiveness themselves for turning their backs on you.' This prayer is not just the Lord's Prayer but *my* prayer and *your* prayer to remind us to ask for forgiveness for ourselves. But it is also the missional prayer to remind us to ask that God would work in the lives of others so they would ask for and receive God's forgiveness.

John Hus was a priest and martyr of the fifteenth-century Protestant Reformation. Hus served in the Bethlehem chapel in Prague. A feature of the chapel was a huge inside well. Legend has it that prostitutes and swindlers had spoiled the local water, in part by making it a burial place for unwanted babies. It was a horrific loss of life and loss of good water. The church was compelled to respond to this very real local need. They dug a well near the pulpit inside the church, adding a side door for access, and it was even available for locals to use during worship services. They also arranged for art to adorn the chapel walls, commemorating the lost local children and other local scenes. The response of Hus and that chapel in Prague urges us to ask: where are we at our best in responding to local and global needs? What is our well?[23] The story also encouraged me to pray for forgiveness on behalf of my neighbourhood, and the world.

Praying for forgiveness for my own sin seems a long enough list. Praying for others may seem exhausting. I'm not suggesting God will forgive others because we ask forgiveness for them, but when I pray this for others I ask that God would help bring people to a place of repentance and forgiveness.

Reconciliation in a Violent World

Forgiveness and reconciliation is an urgent need in our violent world. The default response to violence is retaliatory violence – whether in fights between individuals or wars between nations. A radical part of Jesus' life and message was that he subverted this default response. He urged loving strangers and even enemies, and returning offence with forgiveness. We pray, 'Forgive us our sins, and forgive those who sin against us', and include a plea for forgiveness for our violent tendencies. As we pray 'Forgive *us* our sins', let's pray this on behalf of those who are initiating or responding with violence, and pray for peace and courage in non-violence. Jesus' non-violent ethic is countercultural in a violent world but critically needed. An internet story is circulating about a female CNN journalist who heard about a very old Jewish man who had been going to the Wailing Wall in Jerusalem to pray, twice a day, every day, for a long, long time. She went to the wall, and there he was, walking slowly up to the holy site. She watched him pray, and after about forty-five minutes she interviewed him. 'Pardon me, sir, I'm Rebecca Smith from CNN. What's your name?' 'Morris Feinberg,' he replied. 'Sir, how long have you been coming to the Wailing Wall to pray?' 'For about sixty years.' 'Sixty years! That's amazing! What do you pray for?' 'I pray for peace between the Christians, Jews and the Muslims. I pray for all the wars and all the hatred to stop. I pray for all our children to grow up safely as responsible adults, and to love their fellow man.' 'And how do you feel, sir, after doing this for sixty years?' 'It's like talking to a f*cking brick wall.'

How do we respond, in prayer and activism, to a violent world?

The default response to violence is violence. Christians have even developed justifications for violence, from Augustine's Just War theory to the appeal of Marxist theologians for the necessity of violent revolution. Some Christians adopt pacifism as an alternative and have practised non-resistance. There is, however, a third way of non-violence, and this is more consistent with Jesus' approach and teaching. Walter Wink developed the historical and biblical basis for Christian non-violence in his seminal book *Engaging the Powers* and the later abridged *The Powers That Be*.[24] His biblical scholarship informs non-violent movements globally, advocating for non-violence as Jesus' 'third way' rather than just war or violent liberation. Wink critiques the 'myth of redemptive violence' that is practised by the 'Domination system' that socializes people into believing that violence saves. It is taught in popular culture from cartoons to Hollywood movies, and practised in militarism and foreign policy. Jesus broke the cycle of violence by absorbing it in his flesh, and taught non-violence as a radical new way of living. Despite popular expectations, he refused to lead a violent revolution, rebuked the disciples for wanting to call fire down on inhospitable Samaritans (Luke 9:51–56), and told the disciple using his sword to save Jesus from arrest: 'No more of this' (Luke 22:51). He did not want to simply change the rulers but subvert the rules – and introduce the 'kindom' of God where people and Powers are in harmony. Non-violence is not a soft option. It calls for transformation of society and the challenge of all-inclusive forgiveness of our enemies.[25]

Wink emphasizes, furthermore, that non-violence needs to be grounded in a prayerful spirituality that liberates us from the illusions of the dominant Powers. When exhausted and overcommitted by opposing the Powers and struggling for a better society, we are driven for help beyond ourselves. Through prayer we gain help for the struggle and unmask the spell of the Powers over our lives. Says Wink:

> Prayer is never a private inner act disconnected from day-to-day realities. It is, rather, the interior battlefield where the decisive victory is won before any engagement in the outer world is possible. If we have not undergone that inner liberation in which the individual strands of the nets in which we are caught are severed, one by one, our activism may merely reflect one or another counterideology of some counter-Power. We may simply be caught up in the new collective passion, and fail to discover the possibilities God is pressing for here and now. Unprotected by prayer, our social activism runs the danger of becoming self-justifying good works. As our inner resources atrophy, the wells of love run dry, and we are slowly changed into the likeness of the beast.[26]

Prayer that subverts the myth of redemptive violence begins, at its best, with prayer for forgiveness and the resolve to adopt a posture of forgiveness towards others. Facing a world where violence is the default response to violence, this is where the prayer of Jesus is at its most radical in inspiration and dangerous to the status quo.

Martin Luther King Jr (1929–68) was an American Baptist pastor and leader in the African-American civil rights movement. In the face of mistreatment for his people, King espoused and practised non-violent civil disobedience. He wanted to prevent his people from becoming what they stood against, observing, 'The ultimate weakness of violence is that it is a descending spiral, begetting the very thing it seeks to destroy.'[27] King held a thoroughly theological conviction about the importance of social justice as part of salvation. He said, 'It has been my conviction ever since reading Rauschenbusch that any religion which professes to be concerned about the souls of men and is not concerned about the social and economic conditions that scar the soul is a spiritually moribund religion.'[28] King's echoed his famous 'I Have a Dream' speech in his 1967 Christmas Sermon in which he reiterated his vision for celebrating difference:

> I have a dream that one day men will rise up and come to see that they are made to live together as brothers. I still have a dream this morning that one day every Negro in this country, every colored person in the world, will be judged on the basis of the content of his character rather than the color of his skin, and every man will respect the dignity and worth of human personality.[29]

He challenges me to plead for God's forgiveness for any ways in which society and churches continue to discriminate against people of ethnically different backgrounds, and to plead for forgiveness for how our world so readily responds to offence with anger and violence. He was vocal against violence in America's streets and against the war in Vietnam's forests.[30] Yet King was committed to the practice of non-violent resistance.

Non-violent protest continues to be a valid and proven alternative for revolutionary change. Srdja Popovic was part of the non-violent protest that led to Slobodan Milosevic's downfall in Serbia. Popovic taught and modelled principles of non-violent protest and turning enemies into friends in Serbia, and helped protestors from other contexts think through how to practise non-violent resistance. Nonviolence does not always work, Popovic admits, but it is more likely to succeed than violent revolution (53% compared to 26%).[31] When the default response to violence and oppression is other violence, we desperately need alternative gospel approaches to forgiveness and reconciliation.

Wink learned non-violence in the struggle of apartheid South Africa. Sadly, that country is still a hotbed of ethnic tension. My friends Nigel and Trish Branken have moved with their six children into an apartment block in a troubled area of Johannesburg to live incarnationally. They have opened my eyes to the ongoing struggle for restorative justice and reconciliation in which they are active. As I was finishing this chapter, Nigel wrote an appeal for prayer (used with permission):

The xenophobic attacks are getting horrific. I have been sent videos of necklacings (people burned with petrol while bound inside a tyre) and of brutal murders. People on the streets are angry, hurting, and scared. Many are ready to fight. I have visited communities now all over my city and I am deeply concerned. Last night I witnessed a xenophobic crowd swelling and getting angry. Tonight I met with some Nigerians who live a block from us who said they were ready for a fight. They lamented about how their parents paid taxes to put our current leaders through their universities in their country for free and helped the anti-apartheid struggle. There are now reports of various countries evacuating their citizens from South Africa . . .

Trish asked . . . 'What do we do if our neighbors start getting attacked? What should we do?'

The truth is I don't know. What should we do as Christ followers should we witness this?

Non-violence is not an academic interest for Nigel and Trish and their neighbours, but a courageous option they are advocating.

Beth Barnett has written a prayer of confession that identifies the violence of others as a warning mirror for ourselves:

a liturgy for awful times
the last thing a Christian can do
is look across
at the violence of others
and say
'terrible, unthinkable!
we'd never do that'
or
'there, but for the grace of God go I'

we have a blood-red ledger
there we did go
and the grace of God did not
prevent us from slaughter

We shelled their cities, we gassed their ghettos, we napalmed their villages, we drove their children off a cliff, we burnt their men, we hanged their witch-girls, we blasted their boys, we skewered their women, we buried them in the sand to their necks and kicked them to death

everywhere and in every place
that Christians have gone
we have ridden in on violence

we did it wantonly, we did it deliberately
we did it randomly, we did it vindictively
we did it mindlessly, we did it strategically
we did it biblically

we cannot claim to not comprehend violence
shall we stay silent in shame?
we dare not stay silent in judgement.
let the blood on our hands cry out and condemn us first.[32]

Journaling and Discussion

1. Watch the Common Grace and Bible Society video of Australian indigenous leaders Uncle Graham and Grant Paulson discussing forgiveness and reconciliation. Discuss or journal your response.[33]
2. What does it mean for you to pray, 'Forgive us our sins as we forgive those who sin against us'?
3. What is your experience of God forgiving you?
4. As you pray this prayer for the world, what does it mean for you to be part of the answer to your prayer?
5. What are the implications of this chapter for you? What would you like to stop doing, start doing, or do differently as a result of reading this chapter and reflecting on its implications?
6. Meditate and pray Beth Barnett's prayer above, and expand on it in praying prayers of confession for where the church has not responded to needs around us in the way that Jesus would.
7. Finish by watching and praying through the video of 'Just Prayers – The Lord's Prayer' available online.[34]

5

Discerning Guidance of 'Deliver us'

We are not alone in suffering
Jesus goes before us
We are not alone
He knows our sorrows
He will turn our tears to joy.

I hear the sounds of the suffering
I see the terrors of war
I hear the cry of the homeless and the poor
Does all the suffering and sighing
Just fade into infinite space
Are we alone
As we suffer and groan
Can God feel our pain?
(Ross Langmead, 'We Are Not Alone in Suffering', *from* On the Road, *used with permission*)

Right and Wrong Don't Matter in the Woods

Into the Woods, the 2014 musical fantasy movie produced by Walt Disney, brings a delightful combination of storybook characters together. It's Little Red Riding Hood, Cinderella, Jack and the Beanstalk, and Rapunzel all on quests to fulfil their wishes. Their adventures get tied up with a childless couple, the baker (James Corden) and his wife

(Emily Blunt), who are striving to reverse the curse placed on them by a witch (Meryl Streep). The story has several challenges to potential happily-ever-after endings. Beyond moralistic lessons, it deals with broad ethical questions of self-defence and retribution, parenting, and how it takes a village to raise children. My favourite scene is when the baker's wife finds herself alone in the forest and tempted by Cinderella's prince. The prince flatters her and seeks to seduce the baker's wife. She struggles with the temptation, not of leaving her husband and child, but of seizing the moment with this prince while no one is looking. At first she hesitates, flustered and thinking she is in the wrong story and cannot go through with it.

But Cinderella's prince urges her to explore the opportunity. To her objection that a romance between them is not right, the prince replies with a postmodern posturing about the priority of feelings over values. He urges her to seize the moment. He suggests that for her as a peasant who knows life is unpleasant, she should let herself go with her feelings and not worry about right and wrong.

He kisses her and leaves. Disney softens the event compared to the original Broadway musical (1986) where she and the prince consummate the relationship. Both Broadway and Disney show she is left with longing for the prince yet worried about her family and values. She asserts in song that there are standards and vows as she grapples with her dilemma. She is tempted to consider trying to hold on to her husband for his provision (the baker's bread) and to nurture her child, yet pursue the affair with the prince, but backs away from the temptation of the woods.

With a final 'Never!' she finds fresh resolve to leave the dangerous woods and return to reality and faithfulness to her family. The time in the woods makes her appreciate her old life all the more – the life of fidelity to her family rather than trying to juggle faithfulness with infidelity.[1]

Many of us will identify with the baker's wife. You and I have heard the voices that say, 'Follow your feelings. Don't worry about right and wrong. Do not bother with other people's views of right and wrong when they interfere with what you feel.' In a permissive society, when Hollywood suggests to go with feelings of attraction in the moment, rather than decisions of commitment and faithfulness for a lifetime, we desperately need to understand our needs and revisit our standards in how we express ourselves sexually.

But temptation does not just come our way with a handsome bloke or pretty girl offering moments of ecstasy. Whether or not that is your experience, it is important to underline that temptation is broader than sexuality. We need wholesome and healthy boundaries for sexual expression to enjoy it to its best fulfilment, but when it comes to discerning temptation let's broaden our awareness also to sins that are hidden or subversive.

Not Just Sex

Debra Hirsch, a pastor and activist who has ministered to people of diverse sexualities for two decades, argues that the church is preoccupied with sexual sin. She challenges Christians to healthy and faithful expressions of sexuality, and to celebrate sexuality as part of a holistic spirituality. But she also bemoans 'modesty gone mad' with arbitrary boundaries and unreasonable puritanical rules around relationships, and the hierarchy of sins that is preoccupied with sex more than greed and pride, impatience and rudeness.[2] She queries:

> What is one of the first things we try to get 'cleaned up' when someone decides to follow Jesus? Their sex life. We don't hassle them about how they spend their money, their relationship to the poor, their gossiping or their temper. No, we ask them about what they are doing with their genitals – as if this is the principal thing God is concerned about.[3]

Hirsch says you can see this 'totem poling' in people's reactions to shows and movies. Christian leaders caution against the fantasy show *Game of Thrones* or even the historical episodes of *The Tudors* because of illicit sex scenes. But Hirsch suggested that of more concern is the treachery, malicious gossip, violence and murder – and for the Tudors that was often at the hands of Christian and church leaders.[4]

Where do we turn for help in discerning the real temptations of our society? How do we take our stand of 'Never!' – in the temptation that whispers in our ears when we find ourselves in the woods?

Fortunately, the missional prayer is an all-inclusive prayer. In praying through it we have pleaded for God's purposes to come into the world, asked God for provision (for the present) and forgiveness (for the past), and finally pleaded for protection from future sin: 'And don't let us yield to temptation, but deliver us from the evil one.' I like the way Jim Cotter expresses this part of the prayer:

In the hurts we absorb
from one another, forgive us.
From the trials too great to endure, spare us.
From the grip of all that is evil, free us.[5]

I don't know how vulnerable you feel, but I need this prayer. 'God, keep me from falling' needs to be on my lips. I stumble and do things I should not, and – as I used to confess each Sunday when worshipping in an Anglican church – leave things undone I should have done. I see friends slipping into sin and realize, 'There but for the grace of God go I.' I see evil overcome people in tragic circumstance, and I plead 'God, deliver us from that kind of evil.' I see all kinds of temptations and evils that keep the world from God's dream for us. We have prayed positively, 'Let your kingdom come.' But we also need to pray, 'Keep us from temptations and evils that displace your kingdom.'

Moreover, we can revolutionize the way we pray this prayer by noticing again the pronoun Jesus used. This is still not an individualist plea. We pray for ourselves, but also for one another, and anyone God has an interest in – which is everyone. We need this prayer for those who we are hoping will respond to the gospel and re-orientate their lives around God's dream. We might expand this phrase and plead, 'Please God, let them not yield to the temptation of ignoring you, or being distracted by whatever modern idols keep them preoccupied or feeling like they don't need you. And as we discern the temptations and face the evil in our global systems, please lead us in more life-giving and sustainable directions – away from dehumanization, war and terror.'

In what direction do you focus this prayer? Where do we go for discernment for our prayer? Jesus taught us this dangerous prayer, but he also modelled an answer for us. The episode we can best learn from, in discerning and overcoming temptation, is Jesus' desert time.

Jesus in the Wild

As Matthew tells the gospel, Jesus came to carry out God's big plan to make the way for people to be on friendly terms with God, and bring the world more into line with God's dream for us. Jesus was baptized, to show he was sold out to God (Matthew 3:13–17). Then he went to the desert or wilderness to think quietly about the next part of God's plan for him (Matthew 4:1–11).

In the desert Jesus had to face his demons, literally. He had to stand for the way he was going to fulfil God's purposes. He'd committed to God's purposes, in baptism; he was tested about how he'd pursue God's purposes in the desert. In the same way that Israel as a nation was tempted in the desert to do things their own way – and succumbed, Jesus was tempted – and overcame. It was the original *Man vs Wild* episode. Like a lone *Survivor* competitor, Jesus had to face various tests. *Jesus in the Wild* is a not-to-be-missed episode from the gospels. As we dream about how God wants to use us, and as we plan for how our churches can be missional and transform our neigh-bourhoods, there are powerful lessons here about *how* we do that, and how not to.

Using God for Bread

The first temptation the devil or tempter offered Jesus, after he had been fasting for forty days was, 'If you are the Son of God, tell these stones to become loaves of bread' (Matthew 4:3). The temptation was materialistic self-interest. Jesus' response is self-denial. He quoted from Moses who had led Israel to trust God as the one who would provide for them and who taught, 'People do not live by bread alone, but by every word that comes from the mouth of God' (Matthew 4:4; quoting Deuteronomy 8:3).

Some suggest the temptation here was gluttony. After fasting forty days I hardly think using Jesus' power to make some bread would demonstrate overeating. Gluttony is not just overeating, but prioritizing eating and food too highly. Our needs including food are not inappropriate. What Jesus underlines is that they are to be kept in their proper perspective. He did not want to merely use God's power to provide bread, as if God existed to fulfil his wants and needs. God provided the people of Israel with food – manna from heaven – yet they tragically neglected their loyalty to God. Jesus did not want to repeat that mistake. As people made in God's image, we need to maintain our relationship with God. That includes – or begins with – being attentive to God's words for us.

Dangerous prayer is about what we say to God and listening to what God says to us. In contrast to the solitude of the desert, when we are busy in the world there can be a lot of noise in our day. My day often starts with traffic noise and a clock alarm. Sometimes there are a few alarms in my house as the kids consider the time they need to get ready for school. Television and radio music fills the rooms. Various beeps and programmed sounds alert me as to whether I have an incoming email, Facebook post, text message or mobile call. There is noise all around. What noises are you aware of around you now?

Sometimes Jenni and I take off for a day or a weekend up into the mountains – to escape the noises of the city, and leave our communication devices behind. A technology fast can be as helpful as, and sometimes harder than, abstaining from food. Because of the usual noises in society, and constant communication alerts from friends, family and colleagues, some people cannot stand quiet space. Even in church gatherings, silence can be uncomfortable, perhaps for pastors and worship leaders more than the congregation. Nathan Nettleton, pastor of South Yarra Community Baptist Church, uses ten minutes of silence in every service following the reading of the gospel. They call it the 'sermon of silence'.[6] It takes some getting used to, but people really appreciate the space to reflect personally on what God is saying to them.

For over twenty-five years the Boys' Brigade in Victoria have run an annual solitude retreat for young men aged 16 years and over. They spend three days in the outdoors by themselves with their journal and Bible to listen to God and reassess their lives in light of God's voice. It has been a foundational experience for many of these young men. Two currently serve in my denominational tribe as Baptist youth pastors. Silence is a powerful practice that makes room for God to speak to us and realign our lives.

There are so many competing voices in the world that can drown out Jesus' call to follow him. The fairy tales of modern society, or quotes on Facebook, suggest, 'Follow yourself! Follow your dreams! Be your own person! Don't let anyone tell you what to do!' In the woods or wilderness of contemporary life, there are many calls around us to come and follow the masses: 'Go with the flow!'; or our inner urges: 'If it feels good do it!'; or the latest fads: 'Everyone's doing it!' Joseph Stowell commented: 'Amid the tensions of dozens of voices telling us what to do and how to live, His is the one voice that captures the attention of our hearts.'[7] What is the compassionate voice of God saying to you? N.T. Wright similarly commented, 'It is a central part of the Christian vocation to learn to recognize the voices that whisper attractive lies, to distinguish them from the voice of God, and to use the simple but direct weapons provided in Scripture to rebut the lies with truth.'[8] How long is it since you took quiet space to listen attentively to God's word for you? When did you last read the Bible not for information, but to be open to the living and breathing word of God capturing your imagination?

Three men were talking over coffee. One said, 'I'm concerned about my wife. She talks to herself a lot these days.' The other said, 'Mine does too, but she doesn't know it. She thinks I'm listening.' The third commented, 'My wife said I never listen to what she says, at least I think that's what she said.' Those abysmal comments do not work to make a good marriage. We have to learn to listen attentively to friends and family if we want those relationships to grow, and it is the same with God.

Some parents are fond of telling their children, 'God gave you two ears and only one mouth, so that you would listen twice as much as you talk.' There may be truth in that. Others say it's because God knows listening is twice as hard as talking. As Samuel said, 'Speak, Lord, for your servant is listening' (see 1 Samuel 3:10), let's take time not only to hear but to listen to God. Too often our prayer attitude is, 'Listen, Lord, your servant is talking', rather than, 'Speak, Lord, your servant is listening.' Even worse, our requests might imply, 'Listen, God, you are my servant and I am talking.' Like Moses, and Jesus who quoted him, let's remember that we do not live only by physical bread but by spiritual sustenance. Food and material needs are not bad in themselves, but they are not the only things we need.

Enjoying What Matters

Jesus did not deny himself food because he thought it was bad or a necessary evil. But he set aside time and focus to be attentive to what God was saying to him. In many other scenes of the gospels, Jesus was more often pictured *enjoying* good food and drink than denying himself. I learn this from Jesus – that God provides us with good things which he invites us to enjoy and celebrate. The Talmud says we'll be called to give account for all the good things we have failed to enjoy in the world throughout our life. We don't live on bread alone – but we do need it, and let's enjoy the food and other good gifts God gives us. Sleep, friendships, the satisfaction of work and the restoration of rest are all gifts to enjoy.

Chocolat is a movie which invites people to reflect on the control of Christendom and to celebrate everyday spirituality.[9] Released in 2000, it is set in the imagined French town of Lansquenet in 1959. Vianne Rocher (played by Juliette Binoche) is a young single mother who enters the town as an outsider. She blows in with the wind and, as Lent starts in the traditional Catholic town, opens a chocolaterie. She invites the town to enjoy the sensuality of chocolate, which in a mystical way helps different characters awaken dreams and enrich relationships. Vianne's chocolate, and her friendship and hospitality, help people reclaim unfulfilled dreams, reconcile with estranged friends and relatives, and stand up for a life worth living. She offers permission to indulge with her tasty chocolate creations.

Vianne's invitation to enjoyment and indulgence stands in contrast to the church's teaching of abstinence and denial, especially during Lent. Vianne's nemesis is the town mayor Comte de Reynaud who stands for tradition and moral rigidity. Interestingly, in Joanne Harris's book that the movie is based on, the priest is the opponent and stands for traditional church teaching.[10] In the movie, the priest is a likeable character but the puppet of the mayor, suggestive of Christendom's entanglement of church and state. The mayor and the priest resist Vianne's offer of chocolate, and what it stands for and the changes it brings. Other characters are also dysfunctional and resentful in their response, especially Serge the abusive husband of Josephine whom Vianne helps to stand up for herself, offering her alternative lodging and work in the chocolaterie. Serge reacts vindictively, burning a boat that Vianne's new romantic interest Roux (played by Johnny Depp) has floated into town on.

Worn out and feeling driven away, Vianne feels like moving on. But she comes to a place of mutual understanding with the mayor when he succumbs to scoffing himself with chocolate. Her hope is fully restored when many of her friends surprise her in her kitchen making chocolates for an Easter Sunday 'Grand Festival of Chocolate' celebration. This is when the beautiful message of celebrating creation is integrated with the Easter celebration of redemption. The town has helped bring healing to her, just as she brought more holistic perspectives to the town. Vianne's daughter Anoak is also tired of relocating, and urges Vianne towards stability. She stays, showing she has brought change to the village but also been changed in return.

Vianne beautifully loves life and helps others to love life, laugh often, savour the moment and make life-giving choices. That is a lesson we learn from Jesus too. He practised self-denial, and refused to let the devil tempt him into waving his power around to satisfy and prove himself. Yet Jesus also enjoyed good food and friendship, and providing it for his friends and followers.

Debra Hirsch, teaching about sexuality and spirituality, urges moving on from pedantic rule-keeping. She does not counsel ignoring boundaries but invites us to celebrate the 'permissive' aspect of God's character. It is the nature of God to say, 'Let there be light and life and joy.' Comments Hirsch:

> When discipleship is narrowed down to jumping through behavioural hoops and ticking the right theological boxes, grace is squeezed out and we come to see God as just plain impossible to please, like some nasty first-grade teacher or harsh, authoritarian parent. When we reduce Christianity to a negative system where fasting becomes more sacred than feasting, refraining from embrace, law wins out over grace, and correct theology becomes more important than divine encounter, we in effect become the modern-day Pharisees – whose ministry Jesus was set against.[11]

It is good news that God is permission-giving. God's permission is not about permissiveness to do whatever we want without acknowledging consequences, but a freedom to enjoy the gifts of life God provides.

Celtic contemplatives Ray Simpson and Brent Lyons-Lee explain how the Community of Aidan and Hilda similarly urge the value of enjoying the good gifts God gives us, as part of a simple but not austere lifestyle:

> We are not seeking a life of denial for we thoroughly rejoice in the good things God gives us. Our clothes and furniture should reflect God-given features of our personalities. There is a time to feast and celebrate as well as to fast. Our commitment is to openness. We stand against the influence of the god of mammon in our society by our life-style, by our hospitality, by our intercession, and by regular and generous giving.[12]

It is important to keep 'things' in perspective, and to be accountable for how we use stuff and what we consume. Missional spirituality is engaged fully with all that is good and wholesome in life and in our neighbourhoods. While not hesitating to critique what drains and destroys, it is quick to affirm and recognize where God is fostering life and the kingdom.

In a materialistic society it is easy to be overindulgent. Fasting helps keep our appetites in check. It also gives more time for prayer and reflection. My fitness friends tell me it also has significant and proven health benefits. A Triathlon Club friend explained to me that he fasts two days per week, limiting intake to 500 calories/day, as an exercise in health maintenance. His research, and conversations with his wife who is a medical doctor, shows it delays the onset of dementia and Alzheimer's disease. In our cultural context, we can be indulgent, enjoying everything our eyes see, tasting everything we long for, and thinking we deserve anything our appetites desire. But I am inspired afresh by Jesus and his fasting and focusing on the spiritual side of life. He said 'no' to food while saying 'yes' to waiting on God. In our culture, the practice of self-denial and simplicity which make space for attentiveness to God seems foreign, but so necessary.

Jesus' example cautions me not to be distracted by the materialism of things. Idols come in many shapes and sizes, and in modern Western society it is material things and our pursuit of them that can easily come before God. Jesus' response to the first temptation leads me to echo in prayer, 'Lead us not into that temptation of being preoccupied with what we feel we want, or need and deliver us from materialism.' Rather, let's carefully nurture our relationship with God and listen for God's word for us. Let's enjoy food and things as God's gifts, but also enjoy relationship and service with God as what matters most.

Using God for Fame

For the second temptation, the devil took Jesus from the margins of the wilderness to the centre of Israel's religious and political life – the temple of Jerusalem. There he suggested, 'If you are the Son of God, jump off! For the Scriptures say, "He will order his angels to protect you. And they will hold you up with their hands so you won't even hurt your foot on a stone"' (Matthew 4:6, quoting Psalm 91:11–12). The devil knew the truth that God would protect Jesus. Jesus knew that too. Furthermore, he could see that jumping off the temple and having God's angels protect him would be impressive for everyone who saw it. It would be a sign of God's protection and endorsement. His fame would start and spread right at the centre of religious influence. Yet Matthew tells us Jesus' response was again one of denial, quoting Moses: 'The Scriptures also say, "You must not test the LORD your God"' (Matthew 4:7, quoting Deuteronomy 6:16).

The Jews were hoping for a spectacular deliverer and Jesus could have presented himself as that, but he subverted their expectations. The irony of this scene is that Jesus' destiny was to have all the world and influence. But the way he was to get there was through the cross and resurrection, not the easy route of spectacular miracle-working fame.

This is a temptation I face, to seek my destiny and get in touch with my true self, without being willing to go through my own death experiences. I love shortcuts. As I grew up I wanted to get the most degrees in the shortest time, overlapping and getting cross-credit wherever I could. As I prepared for mission service overseas, I sought out mission organizations who could send me overseas earlier. The devil offered Jesus a great platform to achieve what was, ultimately, God's purpose for him. Offer me that kind of influence with a shortcut to get it, and I'd find it easy to justify.

A Map for Soul-Saving

Recently I read *Immortal Diamond* by Richard Rohr, a spiritual sage who invites his readers to think about deep issues and what really drives us.[13] Rob Bell says of him, '[R]eading Richard Rohr is like sitting around the tribal fire, listening to the village elder give words to that which we've always known to be true, we just didn't know how to

say it . . . in showing us what vibrant, Jesus-centred faith looks like.'
Imagine sitting around the tribal fire, listening to Rohr, who has some
beautiful things to say which help us face the temptation of shortcuts,
achievement and fame.

Rohr says we need to go on a journey of discovering our 'true self'
and leaving our 'false self' behind. Our false self is not something
bad. It's our ego, or the container for our self-image as we grow up.
We accumulate education, money, career, clothing, positions, titles
and even religion, and develop our identity based on these things,
sometimes in comparison with others. But at some stage we need to
leave our reliance on those things behind for our true self to emerge.

The dilemma is that to save our soul, or to find our true self, our
false self has to die. Jesus had to say, 'No, it's not about asserting ourselves as powerful and influential and what's in it for me (WIIFM).'
Later he said, 'I tell you the truth, unless a kernel of wheat is planted
in the soil and dies, it remains alone. But its death will produce many
new kernels – a plentiful harvest of new lives' (John 12:24). Dietrich
Bonhoeffer stated, 'When Christ calls someone, he bids that person
come and die.'[14] Rohr invites us to enter this journey of dying, being
surprised by God's generous love and resurrection power. The journey
does not mean going to Europe to discover this invitation, although
a physical journey may help.

Our true self, our true soul, is who we are in God and who God
is in us. It is our reference point for who we really are as created in
the image of God, the Immortal Diamond that God is fashioning
in us, the ground of our being, our deepest soul. When our true self
emerges, we can be true to who we are created to be. We can be
helped in this by solitude and contemplation, by desert times and
quiet. We allow ourselves to be human beings, not just human doers.
We grow into a whole new awareness of living in God, and God living
in us – not just believing that in our minds but experiencing it in our
souls. When we experience this level of union with God, we will practise our spirituality not as a list of 'shoulds' or moralistic guidelines,
but letting God look out through us on the world so that we have
the same love of life that God demonstrates. That sort of soul-saving

captures my imagination – beginning with my own soul, then help-ing other people let God save their souls; helping people make space for and understand the mystery of God and the overflowing grace and love of Jesus.

Soul-saving, or evangelism, at its best is helping people to get in touch with their true self, letting Jesus save their soul, by discovering what is good in people, naming what is beautiful and in God's image, and inviting people to live in line with God's dream. But becoming one with God, and God's purposes for us, does mean saying no to temptations of gluttony, power and popularity; and 'dying' to those things that might be idols or alternative gods.

That's a journey for a church too – if we are to find our soul and discover our true self. To remember and live into the destiny God has whispered in our ears requires some time in the desert and a willing-ness to say *no* to some things. We need a saviour to show us the way. The church needs soul-saving too.

Churches can be addicted to the status quo and cling to what they have known, enjoying stability and control. They avoid the death of their false selves – all the trappings and forms that made them 'suc-cessful' in the past. Scientism, atheism and secularism can keep people from God, but so too can moralistic boundary markers in religion. Religious practice that is so busy with 'doing church' and providing the answers can crowd out contemplative space for seeking and expe-riencing God. One bishop disparagingly said to Rohr, 'I don't have time for the mystic; we are running a church here.'[15] But a church that embraces action *and* contemplation offers life-giving spirituality to its members and to seekers. Contemplative practice is perhaps one of the best gifts the church can offer Western society.

At AuburnLife, one of our dreams and most basic needs is to de-velop accessible and sustainable approaches to shared spiritual prac-tices – we call it 'the Auburn Way'. Whatever else churches do to look for renewal, it is critical to find contemplative space to listen to God and to rediscover our own soul as a church. Let's ask, 'What is the true self and new life that God wants to birth in us? What is the new life that God wants to breathe into the world through us?'

But as in nature and life, one form has to die for another to come to life. Death is a natural part of life and a necessary precursor to resurrection. We can see in Creation that God is a risk-taker and full of creativity. This is good news for churches facing death. God is full of life and shares resurrection life and hope with people. But we have to go through 'death':

> The only rub, and it is a big one, is that transformation and 'crucifixion' must intervene in between life and Life. Loss always precedes renewal in the physical and biological universe. This is where we all fumble, falter, and fight. Someone needs to personally lead the way, model and path, and say it is 'necessary suffering.' Otherwise we will not trust this counterintuitive path. For Christians, this model and exemplar is Jesus.[16]

Jesus was tempted to bypass that – and go straight to the glory and influence. But he took the way of death and the cross.

As Rohr explores, the invitation is to follow Jesus and enter into the Christ journey of realizing we are loved, entering into the experience of the cross, waiting at the tomb, and looking forward in faith and hope for resurrection.

Jesus' journey is a map for us. Where are you at in the journey? It is helpful to meet Jesus in the desert before we are tempted by glory. Shane Claiborne says that the Simple Way of their community has a guideline written above their front door: 'Today . . . small things with great love (or don't open the door).' They are inspired by Mother Teresa who said, 'We can do no great things, only small things with great love. It is not how much you do but how much love you put into doing it.'[17] Let's pursue God's destiny for each of us, which we will find by following Jesus' example of laying down his life in service. Watch the temptation of shortcuts and being enticed to avoid the Jesus-like steps of the cross, dying to the self and hoping for new life to emerge.

Another element of this temptation is to think that God will do all the work for us. 'God, you want to bring glory to yourself – bring on the miracle.' This is a challenge to me as we think of what it will take to grow our church as a vibrant multicultural mission-shaped church. While transforming the world and cultivating the church as a leadership farm where we grow and cultivate leaders, growing in numbers and influence won't come from throwing ourselves down and letting the angels do it. In the Gospel of Luke it was just after the temptation (Luke 4:1–13) that Jesus declared his mandate of transformation: bringing freedom, banishing oppression, healing the blind and bringing good news to the poor (Luke 4:18–19). Following in his steps, we look to God to do God's work with God, and not leave it to miraculous intervention. I take note of words attributed to St Ignatius Loyola: 'Pray as if everything depended on God and work as if everything depended on you.' If we want to transform our world, we need to pray and advocate, give financially and take action. If we want to share good news, we need to open up the conversations. If we want to be a leadership farm, we need to keep believing in one another and cheering each other on – and look for other people who can flourish within our community. If we want to share the depth of community life and hospitality of our church, we need to reach out to invite people and share life with them. God is a powerful God who works miracles, and God calls us to work diligently to foster God's purposes and rid the world of evil.

Using God for Power

As a third and final attempt at striking Jesus out with temptation, the devil showed Jesus all the world's kingdoms in all their glory and said, 'I will give it all to you . . . if you will kneel down and worship me' (Matthew 4:8–9). It was a temptation of power, prominence, promotion, patriotism, popularity and prestige. It involved all the 'P' temptations that we might be tempted to live for. Whatever the idols are that threaten to distract us, Jesus' answer is instructive, telling the devil where to go: 'Get out of here, Satan . . . For the Scriptures say, "You must worship the LORD your God and serve only him"' (Matthew 4:10, quoting Deuteronomy 6:13).

The devil was not offering Jesus something that Jesus did not deserve (cf. Psalm 2:8; Matthew 28:18). It is Jesus' destiny to receive the worship of all people and to reign over all the world's nations. But the means that the devil was offering to achieve it was subversive of the loyalty that Jesus owed God the Father.

Not many people openly worship the devil, or admit to it. Few people stand openly against God, waving their fist. So what does this temptation mean for us? The temptation is to achieve power, influence and fulfilment, through any means other than God. What are the competing objects of worship that tempt you? What are our society's idols? This is a topic that deserves careful discernment. What is the default way of acquiring power and prominence, popularity and promotion?

Three contenders for high-stakes temptation are money, sex and power. That is why monastic orders invited those signing up for a life of devotion to adopt the monastic vows of poverty, chastity and obedience.[18] It is why the church has told young people to be careful about gold, glory and girls (and guys). These things, though not evil in themselves, can distract us from God's purposes. They can, by default, be the gods we live our lives for. Our society is so focused on money, sex and power that it is difficult to disentangle ourselves from these temptations.

It is obvious when moral boundaries are crossed sexually. Debra Hirsch maintains that the church is well practised at pointing the finger at sexual temptation and sin. We need to pray, 'And don't let us yield to temptation, but deliver us from the evil one' in terms of how we approach sexuality, power and money. But we also need to pray it against temptations which are more subtle and socially acceptable.

Money, sex and power are not the only ways of gaining significance. In what ways are you tempted to place something else before God, or to get significance from a source other than in relationship to God? Some of the insidious temptations that can distract us from loyalty to God which are so common in Western culture today include security and self-reliance, wealth and beauty, selfishness and busyness.

The kissing scene of the show *Into the Woods* alerts us to one temptation. I think about sex most days, but I am not tempted to cross sexual boundaries very often. I don't have 'princesses' throwing themselves into my arms when I go on bushwalks. The healthy relationships I have with many women friends I value too highly to want to turn them into sexual relationships. It is the narrative of another movie that was instructive for me in facing temptations that I often face.

The Devil Wears Prada

Andrea Sachs (played by Anne Hathaway) faces a cocktail of consumerist temptations in the 2006 comedy-drama film *The Devil Wears Prada*. Sachs lands a job in fashion journalism, but distant from her dream writing role. She is second assistant for powerful and ruthless editor Miranda Priestly (Meryl Streep). Sachs learns quickly what it takes to survive and thrive in this new world. Her appearance and image have a makeover, but her relationship with her boyfriend, friends and family suffers. She overworks to try (usually unsuccessfully) to please her demanding boss, but also experiences shallow relationships that elegant fashion and abundant money cannot alleviate. The climax of the movie revolves around what path Sachs follows.

Apart from the obvious temptations in the movie about the idols of appearance and career, there are two other warnings for me.

Firstly, there is the temptation to treat people as things to use rather than relationships to value. The problem of highly aspiring to promote ourselves, building our career, and positioning ourselves to look good is that people around us become tools for our own advancement. Who will we next step on and over to get ahead?

The best antidote against this temptation is to see the image of God in one another. When we esteem people as made in God's image – worthy of attentiveness, nurture and value – then we will cease using people for our purposes and seek to help them to flourish in all God intends for them.

There is a fictional story about an abbot and his monks in a medieval English town who learned this lesson. Their monastery was dwindling. The abbot asked his friend, Rabbi Jacob, for advice. The rabbi comforted him and let him in on a secret. 'There is something you need to know, my brother. We have long known in the Jewish community that the Messiah is one of you.' The abbot was surprised. He returned to the monastery, and as he looked at his brothers over meals and in the chapel, as they shared duties and conversation, he wondered which one of them might be the one. He started treating all of his brothers with a newfound respect and kindness, even awe for who they might be. It became so noticeable that one of the brothers asked him what had changed for him. The brother coaxed the secret from the abbot. Soon word spread: 'The Messiah is one of us.' Before long the whole monastery was full of expectancy and newfound grace, and began to grow and flourish again. The rabbi's secret was: the Messiah is one of us.[19]

When we treat people around us as special before God, it revolutionizes how we treat them. In the Western world, where we are enculturated to value things and use people, we need to flip that right around and right side up: use things in their place and value people. Recall what Quaker Mary Hughes said: 'Once we have said "Our Father" in the morning, we can treat no one as stranger for the rest of the day.'

The image of God in people is more than a doctrinal belief but a powerful motivator for serving others. Charles Taylor says he heard Mother Teresa speaking about her motive for working with those who are abandoned and dying in Calcutta. She explained she tended to their needs because simply they were people created in God's image. As a Catholic philosopher Taylor thought 'I could have said that!' But as a reflective philosopher, he then asked himself, 'But could I have *meant* it?'[20] It is one thing to give verbal assent to the truth of the image of God, but to really mean it and act on it can transform how we serve others in Jesus' name.

Secondly, excessive busyness is another temptation in the corporate world, which is reflected in *The Devil Wears Prada*. I feel this temptation strongly. I admit that in life and ministry I am often driven. I like to achieve, to be significant, to seek and have the approval of others. My friends tell me I simply like to help others – with no other ulterior motive than to be a kind and helpful friend – but that robs me of time and makes me busy. My tendency is to say 'yes' to most of what I am asked to do, rather than discerning where I am called. When I am not careful, my life seems often in transit – trying to get somewhere, driving somewhere, standing in line, waiting for 'that job', tapping my fingers for a meeting to end, trying to get a task completed, worrying about something that might happen, or being angry about something that did happen. Thomas Merton warns about the tyranny of busyness: 'To allow oneself to be carried away by a multitude of conflicting concerns, to surrender to too many demands, to commit oneself to too many projects, to want to help everyone in everything is to succumb to violence. The frenzy of the activist kills the root of inner wisdom which makes work fruitful.'[21]

Busyness in one sense is value-neutral. It is not a sin to be busy. But it is a temptation to find satisfaction and meaning in being busy, and as a result not have the necessary space for who God calls us to be.

Temptation comes from every direction. Martin Luther penned this appeal for prayer: 'our whole life is nothing but temptation by these three, the flesh, the world, the devil. Therefore pray: Father, let not our flesh seduce us, let not the world deceive us, let not the devil cast us down.'[22] Luther was echoing the phrases from the dangerous prayer Jesus taught us: 'And don't let us yield to temptation, but deliver us from the evil one.'

What are the specific temptations Jesus confronted, and what can we learn from them? In the desert Jesus faced and overcame temptations of materialistic self-interest, fame and popularity. Such temptations are not unique to Jesus or his time, so it is worthwhile to look at what Jesus modelled for us.

My remaining question is: how can we cooperate with God in seeing the answer to this prayer?

Out of the Smoking Room

In the classic children's book *The Wind in the Willows* by Kenneth Grahame, Mr Toad is always dangerously joyriding in his car. The other characters – Rat, Mole and Badger – scheme to fix him and 'teach him to be a sensible Toad'. For their mission of mercy, they send him into the 'smoking room' for Badger to tell him some facts about himself and convince him of his wicked ways. Rat is dubious: 'Talking to Toad'll never cure him. He'll say anything.' But Badger preaches well, Toad sobbingly repents, and he commits to a life of abstinence from foolhardy driving.

Once out of the smoking room, Badger asks him to repeat his apology and testimony of conversion. At that place in the story the situation turns:

There was a long, long pause. Toad looked desperately this way and that, while the other animals waited in grave silence. At last he spoke.

'No!' he said, a little sullenly, but stoutly; 'I'm not sorry. And it wasn't folly at all! It was simply glorious!'

'What?' cried the Badger, greatly scandalised. 'You backsliding animal, didn't you tell me just now, in there —'

'Oh, yes, yes, in there,' said Toad impatiently. 'I'd have said anything in there. You're so eloquent, dear Badger, and so moving, and so convincing, and put all your points so frightfully well – you can do what you like with me in there, and you know it. But I've been searching my mind since, and going over things in it, and I find that I'm not a bit sorry or repentant really, so it's no earthly good saying I am; now, is it?'

'Then you don't promise,' said the Badger, 'never to touch a motor-car again?'

'Certainly not!' replied Toad emphatically. 'On the contrary, I faithfully promise that the very first motor-car I see, poop-poop! off I go in it!'[23]

It is easy to commit to all sorts of things within the safety of our church walls. The challenge is following through in everyday life. God's people need resolve against temptation not so much in the confines of the church sanctuary but 'out there' in the world.

Toad did have one thing going for him – there was a community of friends seeking to support him with his temptation. We need one another.

Our need for friends to help stand against temptation is seen in another popular story – *The Lord of the Rings,* and especially *The Fellowship of the Ring.*[24] Frodo is entrusted to carry the ring – the ultimate temptation of power. Smeagol had carried it alone, and it turned him against those around him, twisted his heart with mistrust and ultimately drove him insane as 'Gollum'. But Frodo has his hobbit friends and others in the Fellowship who help him with the burden. His closest companion Samwise even carries it for a time. We all need a community to stand strong in the face of temptation.

Practices in Action

Spiritual practices are helpful in keeping us from temptation and delivering us from evil. Philosopher Michael Polanyi said, 'practical wisdom is more truly embodied in action than expressed in rules of action'.[25] We need practices that guide good actions, not just rules or intentions to avoid bad action. Reality, not rhetoric, is what counts. Toad said all the right things, but what he most needed was the right practices.

James Smith in *Desiring the Kingdom* critiques the tendency of Christians to focus on what we think and the knowledge we accumulate, and urges us instead to focus on what Christians *do* and how our hearts and desires are shaped.[26] For Smith, the important part of worship and education is not adding to knowledge or even having good intentions, but shaping what we love and set our hearts on.

To help us understand how shaped we are by contemporary Western culture rather than the kingdom of God, Smith invites his readers to imagine coming from Mars and looking at our culture as a Martian anthropologist. What underlies our cultural behaviour and its aims? What does it mean to flourish and experience 'the good life'? Smith urges us to admit that we are people of love and passions, but passion needs forming and counter-forming in new directions. As an example, Smith analyses the idolatry of the shopping mall and its unsubtle message that shopping and accumulating belongings is needed to feel good, to match up to others, and to appear successful and beautiful. The practice of 'retail therapy' reinforces our openness to these temptations. Whether it is consumerism, or the military machine, or the workaholism that higher education breeds into many people, we need to be attentive to how our culture and its institutions misshape us by their 'habit-forming, identity-shaping, love-directing rituals that capture our imagination and hence our desire, directing it towards a *telos* [purpose] that is often antithetical to the *telos* envisioned as the kingdom of God'.[27]

What 'practices' can we adopt to help us against temptation and to deliver us from evil? The best practice to combat consumerism is simplicity. Accumulated belongings can clutter our lives so that we have little emotional and physical space for relationships with people and with God. Technology can distance us from the relationships that it is supposed to serve. For example, Facebook, a social media platform I use eagerly and regularly, does have the danger of being loaded with visions of the good life that are antithetical to the kingdom of God. Moreover, it is filled with self-display in a kind of coolness competition where we present ourselves in a particular way. I like its relational connection with my community and tribe. But at its worst it does more for my ego and self-promotion, and little to help me foster reflection and character. With the world at my fingertips, it is appropriate to pray that we don't get carried away: 'Lead us not into iPhone-ization.'[28] Practising simplicity by cutting down the amount of technology we use and reducing the things we have accumulated can make space for attentiveness to God and other relationships. We have to be intentional about using this space for God and others, lest it get filled with some other form of distractedness.

More Danger

Seeing answers to this prayer requires the commitment of humble action and practices, not just inspired rhetoric. Michael Frost saw an example of this in a U2 concert. Bono advocated for action about global poverty. To illustrate the issue he clicked his fingers a few times and said that every second a child died of preventable causes. He called on the audience to take action to make poverty history, declaring 'Together we can do it!' The thousands in the audience cheered. What Frost thought tragic, however, was that after the concert the audience went outside and dodged homeless panhandlers outside the gates, refusing to respond to their requests for help or to even look at them or talk with them. The response to Bono's rally call was strong as a collective intention. But individually in responsive action, outside the gates, there was no reflection of service. The action fell far short of the rhetoric.[29] I don't disparage Bono's appeal. His activism for a better world is inspiring. We need popular artists as well as political leaders who put global poverty on the agenda. But change comes not from cheering at slogans but rolling up our sleeves and responding in service. We need to call one another to move beyond abstract ideals and commit to transforming practices.

Life Well Lived

British philosopher, pacifist and Nobel Prize Laureate in Literature, Bertrand Russell (1872–1970), reflected on his life and whether it was well lived. He commented that pain and suffering kept him grounded and gave him a longing to alleviate evil:

> I have sought knowledge. I have wished to understand the hearts of men. I have wished to know why the stars shine. And I have tried to apprehend the Pythagorean power by which number holds sway above the flux. A little of this, but not much, I have achieved.

Love and knowledge, so far as they were possible, led upward toward the heavens. But always pity brought me back to Earth. Echoes of cries of pain reverberate in my heart. Children in famine, victims tortured by oppressors, helpless old people a burden to their sons, and the whole world of loneliness, poverty, and pain make a mockery of what human life should be. I long to alleviate this evil, but I cannot, and I too suffer.

This has been my life. I have found it worth living, and would gladly live it again if the chance were offered me . . .

I may have thought the road to a world of free and happy human beings shorter than it is proving to be. But I was not wrong in thinking that such a world is possible, and that it is worth while to live with a view of bringing it nearer. I have lived in the pursuit of a vision, both personal and social. Personal: to care for what is noble, for what is beautiful, for what is gentle; to allow moments of insight to give wisdom at more mundane times. Social: to see in imagination the society that is to be created, where individuals grow freely, and where hate and greed and envy die because there is nothing to nourish them. These things I believe, and the world, for all its horrors, has left me unshaken.[30]

Russell did not act from convictions of faith, but I am inspired by his vision to be part of ridding the world of its evils. I suspect the God-image in Russell inspired his desires.

As with other phrases of the Lord's Prayer, the dangerous element here is that as we pray not to be led into temptation and to be delivered from evil, God invites us to be part of the answer to our prayer.

Baptist pastor and CEO of World Vision Australia, Tim Costello, is well known for his prophetic stand against evils in local neighbourhoods and global systems.[31] Respected for his voice on social issues, gambling and global poverty, he is a strong advocate for the church to engage in society's issues and not be content grappling with its own issues:

At present, we have little more than a vision of subcultural existence that leaves everyone isolated in their social ghetto and erects a type of social apartheid. The Church must find its mission in the midst of marginal-ised communities and share its life fully. Too often, it sounds like the exuberant coach shouting instructions about how to play the game from the safety of the boundary line.[32]

Costello says that his faith is bookended by two biblical imperatives: the call to personal transformation from the Great Commission (Matthew 28:18–20), and the mandate for social transformation in Jesus' saying that as we serve people in need we serve him (Matthew 25:31–46). Both expressions of mission work against evil and bring good news to the poor:

> Evil is real and we need both a change of heart to address the evil within and social changes to address the evil without. Sin is the reign of evil and salvation is the overcoming of evil. Sin is expressed in hunger, injustice, sickness and spiritual alienation – in short, all that cripples the image of God. Salvation is expressed in food and justice, health and abundance that heals this crippled image. The good news is that we are called by God to partner with him to put things right.[33]

Working for justice and expressing compassion reflects Jesus' char-acter and God's dream for the world. Costello's challenge is to en-sure we add action to our words, and to integrate activism with our spirituality.

Standing in Hope

Adding action to our words was driven home for me when a young friend, Rekiah O'Donnell, was killed by her boyfriend.[34] At the fu-neral I invited the congregation of 500 to both sit in grief and stand in hope. Rekiah grew up at Aberfeldie Baptist with her parents Craig and Kerryn, and siblings Jesse and Indiana. I was her pastor when she was aged 9 to 12. When she was tragically shot at the age of 22, we were all shocked by the violent injustice.

Rekiah was a unique person, who meant different things to each of us. During the service – in the photos and music, in the stories and sharing – there were some things that made us laugh, some things that made us cry, and many things that reminded us to be thankful: for the beautiful, strong, vibrant, loyal, persistent and passionate young woman that Rekiah was, as a friend, sister, niece, granddaughter, stepdaughter and daughter. She was someone (like many of us) who wrestled with her struggles, but was fierce in her love for her friends and family.

Those gathered brought very mixed emotions and favourite memories. A memory I shared was about a time when I took Rekiah and her friend Bethany (who were our whole teenage youth group) to Mill Valley Camp. I thought I was taking them to ride horses and meet Jesus. The speaker seemed more interested in warning the kids off Harry Potter than warming their hearts about Jesus. The girls were just as interested in meeting boys as Jesus, but they loved Jesus too. At the funeral service, with preplanned speeches and an open mic, many shared their memories of Rekiah. *We sat* gratefully with these memories.

We also bore regrets and griefs; the grief of losing Rekiah, the grief of her struggles and pain, and the inevitable thoughts of what else we might have done. *We sat* with our regrets. I suspect we knew with confidence of Rekiah's appreciation for the care, interest and love that many had shown her. Death, especially so premature, is a reminder of our own limits on life. *We sat* in the presence of eternity, and reflected on what we are living for, and whether we are prepared for life with God. One of the early Facebook posts of Jesse, Rekiah's brother, reminded everyone to love and nurture our friendships and families. *We sat* with that invitation, to love those around us. In the turmoil of our emotions, *we sat* with all this.

But I suspect many of us also sat with anger and rage. We were digging deep for comfort and peace, relying on God and one another for reassurance and grace; with words or tears we struggled with confusion and fear, and the senseless and tragic loss of Rekiah. *We sat* with that, but I prayed – for God's sake and for Rekiah's and for others like her – that we wouldn't just sit, but take a stand for hope.

My eyes were opened to the reality of violence in our society in that at least one woman a week is killed in Australia by a former or current partner. Women in some age brackets are more likely to die from violence than smoking, obesity, drugs or alcohol abuse. Domestic violence is the main cause of homelessness for women and children. Contained in the Australian Institute of Health and Welfare's report, *Specialist Homelessness Services 2011–12*, is the fact that people experiencing domestic or family violence make up one-third of the almost 230,000 Australians who accessed specialist homelessness services, and 78% were female.[35] A running friend, Peter Coburn, is an ambassador for White Ribbon, and he has helped open the eyes of our running group to the reality and tragedy of domestic violence against women.

For these terrible statistics, tears *and* anger are appropriate. This reminded me again of the words quoted in chapter three from St Augustine: 'Hope has two beautiful daughters; their names are Anger and Courage: anger at the way things are, and courage to see that they do not remain as they are.'

Jesse appropriately called us to nurture our relationships; later we called one another to *take a stand* for safer neighbourhoods, for healthy living, for respect for one another – for communities that are more in line with God's dream. We said together '*no*', this is not the way things should be.

We sat at Aberfeldie with memories and grief, with friends and family. But as we left the church, Rekiah's life and her death urged us to *take a stand* for a community that is more hope-ful and safe; a world with justice and respect for all. (I was inspired in this direction by the words of a friend and colleague, Stacey Aslangul, at another recent funeral in similarly tragic circumstances.) Many asked, 'Where is God? Where was God?' That is a very appropriate question. Whether we ask it after Auschwitz or 9/11, after the disaster of hurricanes or accidents, or after murders in our neighbourhoods, we can't answer anything other than 'God is there in the pain.' God is suffering too.

Stacey Wilson, a friend of Rekiah and her mum Kerryn, referred to these words for the occasion of the day:

Beneath the anger
Beneath the fears
Beneath the pain
and silent tears
is a child
loved by God

Within the love
And loyalty
Within the joy
And dream to be free
Is the reflection of
a loving God

As we weep
As we grieve
As we ask questions
No answers relieve
We are embraced
By a wounded God.

We sit in grief, realizing the stark reality of evil in our world. But let's also *take a stand* in prayer and activism to cooperate with God in delivering the world from evil.

Journaling and Discussion

1. Read the lyrics or watch an excerpt from 'Into the Woods – Any Moment' and share your response.[36]
2. What are the temptations that are most obvious in our society and culture?
3. What are the temptations that are less obvious, but perhaps just as dangerous in our society and culture?
4. In what ways can we rely on one another as a community to discern and resist temptation?

5. What evil in the world do you feel most passionately against which is most likely to bring you to tears? How can you and your church pray and act to make a difference about evil, using the missional prayer?

6. What are the implications of this chapter for you? What would you like to stop doing, start doing, or do differently as a result of reading this chapter and reflecting on its implications?

7. Watch the Common Grace and Bible Society video of Ben Meyers, Lecturer in Systematic Theology at United Theological College, discussing the depth of the meaning of praying 'Deliver us from evil', and discuss or journal your response.[37]

8. Finish by rereading and meditating on the reading 'Beneath the Anger' quoted above.

Conclusion: Confident Celebration of the Mission of God

Vatalis

Vatalis was a monk who prayed for the problems and vice of a nearby city. One day, while praying, he heard a voice calling, 'Vatalis, Vatalis.' He answered, 'Yes, Lord', and heard, 'Vatalis, you go down to the city and do something about its problems.' 'You want what, God? Say that again,' replied Vatalis. He was unsure how to respond. Yet, obedient to the heavenly voice, Vatalis moved to the city and met local people. He talked particularly with prostitutes, sometimes in the early hours of the morning when they had time spare from sleep and work. Local religious leaders were suspicious about what the monk was up to, and encouraged him to pursue more respectable avenues of service. Vatalis graciously declined. Yet they were nervous about the reputation of the church. They were concerned about one of their number, a monk in fact, who was being seen in the company of undesirable types. Tensions over Vatalis' ministry increased until one night Vatalis was ambushed and killed to remove his influence. At Vatalis' funeral, first one and then many prostitutes, and others, told of Vatalis' loving concern, and how he had helped change their lives.[1]

While he was praying, Vatalis heard God tell him to get involved in his city. It could happen as we pray too – be careful. Prayer is dangerous business, especially when God calls us to add prayerful action to our prayerful words. It could lead us to be associated with all the 'wrong people' and upset all the 'right ones'. This is particularly valuable for people working with those on the margins. It is important for churches (and parents) as we release our people (and children) to move beyond middle-class expectations and serve among the poor. Sometimes the system that oppresses us is 'expected Christianity' rather than the radical inspiration of Jesus.

What is your response to this Dangerous Prayer we have been exploring? In what ways has it reshaped your life of prayer and prayerful living? You will finish this book soon, but hopefully praying this prayer will never leave you the same.

The entire prayer, including each part of it, is a dangerous prayer. It is dangerous in addressing the discrimination, injustice, selfishness, poverty, violence and consumerism which are rampant in the world. It is dangerous in its countercultural and radical stance, and dangerous because it invites us to be, in part, the answer to our prayers. We look for God's help and seek to cooperate with what God wants to do in our world. But if we pray for God's name to be honoured, and for God's kingdom and will, then we also need to work in those directions. When we pray for daily bread for the world, and reconciliation and deliverance from systems that oppress us, it is our responsibility to live countercultural lives of generosity, forgiveness and holiness that foster God's dream. This is where the prayer is most dangerous – in embracing neighbourhood and global interests beyond ourselves, and in inviting us to live our prayer, and be an answer to the prayer we groan.

We conclude with confidence in celebrating the greatness of God who wants to cooperate with us – or more accurately wants to invite us to cooperate with God's purposes in the world where God sends us: 'For yours is the kingdom, the power and the glory, forever and ever. Amen.' We can pray the breadth and depth that is in this dangerous prayer, entirely because of God's kingdom purposes, the power of what God can do to bring them about, and the glory of who God is.

This phrase was not in the earliest and most reliable manuscripts, but we can expect that Jesus allowed space to add some 'doxology' like this to the end of his prayer. Jews of Jesus' day ended this kind of prayer with spontaneous or set words of praise. Joachim Jeremias commented, 'according to contemporary analogies Jesus must have intended that the Our Father should conclude with a doxology,

but would have left the user to fill it in for [themselves]'.² The early
church added these final words to underline their confidence in the
one they were calling on and to express why they knew God would
answer. Erasmus was probably the original editor, and the Reformers
thought the words were so good they added them to Protestant wor-
ship.³ Echoing the church through the centuries, these words underline our confidence when we pray.

A Kingdom to Hope For

Firstly, we are confident in the kingdom of God. We underline our
prayers, '*Yours is the kingdom*'.

It is the purpose of God's kingdom that we hope in and submit
to. God has a purpose and will fulfil it (Psalm 138:8). God has a
dream for our neighbourhood and is making it happen. We know
there are many competing agendas and kingdoms in the world. But
God's kingdom agenda is the ultimate. Rome did not last, and neither
will oppressive dictatorial systems today. Christendom is disappear-
ing, but the kingdom of God continues to subversively sprout up
in unexpected places on the margins. The idols of this world pale
into insignificance. It is not a particular political system or economic
dream in which we put our hope. It is not materialistic items or am-
bitious goals for which we live and strive. We pray for and submit to
the kingdom of God – this is the ultimate vision.

The kingdom of God frames the whole prayer. We pray, 'Your
kingdom come', and look to God to bring heaven to Hawthorn or
wherever we live. We ask for daily bread for everyone who needs basic
provision – and trust for a more just distribution when the world reflects God's kingdom. Having prayed, 'Lead us not into temptation',
we draw significance from our part in God's kingdom rather than
significance from the temptations of materialism, fame or power.
Neither Caesar nor consumerism is Lord – Jesus is Lord. In his life
and teaching, death and resurrection, we see the kingdom of God
flourishing. When we pray this dangerous prayer, we join Jesus in

his radical rebellion against all that is wrong in the world. We pray it confidently, because the kingdom is God's.

Unfortunately, the world does not always seem as if the kingdom is God's. Painful things happen that are unbearable. Injustice seems to flourish. A generation ago the world hung under the threat of nuclear war. That fear is not absent today. But the growth of terrorism means unprovoked mass violence can happen almost anywhere and at any time.

At a personal level, even for those of us who believe in God, the reality of suffering can take us by sharp surprise. When suffering happens to us it is hard enough. But when those we love suffer, it can drive us to the edge of despair.

Hunter 'Patch' Adams was an unconventional medical student. As depicted in the movie, *Patch*, played by Robin Williams, gathers a group of friends who have volunteered alongside him to set up a clinic offering medical services at no charge to the poor and needy. Sadly, his idealism, humour and compassion were shattered when his girlfriend and fellow medical student, Carin Fisher (Monica Potter), was murdered by a patient whom they were sacrificially helping. The tragedy led Patch to contemplate suicide and question God. He wondered whether it was all worth it, and felt guilty for what he saw as his part in his friend's death. As is so common in human experience in the face of suffering, he questioned God's justice and mercy. From a clifftop he cried out into the sky for an answer to his pain. He was not questioning God's existence but what God was doing and why he had set up the world with such inevitable pain and death. Surely there was space for more compassion, Patch implied. It is natural to question whether God is loving and good when an experience of suffering suggests otherwise. At a crucial moment, Patch saw a butterfly, which reminded him of Carin saying she had wanted to be a caterpillar, so that she could transform herself and fly away from her struggles. The butterfly paused its flight on his medical bag, and then on his colourful shirt, before flying away. There was no audible voice from God or clear answer about the reasons for human suffering. Yet it was a beautiful scene that revived his hope. Patch left, determined to continue his work in Carin's honour.[4]

It is likely there have been circumstances for you when it does not seem God's kingdom is being outworked. Probably you will have had times when life looks far from God's will. Yet that may be when a glimpse of revelation of God's kindness is seen. We can still say, 'Yours is the kingdom', in hope and submission. Malcolm Muggeridge reflects on his personal experience of tragedy and learning of God's goodness in the midst of those times, which echoes the message of the cross of Christ:

> Contrary to what might be expected, I look back on experiences that at the time seemed especially desolating and painful with particular satisfaction. Indeed, I can say with complete truthfulness that everything I have learned in my seventy-five years in this world, everything that has truly enhanced and enlightened my existence, has been through affliction and not through happiness, whether pursued or attained. In other words, if it ever were to be possible to eliminate affliction from our earthly existence by means of some drug or other medical mumbo jumbo . . . the result would not be to make life delectable, but to make it too banal and trivial to be endurable. This, of course, is what the Cross signifies. And it is the Cross, more than anything else, that has called us inexorably to Christ.[5]

I pray that the crosses we experience this side of heaven will help bring heaven to earth. The world needs this kind of transformation. We can pray for it with confidence, because of our confidence in the purposes of God's kingdom that God is outworking.

We live in a world that often seems far from God's kingdom. Even when we are praying and working for the kingdom of God, bad stuff can happen to us and to those close to us. Naturally we'll question God's purposes, and wonder what God is doing. We might be tempted to suggest to God that we could run the world better if we had the power. The movie *Bruce Almighty*, where Bruce takes over God's job, suggests an attractive option for us – it is easy to think we could do a better job than God at setting things right and helping people avoid pain.

However, the good news of Christianity is that we do not have to worry about whether God is good and fair. We do not have the eyes to see everything that God is doing or why. But we confess our confidence in God's overarching purposes. Abraham pleaded with God for the people of Sodom and based his bold confidence in pleading for them on his awareness of God's character when he asked, 'Should not the Judge of all the earth do what is right?' (Genesis 18:25). Naturally God does do what is right. John Walton commented in his commentary on Abraham's encounter with God, 'We don't have to worry about whether God is less fair, less just, less merciful, less loving, or less gracious than we would be.'[6] A primary reason we can be confident that God hears and answers prayers is because it is God's kingdom we hope for and submit to.

Power to Trust In

Secondly, we are confident as we pray this dangerous prayer because of what God can do. We underline our prayers, 'Yours is the kingdom *and the power*'. What does this mean? It is not just God's dream that we hope in, but the ability of God's power that we trust in. We submit to God's kingdom but also rely on God's power.

David in Psalm 139 confidently and beautifully described God as all-knowing, all-present and all-powerful:

O Lord, you have examined my heart
and know everything about me.
You know when I sit down or stand up.
You know my thoughts even when I'm far away . . .
I can never escape from your Spirit!
I can never get away from your presence! . . .
If I ride the wings of the morning,
if I dwell by the farthest oceans,
even there your hand will guide me,
and your strength will support me.

I could ask the darkness to hide me
and the light around me to become night –
but even in darkness I cannot hide from you.
To you the night shines as bright as day.
Darkness and light are the same to you.
(vv. 1–2, 7, 9–12)

It is good news that God's presence and commitment to us as the people of God reaches everywhere, even into the darkest of circumstances. Ours is a God whose power means we can trust God.

One lesson that inspiring saints have learned through history is that when God calls, God provides. For example, George Müller over his lifetime in England cared for over 10,000 orphans, started over a hundred schools and distributed over a million New Testaments. As a pastor he gave up his salary. For the social programmes that he initiated he never requested financial support. God provided sometimes through donors and sometimes through unexpected sources. Once he led the children who were sitting at the meal table to give thanks for their meal, even though they had nothing in the cupboard. As they finished prayer, a baker knocked on the door to offer bread that was enough to feed everyone, and the milkman offered all his fresh milk since his cart had broken down in the street outside the orphanage.[7] Let's not underestimate how God's power is still present and ready to work in our day and age.

This sort of faith in the power of God does not leave everything to God. What do you sense that God might be saying about how the Dangerous Prayer might be answered through you? Be encouraged that God is willing and able to back up your faith. Part of my problem is being aware of God's power and what God might want to do. I know the sort of things God wants to do. I learn from the example of Jesus and the words of this dangerous prayer. When I read the gospels, I get a snapshot of the radical invitation to would-be followers of Jesus. Have a glimpse at a few things Jesus said in Matthew:

'Come, follow me, and I will show you how to fish for people!' (Matthew 4:19)

'God blesses those who are persecuted for doing right, for the Kingdom of Heaven is theirs' (Matthew 5:10).

'Love your enemies! Pray for those who persecute you! In that way, you will be acting as true children of your Father in heaven' (Matthew 5:44–45).

'Do to others whatever you would like them to do to you' (Matthew 7:12).

'Look, I am sending you out as sheep among wolves . . . don't be afraid of those who threaten you . . . Don't be afraid of those who want to kill your body' (Matthew 10:16, 26, 28).

'If you give even a cup of cold water to one of the least of my followers, you will surely be rewarded' (Matthew 10:42).

These are dangerous words. Left to my own will and devices, however, and without the power of God to help me, I prefer my own selfish purposes over God's. I have an inkling of what God might say to me, so I avoid taking time to listen. I have a hunch that Jesus' ways are radical, so I gravitate to conservative alternatives. I'm not proud of that, but I admit that the way I live does not always reflect that the kingdom and power belongs to God.

Annie Dillard marvels at the nonchalance of most Christians when it comes to God's power. Her writing warns me that people in church often have a shallow understanding of what is involved in approaching God:

On the whole, I do not find Christians, outside the catacombs, sufficiently sensible of the conditions. Does anyone have the foggiest idea what sort of power we so blithely invoke? Or, as I suspect, does no one believe a word of it? The churches are children playing on the floor with their chemistry sets, mixing up a batch of TNT to kill a Sunday morning. It is madness to wear ladies' straw hats and velvet hats to church; we should all be wearing crash helmets. Ushers should issue life preservers and signal flares; they should lash us to our pews. For the sleeping god may wake some day and take offense, or the waking god may draw us out to where we can never return.[8]

It is critical to underline the Dangerous Prayer with a word about the power of God – to give us confidence in God's ability to answer our prayer, and to remind us to adopt an appropriate posture of awe as we pray. We begin the prayer with a plea that God's name be respected; we conclude it by confessing God's purposes (yours is the kingdom), abilities (and the power) and also God's awesomeness (and the glory, forever and ever).

Glory to Worship

Thirdly, we are confident as we pray the Dangerous Prayer because of who God is. We hope in the purpose of God's kingdom, trust in the ability of God's power, and worship the awesomeness of God's glory. We underline our prayers, 'Yours is the kingdom and the power *and the glory*'. In the Dangerous Prayer as we say, 'And don't let us yield to temptation, but deliver us from the evil one', we are one breath away from expressing our confidence in God's purpose, ability and awesomeness. It is a helpful addition to remind us that the kingdom and glory does belong to God, and not to us. Our worship and allegiance is firstly, and completely, owed to God.

I love the way David again expresses his recognition of the awesomeness of God in Psalm 103:1–6:

> Let all that I am praise the LORD;
> with my whole heart, I will praise his holy name.
> Let all that I am praise the LORD;
> may I never forget the good things he does for me.
> He forgives all my sins
> and heals all my diseases.
> He redeems me from death

and crowns me with love and tender mercies.
He fills my life with good things.
My youth is renewed like the eagle's!
The LORD gives righteousness
and justice to all who are treated unfairly.

David praises God for all the goodness from God he has experienced for himself – forgiveness, healing, redemption and renewal of life. But I love also the reminder that it is God's character to give justice to those who do not get a fair go from the world around them. He showed compassion to the people of Israel in releasing them from bondage, and he shows mercy to those who suffer today.

It is fitting to honour God's awesomeness. God is intimately interested in people, and Jesus calls us his friends (John 15:15). Nevertheless, we can be too familiar with God's nature. C.S. Lewis depicted the awesomeness of the nature of God in the character of Aslan in the Narnia Chronicles. In one of my favourite scenes from *The Lion, the Witch and the Wardrobe*, Mr Beaver is explaining to Susan who Aslan is:

'Aslan is a lion – the Lion, the great Lion.'

'Ooh,' said Susan. 'I'd thought he was a man. Is he – quite safe? I shall feel rather nervous about meeting a lion.'

. . . 'Safe?' said Mr Beaver . . . 'Who said anything about safe? 'Course he isn't safe. But he's good. He's the King, I tell you.'[9]

Aslan was a dangerous, unconquerable character. Nothing could keep him down – even sacrificial death. The references to Aslan as Christ-like are numerous. There is an awesomeness to respect about Aslan, and about the God we address in the Dangerous Prayer.

Yet God has come near. Joan Osborne ponders in her song 'One of Us' about how we relate to God and how close God is to humanity. The good news of Christian faith is that God has become one of us, to echo Osborne's song. The fourth gospel writer, John, teaches that God engages with people, and explains that we see God's glory as God came near in Jesus: 'So the Word became human and made his home among us. He was full of unfailing love and faithfulness. And we have seen his glory, the glory of the Father's one and only Son' (1:14).

The awesomeness of God's glory is ironically shown most clearly in how God comes close and intimate as a person. Jesus humbles himself to identify with and serve the lowly and poor – he is found on the margins and in the lowermost places. Thielicke describes how we see God's glory most fully not by imagining God in the distant heavens but by meeting God in the closest struggles of our world:

> Manifestly, his purpose in all this is to demonstrate that this is what his Father is like. And the fact is that God did send his Son through the back door of the world, through the stable of Bethlehem. He sent him into the darkness of the earth and let him descend into the deepest pits of human suffering and death. So if you want to see God, you don't lift your eyes to the clouds, as is often portrayed in sentimental pictures of prayer, but rather you must look down. God is always in the depths.[10]

As we look down, in God's upside-down kingdom we see God in all God's glory. Thielicke continues and says that as we pray this dangerous prayer we:

> learn to stand as it were by the side of our brother Jesus, who is praying along with us, testing this prayer and learning from experience that he really does give us our daily bread and forgive us our sins and really can give us a new heart, a heart that is able to forgive others – *before* it begins to dawn on us that we have a Lord who is rich and good and generous and inexhaustible beyond measure, whose is 'the kingdom and the power and the glory'.[11]

The Dangerous Prayer is framed by this posture of worship. It begins with identifying the God to whom we pray. God is not identified in vague terms but in language that suggests both God's personal nature (our Father) and his superior but accessible place in the universe (in heaven). This leads confidently to praying beyond ourselves for God's kingdom and will. Then it invites us to pray for provision, forgiveness and protection. These are prayers for all of life, not just 'sacred compartments', as if God's glory is limited to heaven. It is part of God's glory that God is interested in bringing heaven to earth.

Dangerous Agreement

We pray all of this dangerous prayer, hoping in God's kingdom, trusting in God's power and loving God's glory, then concluding with 'Amen'. This is a declaration of affirmation and agreement. We might say, 'Yes please, God' or 'So be it'. In the 2004 rebooted series of *Battlestar Galactica*, which interweaves spiritual themes in an exodus story of humanity on the run across the universe, all public prayers end with the phrase 'And so say all of us'. The phrase of *Battlestar Galactica*, like the 'Amen' of the Dangerous Prayer, reminds those praying that we all have a part to play in making the prayers real and active.

The whole prayer reflects a declaration of faith and hope in God, and love for God and the things we've prayed for. 'Amen' is a final note of self-giving. It is not enough, as we have repeated throughout the book, to pray this prayer and leave the answer to God. The prayer is at its most dangerous when it invites us to be part of the answer to our prayer.

Shane Claiborne learned this lesson with his community in Philadelphia. He said it started with an interruption. They were mainly students in the suburbs, studying theology, and then saw in the newspaper that homeless families were living in an abandoned Philadelphia cathedral. But the paper said they were being evicted. They were offered two days to get out, and if not gone would be arrested for trespassing on church property. Claiborne explained that at this point he and his students were significantly interrupted. Something was not right. It was one of the times in his life when he threw his hands up at God and said, 'Why don't you do something?' But God's reply was, 'I did, I made you! Get out! You are passing the person on the side of the road struggling in the ditch. Maybe you could be the answer to your own prayer.'[12]

We pray, 'Yours is the kingdom', but we also strive to see it fulfilled.

The 2012 Greenbelt Festival in the United Kingdom offered timely counsel in 'The Lord's Prayer Challenge':

Don't say 'Father' if you do not behave like a son or daughter.

Don't say 'Our' if you only think of your self.

Don't say 'Hallowed' if you do not honour that name.

Don't say 'Your kingdom come' if you are weighed down with material goods.

Don't say 'Thy will be done' if you do not accept the hard bits.

Don't say 'As it is in heaven' if you only think about earthly matters.

Don't say 'Our daily bread' if you have no concern for the hungry or the homeless.

Don't say 'Forgive us our sins' if you remain angry with someone.

Don't say 'Lead us not into temptation' if you intend to continue sinning.

Don't say 'Deliver us from evil' if you are not willing to make a stand against injustice.

Don't say '*Amen*' without considering the words of your prayer![13]

The Dangerous Prayer is never spirituality divorced from action; nor is it driven activism separated from the wellspring of spirituality; it incorporates action *and* contemplation.

Archbishop Oscar Romero Prayer

Prayer inspired by Jesus is dangerous. Archbishop Oscar Romero of El Salvador knew this. In March 1980, Archbishop Romero was assassinated, while saying mass with his church. Romero had been a safe conservative appointment and was expected by the government to keep the status quo and oppose the church's struggle for liberation alongside the people. But a friend of his, a priest, was assassinated for his commitment to social justice, and Romero could not stand neutral. It is hard not to get angry in the face of gross injustice and deception. He preached every week on national radio against repression, and advocated peace and non-violent change, making him an enemy of the government and military. About 75,000 Salvadorians were killed, a million left the country, another million were homeless. Romero, foreseeing his inevitable fate, had said, 'A bishop will die, but the Church of God – the people – will not perish.'[14]

Romero inspires me to thank God for all who stand up for a better world. He challenges me to confess my complicity with systems that avoid truth.

Romero, like Jesus, radically called for Christians not to accept unjust systems. In Melbourne many are homeless, and around the world millions live in urban slums and squatter settlements without clean water and hygiene. Romero challenges me to confess I have ignored the issues; to thank God for those who are working for positive change; and to pray for people affected – their housing and health, and for policies that reduce global poverty.

Romero spoke against human rights abuses, forced migration and politically motivated repression. He challenges me to confess my turning a blind eye; to thank God for human rights advocates; and to pray for an end to practices that violate human rights, promote illicit drugs and foster violence.

Every year millions of people are displaced, and look for a safer home. Many take desperate steps to hop on boats or cross borders with smugglers. I thank God that as a nation Australia has welcomed many from hundreds of countries; but I am sorry for my nation and its injustice against indigenous peoples and lack of hospitality to the most desperate asylum seekers. I pray asking God to please help Australia to respond with compassion and justice, to those who have been in the country thousands of years and those newly arrived.

Romero similarly inspired Bishop Ken Untener of Saginaw, who wrote a homily that included words that have become known as 'The Romero Prayer':[15]

It helps, now and then, to step back and take a long view.
The kingdom is not only beyond our efforts,
it is even beyond our vision.
We accomplish in our lifetime only a tiny fraction
of the magnificent enterprise that is God's work.
Nothing we do is complete, which is a way of saying
that the kingdom always lies beyond us.
No statement says all that could be said.
No prayer fully expresses our faith.
No confession brings perfection.
No pastoral visit brings wholeness.
No program accomplishes the church's mission.
No set of goals and objectives includes everything.
This is what we are about.
We plant the seeds that one day will grow.
We water seeds already planted,
knowing that they hold future promise.
We lay foundations that will need further development.
We provide yeast that produces far beyond our capabilities.
We cannot do everything, and there is a sense of liberation
in realizing that. This enables us to do something,
and to do it very well. It may be incomplete,
but it is a beginning, a step along the way,
an opportunity for the Lord's grace to enter and do the rest.
We may never see the end results, but that is the difference
between the master builder and the worker.
We are workers, not master builders; ministers, not messiahs.
We are prophets of a future not our own.
Amen.
(Bishop Ken Untener of Saginaw)

Oscar Romero, on 24 March 1980, minutes before his assassination, proclaimed:

> God's reign is already present on our earth in mystery. When the Lord comes, it will be brought to perfection. That is the hope of Christians. We know that every effort to better society, especially when injustice and sin are so ingrained, is an effort that God blesses, that God wants, that God demands of us.[16]

Romero was a prophet of a future that was not his own. So much like Jesus, he embodied a life of service and dangerous prayer, and inspires me to pray dangerously and work sacrificially for a more just world:

> Our loving and divine parent, in heaven and close by, you are awesome.
> May your dream for our world happen and your purposes be fulfilled; bring heaven to our world.
> Give us and the world our daily basic needs.
> Please forgive our garbage, as we reflect your love in graciously forgiving others.
> Keep us from giving in to temptations, and rid our world of evil.
> We pray this confident in your purposes, abilities and awesomeness, now and for all time,
> and we agree to be part of the answer to our prayer.

Journaling and Discussion

1. Read the excerpt or watch a video clip about whether Aslan is 'safe', from *The Lion, the Witch and the Wardrobe*. Discuss or journal your response to the video, and to what extent Aslan reflects the character of God.
2. In what ways does a reminder of God's purposes, abilities and awesomeness give you confidence to pray the Dangerous Prayer?

3. What does it mean for you to pray 'Amen' at the end of this prayer? In what ways is God calling you to be an answer to your prayer?

4. What are the implications of this chapter for you? What would you like to stop doing, start doing, or do differently as a result of reading this chapter and reflecting on its implications?

5. Watch the Common Grace and Bible Society video of Tim Costello discussing the implications of this final phrase of the Dangerous Prayer, and discuss or journal your response.[17]

6. Finish by meditating and praying through the prayer of Oscar Romero on the final pages of the chapter.

Versions

The Lord's Prayer can be frozen and meaningless when recited by rote. Included here, to conclude the book, are some different versions to inspire you about different aspects of the prayer, or to inspire you to write your own versions for your current circumstances.

Luke 11:1–4 NRSVA

He was praying in a certain place, and after he had finished, one of his disciples said to him, 'Lord, teach us to pray, as John taught his disciples.' [2] He said to them, 'When you pray, say:

Father,[a] hallowed be your name.

Your kingdom come.[b]

[3] Give us each day our daily bread.[c]

[4] And forgive us our sins,

for we ourselves forgive everyone indebted to us.

And do not bring us to the time of trial.'[d]

a. Luke 11:2 Other ancient authorities read *Our Father in heaven*
b. Luke 11:2 A few ancient authorities read *Your Holy Spirit come upon us and cleanse us.* Other ancient authorities add *Your will be done, on earth as in heaven*
c. Luke 11:3 Or *our bread for tomorrow*
d. Luke 11:4 Or *us into temptation.* Other ancient authorities add *but rescue us from the evil one* (or *from evil*)

New Zealand Prayer Book

Eternal Spirit,
Earth-maker, pain-bearer, life giver,

Source of all that is and that shall be,
Father and mother of us all,
Loving God, in whom is heaven:

The hallowing of your name echo through the universe!
The way of your justice be followed by the peoples of the world!
Your heavenly will be done by all created beings!
Your commonwealth of peace and freedom sustain our hope and
   come on earth.

With the bread we need for today, feed us.
In the hurts we absorb from one another, forgive us.
In times of temptation and test, strengthen us.
From trials too great to endure, spare us.
From the grip of all that is evil, free us.

For you live in the glory of power that is love,
now and forever. Amen.[1]

Roslyn Wright, Australia

Father of love in heaven,
hallowed be your name of love.
Your kingdom of love come.
Your will of love be done,
on earth as it is in heaven.
Give us this day our daily bread of love.
Forgive us for our failure to love,
as we forgive those who have failed to love us.
Lead us not into the temptation of selfish love
But deliver us from the evil that is anti-love
For yours is the kingdom of love
the power of love

and the glory of love
For ever and ever
Amen[2]

Bret Hesla, USA

All Gracious Spirit,
Who loves us like a mother,
Whose realm is blooming among us now. And within.
We pray that your compassion guide us in every action.
Give us what we need for each day,
and help us to be satisfied with the miracle of that alone.
Forgiver, whose embrace brings us to wholeness without our asking,
May we reconcile ourselves to one another in humility.
And may we cancel the crushing debts that imprison our neighbors
So that communities of joy and health may flourish.
May we neither profit from nor ignore evil.
But ever work to thwart it with non-violence
As we co-create the realm of peace in this world.
Now and each day.
Amen.[3]

Luke 11:1–4 NLT

Once Jesus was in a certain place praying. As he finished, one of his disciples came to him and said, 'Lord, teach us to pray, just as John taught his disciples.'

[2] Jesus said, 'This is how you should pray:[a]

'Father, may your name be kept holy.
May your Kingdom come soon.
[3] Give us each day the food we need,[b]

[4] and forgive us our sins,
as we forgive those who sin against us.
And don't let us yield to temptation.[c]'

a. 11:2 Some manuscripts add additional phrases from the Lord's Prayer
as it reads in Matt 6:9–13.
b. 11:3 Or *Give us each day our food for the day*; or *Give us each day our
food for tomorrow*.
c. 11:4 Or *And keep us from being tested*.

Parker J. Palmer, USA

Heavenly Father, heavenly Mother,
Holy and blessed is your true name.
We pray for your reign of peace to come,
We pray that your good will be done,
Let heaven and earth become one.
Give us this day the bread we need,
Give it to those who have none.
Let forgiveness flow like a river between us,
From each one to each one.
Lead us to holy innocence beyond the evil of our days –
Come swiftly Mother, Father, come.
For yours is the power and the glory and the mercy:
Forever your name is All in One. Amen.[4]

Andrew Chua, Australia

Hey Dad
You who I know always wants what is best for us, and have proved
that over and over again already.
I know you are always near and close to us.
Whenever anyone thinks about you let them think about real
justice and a fair go for all.

Help me and others to always live in ways that respects and loves the environment, all other things, each other and ourselves.

Help us appreciate having only what we need to survive, helping us get those needs if they are out of our reach, or to help us make sure others have what they need to survive.

Let us be free from the consequences we deserve when we live in ways that don't respect creation including others, ourselves and you.

Help us to truly let go of any hate, hurt or feelings of revenge we have towards others who haven't treated us as we expect or want.

Help me avoid anything that disrespects others or you.

Keep me focussed on doing things your way, and although you are powerful, you've allowed us to live as we decide because you trust us to see what is best (because you created us with that potential).

We all commit to think and act to make this so.[5]

John Quinley, USA/Thailand

Lord may your Kingdom come, your will be done, on earth as it is in heaven.

Lord, we know there is no poverty or exploitation in heaven.

Help us then discover fulfilling, creative work that will bring provision, joy, and increase of daily bread.

Lord, make us ready to serve one another, forgiving one another as you have forgiven us.

May we be delivered from the temptation to exploit our sisters and brothers, rather to love one another as you have loved us, displaying the glory of your character and the power of your love. Amen.[6]

Luke 11:1–4 *The Message*

One day he was praying in a certain place. When he finished, one of his disciples said, 'Master, teach us to pray just as John taught his disciples.'

So he said, 'When you pray, say,

> Father,
> Reveal who you are.
> Set the world right.
> Keep us alive with three square meals.
> Keep us forgiven with you and forgiving others.
> Keep us safe from ourselves and the Devil.'

Saadi Neil Douglas-Klotz, Scotland, UK

> Prayer of Jesus
> O Birther of the Cosmos,
> focus your light within us,
> make it useful.
> Create your reign of unity now.
> Your one desire then acts with ours,
> as in all light,
> so in all forms.
> Grant us what we need each day in bread and insight:
> loose the cords of mistakes binding us,
> As we release the strands we hold of others' guilt.
> Don't let surface things delude us,
> but free us from what holds us back.
> From you is born all ruling will,
> the power and the life to do,
> the song that beautifies all,
> from age to age it renews,
> I affirm this with my whole being.
> (As translated from the Aramaic by Saadi Neil Douglas-Klotz)[7]

Revd Dr Nancy L. Steeves, Edmonton, Canada

> Ground of all being,
> we honor the many names for our experience of the sacred.

May we build a community
faithful to the dream of heaven on Earth.
May there be food for all who hunger this day.
May we be forgiven for the falseness of what we have done
as we forgive those who have been untrue to us.
May we not feel abandoned in hard times
but find strength to meet each moment.
For the light of life, the vitality of being
is within us and beyond us, now and forever, AMEN.[8]

George Ella Lyon, Lexington, Kentucky, USA

Our Mother Who Art
in the kitchen
cooking us up
hallowed may we see
all that is
Your kingdom here
delivered into our hands
Your will in children
and trees leafing out
on earth
as if it were Heaven.

Give us this day
bread we could feed
the world
and snatch us bald-headed
if we try to swallow it all.

Don't forgive us
till we learn it is all for giving.
That salve you've got in a pot
on the back of the stove
only heals when everybody has some.

And heed us not
if we believe You look like us
and love us best
and gave us the True Truth
with a license to kill Others
writ inside.
Deliver us from this evil.

For it is Yours,
this kitchen we call Universe
where you stir up our favorite treat,
the Milky Way,
folding deep into sweet

our little sphere
with its powerful glory
    of rainforests
    and oceans
    and mountains in feather-boa mist
forever
    if we don't blow it up
and ever
    if we don't tear it down
Amen

(Ah women
Ah children
Ah reckon She's about fed up.
We better make room at the table
for everybody
before She yells 'OUT!'
and turns our table over,
before She calls it off
this banquet we've been hoarding
this paradise

we aim to save
with bombs.)[9]

Matthew 6:9–13 NRSVA

Pray then in this way:

Our Father in heaven,
hallowed be your name.
[10] Your kingdom come.
Your will be done,
on earth as it is in heaven.
[11] Give us this day our daily bread.[a]
[12] And forgive us our debts,
as we also have forgiven our debtors.
[13] And do not bring us to the time of trial,[b]
but rescue us from the evil one.[c]

a. Matthew 6:11 Or *our bread for tomorrow*
b. Matthew 6:13 Or *us into temptation*
c. Matthew 6:13 Or *from evil*. Other ancient authorities add, in some form, *For the kingdom and the power and the glory are yours forever. Amen.*

Saadi Neil Douglas Klotz, Scotland, UK

O Breathing Life, your Name shines everywhere!
Release a space to plant your Presence here.
Imagine your possibilities now.
Embody your desire in every light and form.
Grow through us this moment's bread and wisdom.
Untie the knots of failure binding us,
as we release the strands we hold of others' faults.
Help us not forget our Source,
Yet free us from not being in the Present.

From you arises every Vision, Power and Song
from gathering to gathering.
Amen –
May our future actions grow from here!
(As translated from the Aramaic by Saadi Neil Douglas-Klotz)[10]

Sarah Dylan Breuer, USA

Loving Creator
we honor you,
and we honor all that you have made.
Renew the whole world
in the image of your love.
Give us what we need for today,
and a hunger to see the whole world fed.
Strengthen us for what lies ahead;
heal us from the hurts of the past;
give us courage to follow your call in this moment.
For your love is the only power,
the only home, the only honor we need,
in this world and in the world to come.
Amen.[11]

Andrew Jones: A Blogger's Prayer (UK, 2002)

Our Father who lives above and beyond the dimension of the
   internet
Give us this day a life worth blogging,
The access to words and images that express our journey with
   passion and integrity, And a secure connection to publish your
   daily mercies.

Your Kingdom come into new spaces today,

As we make known your mysteries,
Posting by posting,
Blog by blog.

Give this day,
The same ability to those less privileged,
Whose lives speak louder than ours,
Whose sacrifice is greater,
Whose stories will last longer.

Forgive us our sins,
For blog-rolling strangers and pretending they are friends,
For counting unique visitors but not noticing unique people,
For delighting in the thousands of hits but ignoring the ONE who
    returns,
For luring viewers but sending them away empty handed,
For updating daily but repenting weekly.

As we forgive those who trespass on our sites to appropriate our
    thoughts without reference,
Our images without approval,
Our ideas without linking back to us.
Lead us not into the temptation to sell out our congregation,
To see people as links and not as lives,
To make our blogs look better than our actual story.

But deliver us from the evil of pimping ourselves instead of
    pointing to you,
From turning our guests into consumers of someone else's products,
From infatuation over the toys of technology,
From idolatry over technology
From fame before our time has come.

For Yours is the power to guide the destinies behind the web logs,
To bring hurting people into the sanctuaries of our sites,

To give us the stickiness to follow you, no matter who is watching
　　or reading.
Yours is the glory that makes people second look our sites and our
　　lives,
Yours is the heavy ambience,
For ever and ever,
Amen.[12]

Max Lucado, USA

Our Father
Thank you for adopting me into your family.

who is
Thank you, my Lord.
for being a God of the present tense:
my Jehovah-jireh (the God who provides),
my Jehovah-raah (the caring Shepherd),
my Jehovah-shalom (the Lord is peace),
my Jehovah-rophe (the God who heals),
and my Jehovah-nissi (Lord, my banner)

in heaven,
Your workshop of creation reminds me: If you can make
the skies, you can make sense out of my struggles.

Hallowed be thy name.
Be holy in my heart.
You are a 'cut above' all else.
Enable me to set my sights on you.

Thy Kingdom come,
Come kingdom!
Be present, Lord Jesus!

Have free reign in every corner of my life.

Thy will be done,
Reveal your heart to me, dear Father.
Show me my role in your passion.
Grant me guidance in the following decisions . . .

On earth as it is in heaven.
Thank you that you silence heaven to hear my prayer.
On my heart are the ones you love.
I pray for . . .

Give us this day our daily bread.
I accept your portion for my life today.
I surrender the following concerns
Regarding my well-being . . .

Forgive us our debts,
I thank you for the roof of grace over my head,
Bound together with the timbers and nails of Calvary.
There is nothing I can do to earn or add to your mercy.
I confess my sins to you . . .

As we also have forgiven our debtors;
Treat me, Father, as I treat others.
Have mercy on the following friends
who have wounded me . . .

Lead us not into temptation,
Let my small hand be engulfed in yours.
Hold me, lest I fall.
I ask for special strength regarding . . .

Our Father . . . give us . . . forgive us . . . lead us
Let your kindness be on all your church.

I pray especially for ministers near
and missionaries far away.

Thine – not mine – is the kingdom,
I lay my plans at your feet.

Thine – not mine – is the power,
I come to you for strength.

Thine – not mine – is the glory,
I give you all the credit.
Forever. Amen.

Thine – not mine – is the power. Amen.[13]

Pat Conover, USA

Ah Creator,
Source of all that is and all that is coming,
Thank you for letting us sense your presence.
Help us to harmonize our lives
with all that you are doing
in us, among us, and around us.
Give us the courage to follow where you lead.
Lure us into following you
both in our experience and in our imaginations.
Give us enough bread to live today.
Encourage us to claim your forgiveness and to forgive each
    other.
Guide us away from temptations
and strengthen us in our resistance to all that we know as evil.
We are deeply grateful for the life and world
you have given us and stand in awe
of what you have done and are doing.

We offer again to direct our lives toward your glory
and hope to find rest in your peace. Amen.[14]

The Credo Community Lord's Prayer, Melbourne, Australia

God our creator, provider and carer,
You are the best and fairest;
We are committed to searching you out
and living the way that you want us to;
Help us not to worry about the future,
and to share what we have with others;
Forgive us when we destroy life
and teach us to create life instead;
Give us courage to choose to forgive
those who hurt us;
Be with us in our time of need
and help us not to give up;
Our safety and life is in you. Amen.[15]

Matthew 6:9–13 NLT

Our Father in heaven,
may your name be kept holy.
May your Kingdom come soon.
May your will be done on earth,
as it is in heaven.
Give us today the food we need,
and forgive us our sins,
as we have forgiven those who sin against us.
And don't let us yield to temptation,
but rescue us from the evil one.
For yours is the kingdom and the power and the glory forever.
Amen.

Australian Aboriginal Lord's Prayer – George Rosendale

You are our father, you live in heaven, we talk to you, Father you
are good.
We believe your word, Father, we your children, give us bread
today.
You are our father, you live in heaven, we talk to you, Father you
are good.
We have done wrong, we are sorry, teach us Father not to sin again.
You are our father, you live in heaven, we talk to you, Father you
are good.
Others have done wrong to us and we are sorry for them, Father,
today.
You are our father, you live in heaven, we talk to you, Father you
are good.
Stop us from doing wrong, Father, save us all from the evil one.[16]

Revd Jim Burklo, USA

Dear One,
closer to us than our own hearts,
farther from us than the most distant star,
you are beyond naming.
May your powerful presence become obvious
not only in the undeniable glory of the sky,
but also in the seemingly base
and common processes of the earth.
Give us what we need, day by day,
to keep body and soul together, because
clever as you have made us,
we still owe our existence to you.
We recognize that to be reconciled with you,
we must live peaceably and justly with other human beings,
putting hate and bitterness behind us.

We are torn between our faith in your goodness
and our awareness of the evil in your creation,
so deliver us from the temptation to despair.
Yours alone is the universe and all its majesty and beauty.
So it is. Amen.[17]

Australian Aboriginal Lord's Prayer – Denise Champion

Our Father
Who lives in heaven
Your name is big
Your name is good
Your Holy land is coming
That's the way God does things
On earth and in heaven
Give us today our special bread
Make things right for humankind when we do the wrong thing by
    God
We make things right for others who do the wrong thing against us
Do not take us on the bad road
Give us your helping hand
Do not follow the footprints that made bad tracks along the way
The holy nation belongs to the Most High
The Most High holds us in his hands
The shining greatness of the Most High
Today, yesterday and forever
That's the way it is![18]

Lala Winkley, UK

God, lover of us all
most holy one,
help us to respond to you

to create what you want
for us here on earth.
Give us today enough for our needs;
forgive our weak and
deliberate offences,
just as we must forgive others
when they hurt us.
Help us to resist evil
and to do what is good;
for we are yours,
endowed with your power
to make our world whole.[19]

Student Christian Movement, India

Our God, the father and the mother,
from, through and to whom all lives flow,
Your name is holy
for you water every creature with life.
May your reign of 'waters rolling in justice'
come down and dwell among us
as it is in your presence.

Give us waters sufficient for our living,
and help us to share waters and our resources
with those that are dying in thirst.
Forgive us of our insincerity, insensitivity, irresponsibility
in saving and preserving waters,
and teach us to forgive one another,
and to seek forgiveness for abusing the creation.

Lead us not into the temptation of accumulation,
greed and dominating the waters,
and deliver us from avaricious lifestyles.
For your word is like waters cleansing us from evil;

for your reign is righteousness,
flowing like an ever flowing stream,
dismantling the powers and principalities,
from generation to generation, from history to history,
forever and ever. Amen.[20]

Matthew 6:9–13 TM

Our Father in heaven,
Reveal who you are.
Set the world right;
Do what's best –
as above, so below.
Keep us alive with three square meals.
Keep us forgiven with you and forgiving others.
Keep us safe from ourselves and the Devil.
You're in charge!
You can do anything you want!
You're ablaze in beauty!
Yes. Yes. Yes.

Darren Cronshaw

Our loving and divine parent, in heaven and close by, you are
 awesome.
May your dream for our world happen and your purposes be
 fulfilled; bring heaven to our world.
Give us and the world our daily basic needs.
Please forgive our garbage, as we reflect your love in graciously
 forgiving others.
Keep us from giving into temptations, and rid our world of evil.
We pray this confident in your purposes, abilities and awesomeness,
 now and for all time,
and we agree to be part of the answer to our prayer.

Bibliography

A New Zealand Prayer Book: He Karakia Mihinare o Aotearoa (Auckland: The Anglican Church in Aotearoa, New Zealand and Polynesia).

Anderson, Ray S. *An Emergent Theology for Emerging Churches* (Downers Grove: IVP, 2006).

Australian Government, Australian Institute of Health and Welfare. *Specialist Homelessness Services 2011–12* (Canberra: AIHW, 2012) http://www.aihw.gov.au/publication-detail/?id=60129542549

Baab, Lynne M. *Sabbath Keeping: Finding Freedom in the Rhythms of Rest* (Downers Grove: IVP, 2005).

Baptist World Alliance. 'BWA Urges Action on Nigerian Crisis and Climate Change' (2012). Published electronically 8 July. http://www.bwanet.org/news/news-releases/153-nigerian-crisis

Barnett, Beth. 'A Liturgy for Awful Times.' *multivocality: many voices many friends* (2014). Published electronically 8 August. http://multivocality.wordpress.com/2014/08/08/a-liturgy-for-awful-times/

BBC News. 'Pope Francis Asks Forgiveness for Child Abuse by Clergy' (2014). Published electronically 11 April. http://www.bbc.com/news/world-europe-26989991

Biddulph, Steve. *Manhood* (Sydney: Finch, 1995).

Boff, Leonardo. *Cry of the Earth, Cry of the Poor* (Maryknoll: Orbis, 1997).

Bombeck, Erma. *Eat Less Cottage Cheese and More Ice Cream: Thoughts on Life from Erma Bombeck* (Kansas City: Andrews McMeel, 2003).

Bonhoeffer, Dietrich. *The Cost of Discipleship* (London: SCM, 1959).

Boom, Corrie Ten, with John and Elizabeth Sherrill. *The Hiding Place* (New York: Bantam, 1984).

Bosch, David J. *Transforming Mission: Paradigm Shifts in Theology of Mission* (Maryknoll: Orbis, 1991).

Bray, Gerald. *Yours Is the Kingdom: A Systematic Theology of the Lord's Prayer* (Nottingham: IVP, 2007).

Bread for the World. 'About Global Hunger' http://www.bread.org/hunger/global/

Brussat, Frederic, and Mary Ann Brussat. *Spiritual Literacy: Reading the Sacred in Everyday Life* (New York: Touchstone, 1996).

Buechner, Frederick. *Listening to Your Life: Daily Meditations with Frederick Buechner* (New York: Harper One, 1992).

———. *Wishful Thinking: A Theological ABC* (New York: Harper & Row, 1973).

Carter, Warren. 'The Gospel of Matthew'. Pages 69–104 in *A Postcolonial Commentary on the New Testament Writings* (ed. Fernando F. Segovia and R.S. Sugirtharajah; London: T&T Clark, 2007).

———. *Matthew and the Margins: A Sociopolitical and Religious Reading* (Maryknoll: Orbis, 2000).

Champion, Denise, with Rosemary Dewerse, *Yarta Wandatha: The Land Is Speaking* (Adelaide: Denise Champion, 2014).

Claiborne, Shane. 'Lessons from the Good Samaritan'. *New Urban World*, no. 3 (2013): pp. 37–48.

———. 'Mark 2: Sharing Economic Resources with Fellow Community Members and the Needy among Us'. Pages 26–38 in *School(s) for Conversion: 12 Marks of a New Monasticism* (ed. The Rutba House; Eugene: Cascade, 2005).

Claiborne, Shane, and Jonathan Wilson-Hartgrove. *Becoming the Answer to Our Prayers: Prayer for Ordinary Radicals* (Downers Grove: IVP, 2008).

Claiborne, Shane, Jonathan Wilson-Hartgrove and Enuma Okoro. *Common Prayer: A Liturgy for Ordinary Radicals* (Grand Rapids: Zondervan, 2010).

Climacus, John. *The Ladder of Divine Accent* (trans. Lazarus Moore; New York: Harper, 1959).

Cloud, Henry, and John Townsend. *Boundaries: When to Say Yes, How to Say No to Take Control of Your Life* (Sydney: Strand, 2002).

Coekin, Richard. *Our Father: Enjoying God in Prayer* (Nottingham: IVP, 2009).

Coleridge, Mark. 'Archbishop Coleridge Your Kingdom Come', Common Grace [video], YouTube (uploaded on 24 February 2015) https://www.youtube.com/watch?v=r9Q5Ft82-9M or http://www.lordsprayer.org.au/your_kingdom_come

Collins, Suzanne. *The Hunger Games* (London: Scholastic, 2008).

———. *The Hunger Games: Mockingjay* (Gosford: Scholastic, 2010).

Costello, Tim. *Hope: Moments of Inspiration in a Challenging World* (Melbourne: Hardie Grant, 2012).

———. 'A Passion for Hope and Justice'. Pages 3–22 in *Another Way to Love* (ed. Tim Costello and Rod Yule; Brunswick East: World Vision and Acorn, 2009).

———. 'Rev Tim Costello – Thine Be the Kingdom.' Common Grace [video], YouTube (uploaded on 31 May 2015) https://www.youtube.com/watch?v=8JcUE9nrLGs or http://www.lordsprayer.org.au/yours_is_the_kingdom

———. *Streets of Hope: Finding God in St. Kilda* (St Leonards: Allen & Unwin, 1998).

Cotter, Jim. *Prayer at Night: A Book for the Darkness* (Sheffield: Cairns, 2011).

Cronshaw, Darren. *Credible Witness: Companions, Prophets, Hosts and Other Australian Mission Models* (Melbourne: Urban Neighbours of Hope, 2006).

———. 'Domestic Violence – Where Is God in the Grief?', *Baptists on Mission Blog (BoMb)* (24 November 2016) https://www.buv.com.au/news/domestic-violence-where-is-god-in-the-grief

———. '*Eating Heaven: Spirituality at the Table*, by Simon Carey Holt (Book Review)'. *Journal of Missional Practice* no. 3, Autumn (2013) http://journalofmissionalpractice.com/book-review-eating-heaven-spirituality-at-the-table-by-simon-holt/

———. 'Editorial – Mission and Spirituality'. *Australian Journal of Mission Studies* 2.2 (December 2008): pp. 1–3.

———. '*Everything Must Change: Jesus, Global Crises and a Revolution of Hope*, by Brian D. McLaren (Book Review)'. *Witness: The Voice of Victorian Baptists* 90.10 (2010): p. 20. https://www.buv.com.au/baptistonmission/about-us/what-does-it-mean-to-be-a-baptist

———. 'Improvising a Renewed Story at Auburnlife: Utilising Biblical Narrative for Congregational Transformation'. Pages 225–39 in *Cultural Diversity, Worship, and Australian Baptist Church Life*, New Wineskins, vol. 2 (ed. Darrell Jackson and Darren Cronshaw; Sydney: Morling, 2016).

———. 'Leadership Column (Human Rights)'. *Witness: The Voice of Victorian Baptists* 91.2 (March 2011): p. 7.

———. '*The Leadership Ellipse: Shaping How We Lead by Who We Are*, by Robert A Fryling (Book Review)'. *Witness: The Voice of Victorian Baptists* 90.10 (2010): p. 22. https://www.buv.com.au/baptistonmission/book-reviews/theleadershipellipse

———. '"Lord Let Me Care": Glimpsing Back to Baptist Approaches to Social Justice.' Baptcare-commissioned resource article. https://www.buv.com.au/documents/item/1744

———. 'New Monasticism for Australian Mission: Reflections from "*School(s) for Conversion: 12 Marks of a New Monasticism*"'. *Australian Journal of Mission Studies*, June (2014): pp. 17–25.

———. 'Reenvisioning Theological Education and Missional Spirituality'. *Journal of Adult Theological Education* 9.1 (2012): pp. 9–27.

————. 'Reenvisioning Theological Education, Vocation and the Kingdom of God'. *Zadok Papers* S195 (Summer 2012): pp. 9–16.

————. 'Resisting the Empire in Young Adult Fiction: Lessons from Hunger Games'. In *Re-Naming Sovereignty* (ed. Mark Brett and Monica Melanchthon, forthcoming 2017).

————. 'Review of *Desiring the Kingdom: Worship, Worldview and Cultural Formation*, by James K.A. Smith'. *Journal of Adult Theological Education* 8.2 (2011): pp. 199–200.

————. '*The Road Trip That Changed the World: The Unlikely Theory That Will Change How You View Culture, the Church, and Most Importantly, Yourself*, by Mark Sayers (Book Review)'. *Literature and Theology: An International Journal of Religion, Theory and Culture* 28.4 (December 2014): pp. 491–3.

————. 'Saving Souls and Listening Hearts: Implications for Missional Leaders from Richard Rohr's *Immortal Diamond: The Search for Our True Self*. *Colloquium* 46.2 (November 2014): pp. 242–54.

————. '*The Vertical Self: How Biblical Faith Can Help Us Discover Who We Are in an Age of Self Obsession*, by Mark Sayers (Book Review)'. *EA Equip*, no. 9, June (2011): p. 14. http://www.ea.org.au/site/DefaultSite/filesystem/documents/Equip/EA%20Equip%20Mag%20June11_Web.pdf

Cronshaw, Darren, David Chatelier, Brent Lyons-Lee, Ryan Smith and Anne Wilkinson-Hayes. 'A Contemporary Theology of Local Church Mission, in Global Perspective'. Pages 251–70 in *Congregational Transformation in Australian Baptist Church Life* (ed. Darren Cronshaw and Darrell Jackson; Sydney: Morling, 2015).

Cronshaw, Darren, Stacey Wilson, Meewon Yang, with Ner Dah, Si Khia, Arohn Kuung and Japheth Lian. '"God Called Us Here for a Reason" . . . Karen and Chin Baptist Churches in Victoria: Mission from the Margins of a Diaspora Community'. Pages 263–78 in *We Are Pilgrims: Mission from, in and with the Margins of Our Diverse World* (ed. Darren Cronshaw and Rosemary Dewerse; Melbourne: Urban Neighbours of Hope, 2015).

Crosby, Michael H. *The Prayer That Jesus Taught Us* (Maryknoll: Orbis, 2002).

———. *Thy Will Be Done: Praying the Our Father as Subversive Activity* (Maryknoll: Orbis, 1977).

Crossan, John Dominic. *The Greatest Prayer: Rediscovering the Revolutionary Message of the Lord's Prayer* (London: SPCK, 2011).

Croucher, Rowland. *A Garden of Solitude* (Sutherland: Albatross, 1998).

———. *Rivers in the Desert: Meditations and Prayers for Refreshment* (Sutherland: Albatross, 1991).

———. *Still Waters, Deep Waters: Meditations and Prayers for Busy People* (Sutherland: Albatross, 1987).

d'Alpuget, Blanche. *Robert J. Hawke: A Biography* (Melbourne: Schwartz, 1982).

de Kock, Wynand. *Out of My Mind: Following the Trajectory of God's Redemptive Story* (Eugene: Wipf and Stock, 2014).

de Mello, Anthony. *Taking Flight: A Book of Story Meditations* (New York: Doubleday, 1988).

Dickson, John. 'Rev Dr John Dickson – Give Us Today Our Daily Bread'. Common Grace [video], YouTube (uploaded on 9 March 2015) https://www.youtube.com/watch?v=uQUp6Ll8Ez8 or http://www.lordsprayer.org.au/give_us_today

Dillard, Annie. *Teaching a Stone to Talk: Expeditions and Encounters* (New York: Harper & Row, 1982).

Dillenberger, John, ed. *Martin Luther: Selections from His Writings* (New York: Doubleday, 1962).

Douglas-Klotz, Neil. *Desert Wisdom: A Nomad's Guide to Life's Big Questions from the Heart of the Native Middle East* (Columbus, OH and Edinburgh: ARC Books, 2010).

Duncan, Ann, and Andy Lanford. 'Teen Hero: Life and Death in *The Hunger Games*'. *Christian Century* (4 April 2012): pp. 12–13.

Duncan, Michael. *Alongsiders: Sitting with Those Who Sit Alone* (Melbourne: Urban Neighbours of Hope, 2014).

Dunn, George A., and Nicholas Michaud. 'Introduction: Let the Hunger Games and Philosophy Begin!' Pages 1–5 in *The Hunger Games and Philosophy: A Critique of Pure Treason* (ed. George A. Dunn and Nicholas Michaud; Hoboken: John Wiley & Sons, 2012).

Fernando, Ajith. 'The Uniqueness of Jesus Christ'. Pages 123–37 in *Telling the Truth: Evangelizing Postmoderns* (ed. D.A. Carson; Grand Rapids: Zondervan, 2000).

Fight Slavery Now. 'Child Soldiers' (2010). Published electronically 30 May. http://fightslaverynow.org/why-fight-there-are-27-million-reasons/otherformsoftrafficking/child-soldiers/

Fisher, Max. 'This Map Shows Where the World's 30 Million Slaves Live. There Are 60,000 in the U.S.', *The Washington Post* (2013). Published electronically 17 October. http://www.washingtonpost.com/blogs/worldviews/wp/2013/10/17/this-map-shows-where-the-worlds-30-million-slaves-live-there-are-60000-in-the-u-s/

Forrest Gump. 'Sometimes, I Guess There Just Aren't Enough Rocks' [video], YouTube (uploaded on 20 March 2012) https://www.youtube.com/watch?v=anz91PPMPw8

Foster, Richard. *Prayer: Finding the Heart's True Home* (New York: HarperCollins, 1992).

————. *Streams of Living Water: Celebrating the Great Traditions of Christian Faith* (London: HarperCollins, 1999).

Frost, Michael. *Exiles: Living Missionally in a Post-Christian Culture* (Peabody: Hendrickson, 2006).

————. *Incarnate: The Body of Christ in an Age of Disengagement* (Downers Grove: IVP, 2014).

————. *Jesus the Fool: The Mission of the Unconventional Christ* (Melbourne: Urban Neighbours of Hope, 2007).

Frost, Michael, and Alan Hirsch. *The Shaping of Things to Come: Innovation and Mission for the 21st-Century Church* (Peabody: Hendrickson, 2003).

Fryling, Robert A. *The Leadership Ellipse: Shaping How We Lead by Who We Are* (Downers Grove: IVP, 2010).

Gandhi, Mahatma. '364. Wanted a Manifestation of Christ in Daily Life'. Pages 327–8 in *The Collected Works of Mahatma Gandhi*, vol. 63 (18 January – 19 May 1934). GandhiServe Foundation http://www.gandhiserve.org/cwmg/VOL063.PDF

'George Müller.' *Wikipedia* http://en.wikipedia.org/wiki/George_M%C3%BCller#cite_ref-12

Grahame, Kenneth. *The Wind in the Willows* (Ware: Wordsworth, 1993).

Greenwood, Adrian. 'A Social Justice Grace?', *more>praxis.org.au* (2009). Published electronically 17 September. http://morepraxis.org.au/a-social-justice-grace/

Grey, Jacqueline. 'Rev Dr Jacqueline Grey – Our Father'. Common Grace [video], YouTube (uploaded on 19 February 2015) https://www.youtube.com/watch?v=_sEHF3kBn2w or http://www.lords-prayer.org.au/our_father_in_heaven

Hamilton, Clive. *Affluenza: When Too Much Is Never Enough* (Crows Nest: Allen & Unwin, 2006).

Hammond, Kim, and Darren Cronshaw. *Sentness: Six Postures of Missional Christians* (Downers Grove: IVP, 2014).

Hand, Karl. 'Come Now, Let Us Treason Together: Conversion and Revolutionary Consciousness in Luke 22:35–38 and The Hunger Games Trilogy'. *Literature and Theology: An International Journal of Religion, Theory and Culture* 29.3 (2015): pp. 348–65.

Hare, Douglas R.A. *Matthew* (Louisville: John Knox, 1993).

Harris, Joanne. *Chocolat* (London: Transworld, 1999).

Hawke, Bob. *The Hawke Memoirs* (London: Heinemann, 1994).

Hawkins, Tim. 'Tim Hawkins Comedy – Worship & Prayer'. http://www.youtube.com/watch?v=iz17Ugnz6rg

Helland, Roger, and Leonard Hjalmarson. *Missional Spirituality: Embodying God's Love from the Inside Out* (Downers Grove: IVP, 2011).

Hirsch, Debra. *Redeeming Sex: Naked Conversations about Sexuality and Spirituality* (Downers Grove: IVP, 2015).

Holt, Simon Carey. *Eating Heaven: Spirituality at the Table* (Brunswick East: Acorn, 2013).

Huggett, Joyce. *Conflict: Understanding, Managing & Growing through Conflict* (Guildford: Eagle, 1998).

Hughes, Philip, and Darren Cronshaw. *Baptists in Australia: A Church with a Heritage and a Future* (Melbourne: Christian Research Association, 2013).

Hybels, Bill. 'Power: Preaching for Total Commitment'. Pages 113–25 in *Mastering Contemporary Preaching* (ed. Stuart Briscoe, Bill Hybels and Haddon Robinson; Portland: Multnomah, 1989).

———. *Too Busy Not to Pray: Slowing Down to Be with God* (Downers Grove: IVP, 2008).

Jeyaratnam, Chrishan. 'Chrishan Jeyaratnam – Your Will Be Done'. Common Grace [video], YouTube (uploaded on 3 March 2015) https://www.youtube.com/watch?v=r9r59qocaJ4 or http://www.lordsprayer.org.au/your_will_be_done

Jones, Barry D. *Dwell: Life with God for the World* (Downers Grove: IVP, 2014).

Jones, David, and Russell Woodbridge. *Health, Wealth & Happiness: Has the Prosperity Gospel Overshadowed the Gospel of Christ?* (Grand Rapids: Kregel, 2011).

Jones, Tony. 'Hopeful Activism'. Pages 245–6 in *An Emergent Manifesto of Hope* (ed. Doug Pagitt and Tony Jones; Grand Rapids: Baker, 2007).

King Jr, Martin Luther. 'A Christmas Sermon on Peace' (1967). http://www.ecoflourish.com/Primers/education/Christmas_Sermon.html

———. 'Remaining Awake through a Great Revolution'. Delivered at the National Cathedral, Washington, DC, 1968.

———. *Stride towards Freedom* (New York: Harper & Row, 1958).

Lagos-Schuffenegger, Roberto. 'Human Rights in South America'. In Commission on Social and Environmental Justice, unpublished paper, Baptist World Alliance annual gathering, Santiago, Chile, 2012.

Langmead, Ross. 'Theological Reflection in Ministry and Mission'. *Ministry Society and Theology* 18 (2004): pp. 9–28.

Lester, Muriel. *Ambassador of Reconciliation: A Muriel Lester Reader* (Philadelphia: New Society, 1991).

Leunig, Michael. *Common Prayer Collection* (North Blackburn: HarperCollins, 1993).

Lewis, C.S. *The Lion, the Witch and the Wardrobe*. The Chronicles of Narnia, Book Two (New York: HarperCollins, 2002).

———. *The Weight of Glory and Other Addresses* (Grand Rapids: Eerdmans, 1965).

Lewis, Peter. *The Lord's Prayer: The Greatest Prayer in the World* (Milton Keynes: Paternoster, 2008).

Linklater, Andro. *Owning the Earth: The Transforming History of Land Ownership* (New York: Bloomsbury, 2013).

Linn, Dennis, Sheila Fabricant Linn and Matthew Linn. *Don't Forgive Too Soon: Extending the Two Hands That Heal* (New York: Paulist, 1997).

Llosa, Mario Vargas. *The Temptation of the Impossible: Victor Hugo and* Les Misérables (Princeton: Princeton University Press, 2007).

'The Lord's Prayer'. Common Grace and the Bible Society http://www.lordsprayer.org.au/

Lucado, Max. *God Will Use This for Good: Surviving the Mess of Life* (Nashville: Thomas Nelson, 2013).

———. *The Great House of God: A Home for Your Heart* (Dallas: Word, 1997).

Luz, Ulrich. *Matthew 1 – 7: A Continental Commentary* (Minneapolis: Fortress, 1989).

Mancini, Will. *Church Unique: How Missional Leaders Cast Vision, Capture Culture, and Create Movement* (San Francisco: Jossey-Bass, 2008).

Mandela, Nelson. *Long Walk to Freedom* (London: Abacus, 1994).

Mandryk, Jason. *Operation World: The Definitive Prayer Guide to Every Nation* (Downers Grove: IVP, 2010).

McKenna, Jarrod. 'Jarrod McKenna – Teach Us to Pray'. Common Grace [video], YouTube (uploaded on 17 February 2015) https://www.youtube.com/watch?v=c9J3ItajSiY or http://www.lordsprayer.org.au/introductory_video

McLaren, Brian D. *Everything Must Change: Jesus, Global Crises and a Revolution of Hope* (Nashville: Thomas Nelson, 2007).

———. *The Secret Message of Jesus: Uncovering the Truth That Could Change Everything* (Nashville: Thomas Nelson, 2006).

Meier, Paul. *Don't Let Jerks Get the Best of You: Advice for Dealing with Difficult People* (Nashville: Thomas Nelson, 1993).

Merton, Thomas. *Conjectures of a Guilty Bystander* (New York: Doubleday, 1966).

———. *Contemplative Prayer* (London: Darton, Longman & Todd, 1969).

Messer, Donald. *Contemporary Images of Christian Ministry* (Nashville: Abingdon, 1989).

Miller, Donald. *Blue Like Jazz: Nonreligious Thoughts on Christian Spirituality* (Nashville: Thomas Nelson, 2003).

Moltmann, Jürgen. *The Crucified God: The Cross of Christ as the Foundation and Criticism of Christian Theology* (London: SCM, 1974).

———. *The Gospel of Liberation* (Waco: Word, 1973).

Moore, James W. *Yes Lord, I Have Sinned, but I Have Several Good Excuses* (Nashville: Abingdon, 1991).

Morris, Leon. *The Gospel According to Matthew* (Grand Rapids: Eerdmans, 1992).

Moynagh, Michael. *Emergingchurch.Intro* (Oxford: Monarch, 2004).

Muggeridge, Malcolm. *A Twentieth Century Testimony* (Nashville: Thomas Nelson, 1978).

Myers, Ben. 'Dr Ben Myers – Deliver Us from Evil'. Common Grace [video], YouTube (uploaded on 24 March 2015) https://www.youtube.com/watch?v=1nZnquVyfJs

Nelson-Pallmeyer, Jack and Bret Hesla. *Worship in the Spirit of Jesus: Theology, Liturgy and Songs without Violence* (Eugene: Wipf and Stock, 2004).

Nettleton, Nathan. 'South Yarra Baptist Weekly Worship' http://laughingbird.net/sycb/SouthYarraBaptist/Weekly_Worship.html

Newbigin, Lesslie. *The Good Shepherd: Meditations on Christian Ministry in Today's World* (London: Mowbray, 1977).

———. *The Open Secret: Sketches for a Missionary Theology* (Grand Rapids: Eerdmans, 1978).

Nouwen, Henri. *Reaching Out: The Three Movements of the Spiritual Life* (New York: Doubleday, 1975).

Nouwen, Henri J.M., with Michael J. Christensen and Rebecca J. Laird. *Discernment: Reading the Signs of Daily Life* (London: SPCK, 2013).

Ortberg, John. *The Life You've Always Wanted: Spiritual Disciplines for Ordinary People* (Grand Rapids: Zondervan, 2002).

Owen, Jon. *Muddy Spirituality: Bringing It All Down to Earth* (Dandenong: U N of Hope, 2011).

Palmer, Parker J. *Let Your Life Speak: Listening for the Voice of Vocation* (San Francisco: Jossey-Bass, 2000).

———. *The Promise of Paradox: A Celebration of Contradictions in the Christian Life* (San Francisco: Jossey-Bass, 2008).

Patch Adams. 'Patch Adams Butterfly Omen' [video], YouTube (uploaded on 23 October 2011) https://www.youtube.com/watch?v=30rGicdlWm0

Paulsell, Stephanie. 'Spiritual Formation and Intellectual Work in Theological Education'. *Theology Today* 55.2, July (1998): pp. 229–34.

Paulson, Graham, and Grant Paulson. 'Uncle Graham & Grant Paulson – Forgive Us Our Sins'. Common Grace [video], YouTube (uploaded on 17 May 2015) https://www.youtube.com /watch?v=YIUcZ_HBktU   or   http://www.lordsprayer.org.au/and_forgive_us_our_debts

Percival, Kevin. 'Not Just the Task of the Church to Preach the Gospel, but to Serve Those in Need'. Final year thesis (Baptist College of New South Wales, c. 1976).

Peterson, Eugene H. *Christ Plays in Ten Thousand Places: A Conversation in Spiritual Theology* (London: Hodder & Stoughton, 2005).

———. *Five Smooth Stones for Pastoral Work* (Grand Rapids: Eerdmans, 1992).

———. *Working the Angles: The Shape of Pastoral Integrity* (Grand Rapids: Eerdmans, 1987).

Phillips, J.B. *Your God Is Too Small* (New York: Touchstone, 1997).

Pike, Eunice V. 'The Concept of Limited Good and the Spread of the Gospel'. *Missiology: An International Review* 8.4 (October 1980): pp. 449–54.

Pitts, Bill. 'Christianity and the Social Crisis'. *Baptist History and Heritage* (Summer/Fall 2006): pp. 35–48.

Polanyi, Michael. *Personal Knowledge: Towards a Post-Critical Philosophy* (London: Routledge & Kegan Paul, 1962).

Pope John Paul II. 'Nova Millennio Ineunte' (6 January 2001).

Popovic, Srdja, with Matthew Miller. *Blueprint for Revolution: How to Use Rice Pudding, Lego Men, and Other Nonviolent Techniques to*

Galvanize Communities, Overthrow Dictators, or Simply Change the World (New York: Random House, 2015).

Porter, Muriel. *Land of the Spirit? The Australian Religious Experience* (Geneva: World Council of Churches, 1990).

Postema, Don. *Space for God: Study and Practice of Spirituality and Prayer* (Grand Rapids: Faith Alive Christian Resources, 1997).

Quinley Jr, John H., with John H. Quinley III, 'Urban Economic Shalom: Possible Place of Peace and Economic Growth'. Pages 51–69 in *Seeking Urban Shalom: Integral Urban Mission in a New Urban World* (ed. Darren Cronshaw; Melbourne: International Society for Urban Mission, 2014).

Raiter, Michael. *Stirrings of the Soul: Evangelicals and the New Spirituality* (Sydney: Matthias, 2003).

Reeves, Nancy. *Spirituality for Extroverts (and Tips for Those Who Love Them)* (Nashville: Abingdon, 2008).

Rhyder, Julia, and Darren Cronshaw. 'Mustard Tree Aspirations (Luke 13:18–19)'. *W!tness* (10 July 2014, reproduced 3 November 2016). https://www.buv.com.au/news/mustard-tree-aspirations-luke-1318-19

Roddan, Michael. 'Domestic Violence: Telling It Like It Is'. *The Citizen* (2013). Published electronically 27 September. http://thecitizen.org.au/features/domestic-violence-telling-it-it

Rohr, Richard. *Immortal Diamond: The Search for Our True Self* (London: SPCK, 2013).

———. *The Naked Now: Learning to See How the Mystics See* (New York: Crossroad, 2009).

Romero, Robert Chao. *Jesus for Revolutionaries: An Introduction to Race, Social Justice, and Christianity* (Christian Ethnic Studies, 2013).

Rosendale, George. 'Breaking Open the Word for Aborigines'. *Compass: A Review of Topical Theology* 37.3 (Spring 2003) http://compassreview.org/spring03/2.html

Rudd, Kevin. 'Apology to Australia's Indigenous Peoples' (2008). http://www.australia.gov.au/about-australia/our-country/our-people/apology-to-australias-indigenous-peoples

Rupp, Joyce. *The Open Door: A Journey to the True Self* (Notre Dame: Sorin, 2008).

Russell, Bertrand. *The Autobiography of Bertrand Russell, 1872–1914*, vol. 1 (London: George Allen & Unwin, 1967).

———. *The Autobiography of Bertrand Russell, 1944–1967*, vol. 3 (London: George Allen & Unwin, 1969).

Sayers, Mark. *The Road Trip That Changed the World: The Unlikely Theory That Will Change How You View Culture, the Church, and Most Importantly, Yourself* (Chicago: Moody, 2012).

———. *The Vertical Self: How Biblical Faith Can Help Us Discover Who We Are in an Age of Self Obsession* (Nashville: Thomas Nelson, 2010).

Seamands, David A. *Healing Grace: Finding a Freedom from the Performance Trap* (Wheaton: Victor, 1989).

Shomanah, Musa W. Dube. 'Praying the Lord's Prayer in a Global Economic Era'. *Ecumenical Review* 49 (1997): pp. 439–50.

Simpson, Ray, and Brent Lyons-Lee. *Emerging Downunder: Creating New Monastic Villages of God* (Adelaide: ATF, 2008).

Smith, C. Christopher, and John Pattison. *Slow Church: Cultivating Community in the Patient Way of Jesus* (Downers Grove: IVP, 2014).

Smith, James K.A. *Desiring the Kingdom: Worship, Worldview and Cultural Formation* (Grand Rapids: Baker, 2009).

Smith, John. *Advance Australia Where?* (Homebush West: ANZEA, 1988).

Smith, Mitzi J. '"Knowing More Than Is Good for One": A Womanist Interrogation of the Matthean Great Commission'. Pages 127–56 in *Teaching All Nations: Interrogating the Matthean Great Commission* (ed. Mitzi J. Smith and Jayachitra Lalitha; Minneapolis: Fortress, 2014).

Sondheim, Stephen. 'Into the Woods–Any Moment Lyrics'. *MetroLyrics* http://www.metrolyrics.com/into-the-woods-any-moment-lyrics-broadways.html

Soon, Wong Young. Keynote conference talk, at Signs of Hope in the City, International Society for Urban Mission Summit, Kuala Lumpur, 1 July 2014.

St Cyprian. *The 'Our Father'* (Dublin: Clonmore & Reynolds, 1953).

St John of the Cross. *Dark Night of the Soul* (trans. E. Allison Peers; London: Catholic Way, 2013).

Steer, Roger. *George Müller: Delighted in God* (Tain: Christian Focus, 1997).

Stevenson, Kenneth W. *The Lord's Prayer: A Text in Tradition* (Minneapolis: Fortress, 2004).

Stowell, Joseph M. *Following Christ: Experiencing Life the Way It Was Meant to Be* (Grand Rapids: Zondervan, 1996).

Tacey, David. *Remaking Men: The Revolution in Masculinity* (Ringwood: Viking, 1997).

Thielicke, Helmut. *The Prayer That Spans the World: Sermons on the Lord's Prayer* (London: Lutterworth, 1988).

Tolkien, J.R.R. *The Lord of the Rings* (Boston: HarperCollins, 2005).

Tolstoy, Leo. 'How Much Land Does One Man Need?' http://www.online-literature.com/tolstoy/2738/

Tutu, Desmond. *No Future without Forgiveness* (New York: Image Doubleday, 1999).

Tyler, Tim. 'Global Crisis Wrap-up (Global Crisis Series)' (2012). Published electronically 3 March. http://planetsave.com/2012/03/03/global-crisis-wrap-up-global-crisis-series/

Untener, Bishop Ken of Saginaw. 'Archbishop Oscar Romero Prayer: A Step along the Way' (1979). http://www.usccb.org/prayer-and-worship/prayers-and-devotions/prayers/archbishop_romero_prayer.cfm van de Kamp, Bert. *And They Called Him Bono* (lulu.com, 2012).

Vanier, Jean. *Befriending the Stranger* (Mahwaj: Paulist, 2010).

Volf, Miroslav. *A Public Faith: How Followers of Christ Should Serve the Common Good* (Grand Rapids: Brazos, 1996).

Walk Free. 'Learn More about Modern Slavery'. http://www.walkfree. org/learn/

Walters, Dorothy. *Marrow of Flame: Poems of the Spiritual Journey* (Boulder: Poetry Chaikhana, 2nd edn, 2015).

Walton, John H. *Genesis: The NIV Application Commentary* (Grand Rapids: Zondervan, 2001).

Water Aid Australia. 'Statistics'. http://www.wateraidaustralia.org

Weil, Simone. *Waiting for God* (trans. Emma Craufurd; New York: Harper Perennial, 1951).

Weinandy, Thomas G. *Does God Suffer?* (Notre Dame: University of Notre Dame, 2000).

Wells, David. 'Prayer: Rebelling against the Status Quo'. Pages 142–4 in *Perspectives on the World Christian Movement: A Reader* (ed. Ralph D. Winter and Steven C. Hawthorne; Pasadena: William Carey Library, 1999).

Wilkinson-Hayes, Anne. 'Living Our Prayer (Matthew 5:13)'. Aberfeldie Baptist Church sermon, 6 February 2005.

Willard, Dallas. *The Divine Conspiracy: Rediscovering Our Hidden Life in God* (San Francisco: HarperSanFrancisco, 1998).

Williamson, Marianne. *A Return to Love: Reflections on the Principles of* A Course in Miracles (New York: HarperCollins, 1992).

Willimon, William H., and Stanley Hauerwas. *Lord, Teach Us: The Lord's Prayer and the Christian Life* (Nashville: Abingdon, 1996).

Wink, Walter. *Engaging the Powers: Discernment and Resistance in a World of Domination* (Minneapolis: Fortress, 1992).

———. *The Powers That Be: Theology for a New Millennium* (New York: Galilee, 1999).

Woodward, J.R. *Creating a Missional Culture: Equipping the Church for the Sake of the World* (Downers Grove: IVP, 2012).

Work, Telford. *Ain't Too Proud to Beg: Living through the Lord's Prayer* (Grand Rapids: Eerdmans, 2007).

Wright, Christopher J.H. *The Mission of God: Unlocking the Bible's Grand Narrative* (Nottingham: IVP, 2006).

Wright, N.T. *Jesus and the Victory of God* (London: SPCK, 1996).

———. *Surprised by Hope* (New York: HarperOne, 2008).

Wright, Tom. *The Lord and His Prayer* (London: Triangle, 1996).

———. *Luke for Everyone* (London: SPCK, 2001).

———. *Simply Christian* (London: SPCK, 2006).

Yancey, Philip. *What's So Amazing about Grace?* (Grand Rapids: Zondervan, 1997).

Zehr, Howard. *Changing Lenses: A New Focus for Crime and Justice* (Scottdale: Herald, 1990).

Notes

Foreword

[1] Barry D. Jones, *Dwell: Life with God for the World* (Downers Grove: IVP, 2014), p. 135.

Preface

[1] Darren Cronshaw et al., "'God Called Us Here for a Reason' . . . Karen and Chin Baptist Churches in Victoria: Mission from the Margins of a Diaspora Community', in *We Are Pilgrims: Mission from, in and with the Margins of Our Diverse World*; (ed. Darren Cronshaw and Rosemary Dewerse; Melbourne: Urban Neighbours of Hope, 2015), pp. 263–78.

[2] https://www.baptistworldaid.org.au/

Introduction: 'Lord, teach us to pray *glocally*'

[1] Michael Leunig, *When I Talk to You* (North Blackburn: HarperCollins, 2014), p. 16. Copyright © Michael Leunig 2014. Used by permission www.harpercollins.com.au. Leunig is a popular creative Australian artist whose poems and prayers comment on the mystery and challenges of life in its everyday forms. I reflected on Leunig's spirituality in Darren Cronshaw, *Credible Witness: Companions, Prophets, Hosts and Other Australian Mission Models* (Melbourne: Urban Neighbours of Hope, 2006), pp. 32–7.

[2] Shane Claiborne and Jonathan Wilson-Hartgrove, *Becoming the Answer to Our Prayers: Prayer for Ordinary Radicals* (Downers Grove: IVP, 2008).

[3] Ajith Fernando, 'The Uniqueness of Jesus Christ', in *Telling the Truth: Evangelizing Postmoderns* (ed. D.A. Carson; Grand Rapids: Zondervan, 2000), p. 133.

4   St John of the Cross, *Dark Night of the Soul* (trans. E. Allison Peers; London: Catholic Way, 2013).

5   Dorothy Walters, *Marrow of Flame: Poems of the Spiritual Journey* (Boulder: Poetry Chaikhana, 2nd edn, 2015).

6   Joyce Rupp, *The Open Door: A Journey to the True Self* (Notre Dame: Sorin, 2008), pp. 58–60.

7   Leon Morris, *The Gospel According to Matthew* (Grand Rapids: Eerdmans, 1992), p. 141.

8   Taken from Mark Sayers, *The Vertical Self: How Biblical Faith Can Help Us Discover Who We Are in an Age of Self Obsession* (Nashville: Thomas Nelson, 2010), p. 19; copyright © 2010 by Mark Sayers. Used by permission of Thomas Nelson. www.thomasnelson.com. See my review in *EA Equip*, no. 9, June (2011): p. 14. http://www.ea.org.au/site/DefaultSite/filesystem/documents/Equip/EA%20Equip%20Mag%20June11_Web.pdf

9   Sayers, *Vertical Self*, p. 19.

10 Robert A. Fryling, *The Leadership Ellipse: Shaping How We Lead by Who We Are* (Downers Grove: IVP, 2010), p. 46; from my review in *Witness: The Voice of Victorian Baptists* 90.10 (2010): p. 22; https://www.buv.com.au/baptistonmission/book-reviews/theleadershipellipse.

11 E.g. Douglas R.A. Hare, *Matthew* (Louisville: John Knox, 1993).

12 Helmut Thielicke, *The Prayer That Spans the World: Sermons on the Lord's Prayer* (London: Lutterworth, 1988).

13 John Dominic Crossan, *The Greatest Prayer: Rediscovering the Revolutionary Message of the Lord's Prayer* (London: SPCK, 2011).

14 Eugene H. Peterson, *Working the Angles: The Shape of Pastoral Integrity* (Grand Rapids: Eerdmans, 1987), p. 40.

15 Bill Hybels, *Too Busy Not to Pray: Slowing Down to Be with God* (Downers Grove: IVP, 2008).

16 Cf. Lynne M. Baab, *Sabbath Keeping: Finding Freedom in the Rhythms of Rest* (Downers Grove: IVP, 2005).

17 Kim Hammond and Darren Cronshaw, *Sentness: Six Postures of Missional Christians* (Downers Grove: IVP, 2014), pp. 93–4.

18 Darren Cronshaw, 'Reenvisioning Theological Education and Missional Spirituality', *Journal of Adult Theological Education* 9.1 (2012): p. 19; drawing on Nancy Reeves, *Spirituality for Extroverts (and Tips for Those Who Love Them)* (Nashville: Abingdon, 2008); expanded in Hammond and Cronshaw, *Sentness*, pp. 91–3.

19 Roger Helland and Leonard Hjalmarson, *Missional Spirituality: Embodying God's Love from the Inside Out* (Downers Grove: IVP, 2011).

[20] Lesslie Newbigin, *The Good Shepherd: Meditations on Christian Ministry in Today's World* (London: Mowbray, 1977), pp. 96–9; discussed previously in Darren Cronshaw, 'Editorial – Mission and Spirituality', *Australian Journal of Mission Studies* 2.2 (2008): pp. 1–3.

[21] David J. Bosch, *Transforming Mission: Paradigm Shifts in Theology of Mission* (Maryknoll: Orbis, 1991), p. 212.

[22] Michael Frost and Alan Hirsch, *The Shaping of Things to Come: Innovation and Mission for the 21st-Century Church* (Peabody: Hendrickson, 2003), p. 126.

[23] Frost and Hirsch, *Shaping of Things to Come*, p. 116.

[24] E.g. Mark 1:9–39; Cronshaw, 'Missional Spirituality', p. 19; Hammond and Cronshaw, *Sentness*, p. 105.

[25] Cronshaw, 'Missional Spirituality', p. 19.

[26] Ross Langmead, 'Theological Reflection in Ministry and Mission', *Ministry Society and Theology* 18 (2004): pp. 25–6; drawing on Donald Messer, *Contemporary Images of Christian Ministry* (Nashville: Abingdon, 1989).

[27] Langmead, 'Theological Reflection', pp. 12–13; discussed in Hammond and Cronshaw, *Sentness*, p. 93.

[28] Richard Rohr, *The Naked Now: Learning to See How the Mystics See* (New York: Crossroad, 2009), p. 180.

[29] Thomas Merton, *Contemplative Prayer* (London: Darton, Longman & Todd, 1969), p. 23; discussed in Cronshaw, 'Missional Spirituality', pp. 16–17; Hammond and Cronshaw, *Sentness*, p. 105.

[30] Inspired by Telford Work, *Ain't Too Proud to Beg: Living through the Lord's Prayer* (Grand Rapids: Eerdmans, 2007), pp. xv–xvi.

[31] John Climacus, *The Ladder of Divine Accent* (trans. Lazarus Moore; New York: Harper, 1959), p. 203; in Henri Nouwen, *Reaching Out: The Three Movements of the Spiritual Life* (New York: Doubleday, 1975), p. 16.

[32] William H. Willimon and Stanley Hauerwas, *Lord, Teach Us: The Lord's Prayer and the Christian Life* (Nashville: Abingdon, 1996), p. 18.

[33] Willimon and Hauerwas, *Lord, Teach Us*, p. 11.

[34] Kenneth W. Stevenson, *The Lord's Prayer: A Text in Tradition* (Minneapolis: Fortress, 2004), p. vii.

[35] Richard Coekin, *Our Father: Enjoying God in Prayer* (Nottingham: IVP, 2009), p. 23.

[36] Quoted in *Martin Luther: Selections from His Writings* (ed. John Dillenberger; New York: Doubleday, 1962), p. 226; from Work, *Ain't Too Proud to Beg*, p. xiv.

[37] Hammond and Cronshaw, *Sentness*, pp. 11–12.

[38] Jarrod McKenna, 'Jarrod McKenna – Teach Us to Pray', Common Grace [video], YouTube (uploaded on 17 February 2015) https://www.youtube.com/watch?v=c9J3ItajSiY or http://www.lordsprayer.org.au/introductory_video; see also 'The Lord's Prayer', Common Grace and the Bible Society http://www.lordsprayer.org.au/. Used with permission.

1. Radical Inclusion of 'Our Father'

[1] Darren Cronshaw, 'Leadership Column (Human Rights)', *Witness: The Voice of Victorian Baptists* 91.2 (2011): p. 7.

[2] Walk Free, 'Learn More about Modern Slavery' http://www.walkfree.org/learn/

[3] Max Fisher, 'This Map Shows Where the World's 30 Million Slaves Live. There Are 60,000 in the U.S.', *The Washington Post* (2013) http://www.washingtonpost.com/blogs/worldviews/wp/2013/10/17/this-map-shows-where-the-worlds-30-million-slaves-live-there-are-60000-in-the-u-s/

[4] Fight Slavery Now, 'Child Soldiers' (2010) http://fightslaverynow.org/why-fight-there-are-27-million-reasons/otherformsoftrafficking/child-soldiers/

[5] Cronshaw, 'Human Rights', p. 7.

[6] John Dominic Crossan, *The Greatest Prayer: Rediscovering the Revolutionary Message of the Lord's Prayer* (London: SPCK, 2011), pp. 40–41.

[7] Nelson Mandela, *Long Walk to Freedom* (London: Abacus, 1994), p. 438.

[8] Marianne Williamson, *A Return to Love: Reflections on the Principles of A Course in Miracles* (New York: HarperCollins, 1992), pp. 190–92.

[9] E.g. Steve Biddulph, *Manhood* (Sydney: Finch, 1995).

[10] On the loss and recovery of a Heavenly Father archetype and the religious dimensions of father absence, see David Tacey, *Remaking Men: The Revolution in Masculinity* (Ringwood: Viking, 1997), pp. 17–67.

[11] Inspired by Max Lucado, *The Great House of God: A Home for Your Heart* (Dallas: Word, 1997), pp. 136–7.

[12] N.T. Wright, *Jesus and the Victory of God* (London: SPCK, 1996), pp. 612–53.

[13] David A. Seamands, *Healing Grace: Finding a Freedom from the Performance Trap* (Wheaton: Victor, 1989), p. 26.

[14] J.B. Phillips, *Your God Is Too Small* (New York: Touchstone, 1997).

[15] Telford Work, *Ain't Too Proud to Beg: Living through the Lord's Prayer* (Grand Rapids: Eerdmans, 2007), p. 27.

[16] Darren Cronshaw, *Credible Witness: Companions, Prophets, Hosts and Other Australian Mission Models* (Melbourne: Urban Neighbours of Hope, 2006), pp. 44–7.

[17] John Smith, *Advance Australia Where?* (Homebush West: ANZEA, 1988), p. 225; discussed in Cronshaw, *Credible Witness*, p. 104.

[18] Richard Foster, *Prayer: Finding the Heart's True Home* (New York: HarperCollins, 1992), p. 9.

[19] Helmut Thielicke, *Prayer That Spans the World: Sermons on the Lord's Prayer* (London: Lutterworth, 1988), p. 40.

[20] St Cyprian, *The 'Our Father'* (Dublin: Clonmore & Reynolds, 1953), p. 15.

[21] E.g. Martin Luther King Jr, 'Remaining Awake through a Great Revolution' (delivered at the National Cathedral, Washington, DC, 1968).

[22] Anthony de Mello, *Taking Flight: A Book of Story Meditations* (New York: Doubleday, 1988).

[23] Warren Carter, 'The Gospel of Matthew', in *A Postcolonial Commentary on the New Testament Writings* (ed. Fernando F. Segovia and R.S. Sugirtharajah; London: T&T Clark, 2007), p. 71.

[24] Carter, 'The Gospel of Matthew', pp. 100–01.

[25] Warren Carter, *Matthew and the Margins: A Sociopolitical and Religious Reading* (Maryknoll: Orbis, 2000), p. 164.

[26] Muriel Lester, *Ambassador of Reconciliation: A Muriel Lester Reader* (Philadelphia: New Society, 1991), p. ix.

[27] Lester, *Ambassador of Reconciliation*, pp. 133–70.

[28] Mahatma Gandhi, '364. Wanted a Manifestation of Christ in Daily Life', in *The Collected Works of Mahatma Gandhi*, vol. 63 (18 January – 19 May 1934), p. 327, GandhiServe Foundation http://www.gandhiserve.org/cwmg/VOL063.PDF

[29] Anne Wilkinson-Hayes, 'Living Our Prayer (Matthew 5:13)', Aberfeldie Baptist Church sermon, 6 February 2005; Lester, *Ambassador of Reconciliation*; Darren Cronshaw, '"Lord Let Me Care": Glimpsing Back to Baptist Approaches to Social Justice', Baptcare-commissioned resource article; https://www.buv.com.au/documents/item/1744

[30] Jürgen Moltmann, *The Crucified God: The Cross of Christ as the Foundation and Criticism of Christian Theology* (London: SCM, 1974), pp. 273–4.

[31] Thomas G. Weinandy, *Does God Suffer?* (Notre Dame: University of Notre Dame, 2000), p. 3, cf. p. 282.

[32] Moltmann, *Crucified God*, p. 274.

[33] Thielicke, *Prayer That Spans the World*, p. 28.

[34] Thielicke, *Prayer That Spans the World*, p. 98.

[35] Tim Costello, 'A Passion for Hope and Justice', in *Another Way to Love* (ed. Tim Costello and Rod Yule; Brunswick East: World Vision and Acorn, 2009), pp. 4–7.

[36] Tom Wright, *The Lord and His Prayer* (London: Triangle, 1996), p. 21.

[37] Wright, *Lord and His Prayer*, pp. 19–20; cf. Michael Frost, *Exiles: Living Missionally in a Post-Christian Culture* (Peabody: Hendrickson, 2006), pp. 180–84.

[38] Thielicke, *Prayer That Spans the World*, pp. 20–21.

[39] Tom Wright, *Simply Christian* (London: SPCK, 2006), pp. 52–9, 138–40.

[40] Thielicke, *Prayer That Spans the World*, p. 36.

[41] Inspired by Lucado, *Great House of God*, p. 50.

[42] Mark Sayers, *The Road Trip That Changed the World: The Unlikely Theory That Will Change How You View Culture, the Church, and Most Importantly, Yourself* (Chicago: Moody, 2012), pp. 205–6; reviewed by me in *Literature and Theology: An International Journal of Religion, Theory and Culture* 28.4 (2014): pp. 491–3.

[43] Sayers, *Road Trip*, p. 87.

[44] *Road Trip*, pp. 205–6.

[45] Wright, *Lord and His Prayer*, p. 7.

[46] Don Postema, *Space for God: Study and Practice of Spirituality and Prayer* (Grand Rapids: Faith Alive Christian Resources, 1997).

[47] Leon Morris, *The Gospel According to Matthew* (Grand Rapids: Eerdmans, 1992), p. 144.

[48] Thielicke, *Prayer That Spans the World*, p. 43.

[49] Richard Foster, *Streams of Living Water: Celebrating the Great Traditions of Christian Faith* (London: HarperCollins, 1999), p. 49.

[50] N.T. Wright, *Surprised by Hope* (New York: HarperOne, 2008), p. 170.

[51] Simone Weil, *Waiting for God* (trans. Emma Craufurd; New York: Harper Perennial, 1951), pp. 57, 64; Stephanie Paulsell, 'Spiritual Formation and Intellectual Work in Theological Education', *Theology Today* 55.2 (1998): p. 232; discussed in Kim Hammond and Darren Cronshaw, *Sentness: Six Postures of Missional Christians* (Downers Grove: IVP, 2014), p. 105.

[52] Wright, *Lord and His Prayer*, p. 22.

[53] Crossan, *Greatest Prayer*, p. 49.

[54] Tim Hawkins, 'Tim Hawkins Comedy – Worship & Prayer' http://www.youtube.com/watch?v=iz17Ugnz6rg. Copyright © Tim Hawkins. Used with permission. www.timhawkins.net

[55] Jacqueline Grey, 'Rev Dr Jacqueline Grey – Our Father', Common Grace [video], YouTube (uploaded on 19 February 2015) https://www. youtube.com/watch?v=_sEHF3kBn2w or http://www.lordsprayer.org. au/our_father_in_heaven. Used with permission.

[56] Rowland Croucher, *Still Waters, Deep Waters: Meditations and Prayers for Busy People* (Sutherland: Albatross, 1987), p. 112.

2. Subversive Justice of 'Your kingdom come'

[1] Frederick Buechner, *Listening to Your Life: Daily Meditations with Frederick Buechner* (New York: Harper One, 1992); cited in William H. Willimon and Stanley Hauerwas, *Lord, Teach Us: The Lord's Prayer and the Christian Life* (Nashville: Abingdon, 1996), p. 9.

[2] E.g. Mitzi J. Smith, '"Knowing More Than Is Good for One": A Womanist Interrogation of the Matthean Great Commission', in *Teaching All Nations: Interrogating the Matthean Great Commission* (ed. Mitzi J. Smith and Jayachitra Lalitha; Minneapolis: Fortress, 2014), p. 147.

[3] Roberto Lagos-Schuffenegger, 'Human Rights in South America', in Commission on Social and Environmental Justice, unpublished paper, Baptist World Alliance annual gathering, Santiago, Chile, 2012.

[4] Baptist World Alliance, 'BWA Urges Action on Nigerian Crisis and Climate Change' (8 July 2012) http://www.bwanet.org/news/ news-releases/153-nigerian-crisis

[5] http://www.joshuaproject.net/; see also Jason Mandryk, *Operation World: The Definitive Prayer Guide to Every Nation* (Downers Grove: IVP, 2010).

[6] Taken from Max Lucado, *God Will Use This for Good: Surviving the Mess of Life* (Nashville: Thomas Nelson, 2013), pp. vii–ix. Copyright © 2013 by Max Lucado. Used by permission of Thomas Nelson. www. thomasnelson.com.

[7] Dallas Willard, *The Divine Conspiracy: Rediscovering Our Hidden Life in God* (San Francisco: HarperSanFrancisco, 1998), pp. 29–70.

[8] Cited in Michael Moynagh, *Emergingchurch.Intro* (Oxford: Monarch, 2004), p. 135.

[9] Moynagh, *Emergingchurch.Intro*, p. 139.

[10] Lesslie Newbigin, *The Open Secret: Sketches for a Missionary Theology* (Grand Rapids: Eerdmans, 1978), p. 110.

[11] Brian D. McLaren, *The Secret Message of Jesus: Uncovering the Truth That Could Change Everything* (Nashville: Thomas Nelson, 2006), p. 82.

[12] Tim Costello, *Hope: Moments of Inspiration in a Challenging World* (Melbourne: Hardie Grant, 2012), pp. 207–8.

[13] N.T. Wright, *Surprised by Hope* (New York: HarperOne, 2008), pp. 111, 211–15, 236.

[14] Helmut Thielicke, *Prayer That Spans the World: Sermons on the Lord's Prayer* (London: Lutterworth, 1988), p. 62.

[15] Telford Work, *Ain't Too Proud to Beg: Living through the Lord's Prayer* (Grand Rapids: Eerdmans, 2007), pp. 76–7.

[16] Michael H. Crosby, *Thy Will Be Done: Praying the Our Father as Subversive Activity* (Maryknoll: Orbis, 1977), pp. 59–60.

[17] Crosby, *Thy Will Be Done*, p. 73.

[18] Cf. Jürgen Moltmann, *The Gospel of Liberation* (Waco: Word, 1973), p. 99; Crosby, *Thy Will Be Done*, p. 70.

[19] David Wells, 'Prayer: Rebelling against the Status Quo', in *Perspectives on the World Christian Movement: A Reader* (ed. Ralph D. Winter and Steven C. Hawthorne; Pasadena: William Carey Library, 1999), pp. 142–4.

[20] Max Lucado, *The Great House of God: A Home for Your Heart* (Dallas: Word, 1997), pp. 62–6.

[21] Paul Meier, MD, *Don't Let Jerks Get the Best of You: Advice for Dealing with Difficult People* (Nashville: Thomas Nelson, 1993).

[22] Lucado, *Great House of God*, p. 66.

[23] Michael Raiter, *Stirrings of the Soul: Evangelicals and the New Spirituality* (Sydney: Matthias, 2003), p. 182.

[24] John Ortberg, *The Life You've Always Wanted: Spiritual Disciplines for Ordinary People* (Grand Rapids: Zondervan, 2002).

[25] Walter Wink, *The Powers That Be: Theology for a New Millennium* (New York: Galilee, 1999), p. 186.

[26] Ortberg, *Life You've Always Wanted*; Wink, *Powers That Be*, p. 186.

[27] C.S. Lewis, *The Weight of Glory and Other Addresses* (Grand Rapids: Eerdmans, 1965), pp. 1–2.

[28] The remainder of this section draws from Julia Rhyder and Darren Cronshaw, 'Mustard Tree Aspirations (Luke 13:18–19)', *W!tness* (10 July 2014, reproduced 3 November 2016) https://www.buv.com.au/news/mustard-tree-aspirations-luke-1318-19; also in Darren Cronshaw, 'Improvising a Renewed Story at Auburnlife: Utilising Biblical Narrative for Congregational Transformation', in *Cultural Diversity, Worship, and Australian Baptist Church Life*, New Wineskins, vol. 2 (ed. Darrell Jackson and Darren Cronshaw; Sydney: Morling, 2016), pp. 225–39.

29 Jean Vanier, *Befriending the Stranger* (Mahwaj: Paulist, 2010), p. 12.

30 C. Christopher Smith and John Pattison, *Slow Church: Cultivating Community in the Patient Way of Jesus* (Downers Grove: IVP, 2014).

31 Christopher J.H. Wright, *The Mission of God: Unlocking the Bible's Grand Narrative* (Nottingham: IVP, 2006), p. 534.

32 Cited in Robert A. Fryling, *The Leadership Ellipse: Shaping How We Lead by Who We Are* (Downers Grove: IVP, 2010), p. 47.

33 Frederick Buechner, *Wishful Thinking: A Theological ABC* (New York: Harper & Row, 1973), p. 95; cited in Parker J. Palmer, *Let Your Life Speak: Listening for the Voice of Vocation* (San Francisco: Jossey-Bass, 2000), p. 16.

34 Bert van de Kamp, *And They Called Him Bono* (lulu.com, 2012), p. 67.

35 Musa W. Dube Shomanah, 'Praying the Lord's Prayer in a Global Economic Era', *Ecumenical Review* 49 (1997): p. 447; in Michael H. Crosby, *The Prayer That Jesus Taught Us* (Maryknoll: Orbis, 2002).

36 Tom Wright, *The Lord and His Prayer* (London: Triangle, 1996), p. 31.

37 Wright, *Lord and His Prayer*, p. 32.

38 Wright, *Lord and His Prayer*, pp. 34–5.

39 Crosby, *Thy Will Be Done*, p. 1.

40 Fryling, *Leadership Ellipse*; and drawing on my review.

41 Eugene H. Peterson, *Christ Plays in Ten Thousand Places: A Conversation in Spiritual Theology* (London: Hodder & Stoughton, 2005), p. 229.

42 Anne Wilkinson-Hayes, 'Living Our Prayer (Matthew 5:13)', Aberfeldie Baptist Church sermon, 6 February 2005.

43 Crosby, *Thy Will Be Done*, p. 35.

44 John Dominic Crossan, *The Greatest Prayer: Rediscovering the Revolutionary Message of the Lord's Prayer* (London: SPCK, 2011), p. 10.

45 Crossan, *Greatest Prayer*, p. 155.

46 Jon Owen, *Muddy Spirituality: Bringing It All Down to Earth* (Dandenong: Urban Neighbours of Hope, 2011), p. 134; discussed in Kim Hammond and Darren Cronshaw, *Sentness: Six Postures of Missional Christians* (Downers Grove: IVP, 2014), pp. 114–15.

47 Chrishan Jeyaratnam, 'Chrishan Jeyaratnam – Your Will Be Done', Common Grace [video], YouTube (uploaded on 3 March 2015) https://www.youtube.com/watch?v=r9r59qocaJ4 or http://www.lordsprayer.org.au/your_will_be_done. Used with permission.

48 Mark Coleridge, 'Archbishop Coleridge Your Kingdom Come', Common Grace [video], YouTube (uploaded on 24 February 2015) https://www.youtube.com/watch?v=r9Q5Ft82-9M or http://www.lordsprayer.org.au/your_kingdom_come. Used with permission.

[49] Tony Cupit, in *Rivers in the Desert: Meditations and Prayers for Refreshment* (ed. Rowland Croucher; Sutherland: Albatross, 1991), p. 88.

3. Integral Mission of 'our daily bread'

[1] Cf. Michael Frost, *Jesus the Fool: The Mission of the Unconventional Christ* (Melbourne: Urban Neighbours of Hope, 2007), pp. 22–6.

[2] Michael Frost, *Exiles: Living Missionally in a Post-Christian Culture* (Peabody: Hendrickson, 2006), p. 168.

[3] Michael Frost's teaching.

[4] David Jones and Russell Woodbridge, *Health, Wealth & Happiness: Has the Prosperity Gospel Overshadowed the Gospel of Christ?* (Grand Rapids: Kregel, 2011).

[5] Bill Hybels, 'Power: Preaching for Total Commitment', in *Mastering Contemporary Preaching* (ed. Stuart Briscoe, Bill Hybels and Haddon Robinson; Portland: Multnomah, 1989), pp. 120–21.

[6] Clive Hamilton, *Affluenza: When Too Much Is Never Enough* (Crows Nest: Allen & Unwin, 2006).

[7] Leonardo Boff, *Cry of the Earth, Cry of the Poor* (Maryknoll: Orbis, 1997).

[8] Eunice V. Pike, 'The Concept of Limited Good and the Spread of the Gospel', *Missiology: An International Review* 8.4 (1980): pp. 449–54.

[9] Eugene H. Peterson, *Five Smooth Stones for Pastoral Work* (Grand Rapids: Eerdmans, 1992), pp. 216–17.

[10] Leo Tolstoy, 'How Much Land Does One Man Need?' http://www.online-literature.com/tolstoy/2738/

[11] Andro Linklater, *Owning the Earth: The Transforming History of Land Ownership* (New York: Bloomsbury, 2013).

[12] Wong Young Soon, keynote conference talk, at Signs of Hope in the City, International Society for Urban Mission Summit, Kuala Lumpur, 1 July 2014.

[13] Frost, *Exiles*, p. 323.

[14] Brian D. McLaren, *Everything Must Change: Jesus, Global Crises and a Revolution of Hope* (Nashville: Thomas Nelson, 2007); reviewed by me in *Witness: The Voice of Victorian Baptists* 90.10 (2010): p. 20; https://www.buv.com.au/baptistonmission/book-reviews/everything-must-change

[15] Parker J. Palmer, *The Promise of Paradox: A Celebration of Contradictions in the Christian Life* (San Francisco: Jossey-Bass, 2008), p. 114.

[16] John Dominic Crossan, *The Greatest Prayer: Rediscovering the Revolutionary Message of the Lord's Prayer* (London: SPCK, 2011), p. 136.

[17] Ulrich Luz, *Matthew 1 – 7: A Continental Commentary* (Minneapolis: Fortress, 1989), p. 383.

[18] Michael H. Crosby, *The Prayer That Jesus Taught Us* (Maryknoll: Orbis, 2002), p. 119.

[19] Musa W. Dube Shomanah, 'Praying the Lord's Prayer in a Global Economic Era', *Ecumenical Review* 49 (1997): p. 447.

[20] Tim Tyler, 'Global Crisis Wrap-up (Global Crisis Series)' (2012) http://planetsave.com/2012/03/03/global-crisis-wrap-up-global-crisis-series/

[21] Bread for the World, 'About Global Hunger' http://www.bread.org/hunger/global/

[22] Kim Hammond and Darren Cronshaw, *Sentness: Six Postures of Missional Christians* (Downers Grove: IVP, 2014), p. 36.

[23] Ray S. Anderson, *An Emergent Theology for Emerging Churches* (Downers Grove: IVP, 2006), p. 196.

[24] Frost, *Exiles*, p. 158.

[25] Frost, *Exiles*, pp. 162–3.

[26] Simon Carey Holt, *Eating Heaven: Spirituality at the Table* (Brunswick East: Acorn, 2013), p. 150. This section draws on my review in *Journal of Missional Practice*, no. 3, Autumn (2013) http://themissionalnetwork.com/index.php/tmn-journal

[27] Adrian Greenwood, 'A Social Justice Grace?', *more>praxis.org.au* (2009) http://morepraxis.org.au/a-social-justice-grace/. Used with permission.

[28] From Shane Claiborne, 'Mark 2: Sharing Economic Resources with Fellow Community Members and the Needy among Us', in *School(s) for Conversion: 12 Marks of a New Monasticism* (ed. The Rutba House; Eugene: Cascade, 2005), pp. 26–38; Darren Cronshaw, 'New Monasticism for Australian Mission: Reflections from "*School(s) for Conversion: 12 Marks of a New Monasticism*"', *Australian Journal of Mission Studies*, June (2014): pp. 17–25.

[29] Pope John Paul II, 'Nova Millennio Ineunte' (2001); Crosby, *Prayer That Jesus Taught Us*, p. 136.

[30] J.R. Woodward, *Creating a Missional Culture: Equipping the Church for the Sake of the World* (Downers Grove: IVP, 2012), p. 196.

[31] Water Aid Australia, 'Statistics' http://www.wateraidaustralia.org.

[32] Tony Jones, 'Hopeful Activism', in *An Emergent Manifesto of Hope* (ed. Doug Pagitt and Tony Jones; Grand Rapids: Baker, 2007), p. 245.

[33] Tim Costello, *Hope: Moments of Inspiration in a Challenging World* (Melbourne: Hardie Grant, 2012), p. 34.

[34] Muriel Porter, *Land of the Spirit? The Australian Religious Experience* (Geneva: World Council of Churches, 1990), p. 100.

[35] Bob Hawke, *The Hawke Memoirs* (London: Heinemann, 1994), pp. 20–22; Darren Cronshaw, *Credible Witness: Companions, Prophets, Hosts and Other Australian Mission Models* (Melbourne: Urban Neighbours of Hope, 2006), p. 120.

[36] Blanche d'Alpuget, *Robert J. Hawke: A Biography* (Melbourne: Schwartz, 1982), pp. 46–7; Cronshaw, *Credible Witness*, pp. 120–21.

[37] Cronshaw, *Credible Witness*, pp. 123–4.

[38] Frost, *Exiles*, p. 16.

[39] Desmond Tutu, *No Future Without Forgiveness* (New York: Image Doubleday, 1999), p. 31.

[40] Suzanne Collins, *The Hunger Games* (London: Scholastic, 2008), p. 21. This section draws on Darren Cronshaw, 'Resisting the Empire in Young Adult Fiction: Lessons from Hunger Games', in *Re-Naming Sovereignty* (ed. Mark Brett and Monica Melanchthon [forthcoming 2017]), and talks at Carey Baptist Grammar School chapels, 8–12 September 2014.

[41] Ann Duncan and Andy Lanford, 'Teen Hero: Life and Death in *The Hunger Games*', *Christian Century* (2012): pp. 12–13.

[42] Suzanne Collins, *The Hunger Games: Mockingjay* (Gosford: Scholastic, 2010), pp. 101–18; discussed in Karl Hand, 'Come Now, Let Us Treason Together: Conversion and Revolutionary Consciousness in Luke 22:35–38 and The Hunger Games Trilogy', *Literature and Theology: An International Journal of Religion, Theory and Culture* 29:3 (2015).

[43] George A. Dunn and Nicolas Michaud, 'Introduction: Let the Hunger Games and Philosophy Begin!', in *The Hunger Games and Philosophy: A Critique of Pure Treason* (ed. George A. Dunn and Nicolas Michaud; Hoboken: John Wiley & Sons, 2012), pp. 4–5.

[44] Hand, 'Come Now, Let Us Treason Together'.

[45] http://www.youtube.com/watch?v=6HXzRwiIaC4

[46] John Dickson, 'Rev Dr John Dickson – Give Us Today Our Daily Bread', Common Grace [video], YouTube (uploaded on 9 March 2015) https://www.youtube.com/watch?v=uQUp6Ll8Ez8 or http://www.lordsprayer.org.au/give_us_today. Used with permisison.

[47] Rowland Croucher, *A Garden of Solitude* (Sutherland: Albatross, 1998), p. 292.

4. Countercultural Reconciliation of 'Forgive us'

[1] Miroslav Volf, *A Public Faith: How Followers of Christ Should Serve the Common Good* (Grand Rapids: Brazos, 1996), p. 114.

2 Mario Vargas Llosa, *The Temptation of the Impossible: Victor Hugo and Les Misérables* (Princeton: Princeton University Press, 2007), pp. 63–4.

3 Erma Bombeck, *Eat Less Cottage Cheese and More Ice Cream* © 1979, Erma Bombeck. Published by Andrews McMeel Publishing (Kansas City 2003). Used with permission.

4 James W. Moore, *Yes Lord, I Have Sinned, but I Have Several Good Excuses* (Nashville: Abingdon, 1991).

5 Prime Minister Kevin Rudd, 'Apology to Australia's Indigenous Peoples' (2008) http://www.australia.gov.au/about-australia/our-country/our-people/apology-to-australias-indigenous-peoples

6 E.g. BBC News, 'Pope Francis Asks Forgiveness for Child Abuse by Clergy' (2014) http://www.bbc.com/news/world-europe-26989991

7 Donald Miller, *Blue Like Jazz: Nonreligious Thoughts on Christian Spirituality* (Nashville: Thomas Nelson, 2003).

8 Tom Wright, *The Lord and His Prayer* (London: Triangle, 1996), pp. 49–51.

9 Wright, *Lord and His Prayer*, p. 63.

10 Wright, *Lord and His Prayer*, pp. 59–60.

11 Douglas R.A. Hare, *Matthew* (Louisville: John Knox, 1993), p. 69.

12 Walter Wink, *The Powers That Be: Theology for a New Millennium* (New York: Galilee, 1999), pp. 98–111.

13 Dennis Linn, Sheila Fabricant Linn and Matthew Linn, *Don't Forgive Too Soon: Extending the Two Hands That Heal* (New York: Paulist, 1997), pp. 28–96.

14 Michael Duncan, *Alongsiders: Sitting with Those Who Sit Alone* (Melbourne: Urban Neighbours of Hope, 2014), pp. 65–6; drawing on Joyce Hugget, *Conflict: Understanding, Managing and Growing through Conflict* (Guildford: Eagle, 1998), p. 163.

15 Henry Cloud and John Townsend, *Boundaries: When to Say Yes, How to Say No to Take Control of Your Life* (Sydney: Strand, 2002).

16 Forrest Gump, 'Sometimes, I Guess There Just Aren't Enough Rocks' [video], YouTube (uploaded on 20 March 2012) https://www.youtube.com/watch?v=anz91PPMPw8

17 Telford Work, *Ain't Too Proud to Beg: Living through the Lord's Prayer* (Grand Rapids: Eerdmans, 2007), pp. 168–9.

18 Corrie Ten Boom, with John and Elizabeth Sherrill, *The Hiding Place* (New York: Bantam, 1984).

19 Howard Zehr, *Changing Lenses: A New Focus for Crime and Justice* (Scottdale: Herald, 1990), p. 47.

[20] Philip Yancey, *What's So Amazing about Grace?* (Grand Rapids: Zondervan, 1997).

[21] Helmut Thielicke, *Prayer That Spans the World: Sermons on the Lord's Prayer* (London: Lutterworth, 1988).

[22] J.R. Woodward, *Creating a Missional Culture: Equipping the Church for the Sake of the World* (Downers Grove: IVP, 2012), pp. 158–9.

[23] Will Mancini, *Church Unique: How Missional Leaders Cast Vision, Capture Culture, and Create Movement* (San Francisco: Jossey-Bass, 2008), p. 86; Darren Cronshaw et al., 'A Contemporary Theology of Local Church Mission, in Global Perspective', in *Congregational Transformation in Australian Baptist Church Life* (ed. Darren Cronshaw and Darrell Jackson; Sydney: Morling, 2015), pp. 251–70.

[24] Walter Wink, *Engaging the Powers: Discernment and Resistance in a World of Domination* (Minneapolis: Fortress, 1992); Wink, *Powers That Be*.

[25] Wink, *Powers That Be*, pp. 11, 42–62, 68–9, 81, 142.

[26] Wink, *Powers That Be*, p. 181.

[27] Wink, *Powers That Be*, p. 124.

[28] Martin Luther King Jr, *Stride Toward Freedom* (New York: Harper & Row, 1958), p. 73; cited in Bill Pitts, 'Christianity and the Social Crisis', *Baptist History and Heritage* (2006): p. 45.

[29] Martin Luther King Jr, 'A Christmas Sermon on Peace' (1967) http://www.ecoflourish.com/Primers/education/Christmas_Sermon.html

[30] Darren Cronshaw, '"Lord Let Me Care": Glimpsing Back to Baptist Approaches to Social Justice', Baptcare-commissioned resource article; https://www.buv.com.au/documents/item/1744

[31] Srdja Popovic with Matthew Miller, *Blueprint for Revolution: How to Use Rice Pudding, Lego Men, and Other Nonviolent Techniques to Galvanize Communities, Overthrow Dictators, or Simply Change the World* (New York: Random House, 2015).

[32] Beth Barnett, 'A Liturgy for Awful Times', *multivocality: many voices many friends* (2014) http://multivocality.wordpress.com/2014/08/08/a-liturgy-for-awful-times/. Used with permission.

[33] Graham Paulson and Grant Paulson, 'Uncle Graham & Grant Paulson – Forgive Us Our Sins' Common Grace [video], YouTube (uploaded on 17 May 2015) https://www.youtube.com/watch?v=YIUcZ_HBktU or http://www.lordsprayer.org.au/and_forgive_us_our_debts. Used with permission.

[34] 'Just Prayers – The Lord's Prayer (No Subtitles)' (Exposure 2012) https://vimeo.com/64971148

5. Discerning Guidance of 'Deliver us'

[1] Stephen Sondheim, 'Into the Woods – Any Moment Lyrics', *MetroLyrics* http://www.metrolyrics.com/into-the-woods-any-moment-lyrics-broad-ways.html

[2] Debra Hirsch, *Redeeming Sex: Naked Conversations about Sexuality and Spirituality* (Downers Grove: IVP, 2015), pp. 32–48.

[3] Hirsch, *Redeeming Sex*, p. 42.

[4] Hirsch, *Redeeming Sex*, pp. 42–3.

[5] Lord's Prayer in 'Night Prayer', *A New Zealand Prayer Book: He Karakia Mihinare o Aotearoa* (Auckland: The Anglican Church in Aotearoa, New Zealand and Polynesia), p. 181; http://anglicanprayerbook. nz/167.html. Used with permission. Adapted from Jim Cotter's prayer. See also Jim Cotter, *Prayer at Night: A Book for the Darkness* (Sheffield: Cairns, 2011).

[6] Nathan Nettleton, 'South Yarra Baptist Weekly Worship' http://laughingbird.net/sycb/SouthYarraBaptist/Weekly_Worship.html

[7] Joseph M. Stowell, *Following Christ: Experiencing Life the Way It Was Meant to Be* (Grand Rapids: Zondervan, 1996), p. 22.

[8] Tom Wright, *Luke for Everyone* (London: SPCK, 2001), p. 44.

[9] Discussed in Kim Hammond and Darren Cronshaw, *Sentness: Six Postures of Missional Christians* (Downers Grove: IVP, 2014), pp. 70–71.

[10] Joanne Harris, *Chocolat* (London: Transworld, 1999).

[11] Hirsch, *Redeeming Sex*, pp. 46–7.

[12] Ray Simpson and Brent Lyons-Lee, *Emerging Downunder: Creating New Monastic Villages of God* (Adelaide: ATF, 2008), p. 114.

[13] Richard Rohr, *Immortal Diamond: The Search for Our True Self* (London: SPCK, 2013); discussed previously in Darren Cronshaw, 'Saving Souls and Listening Hearts: Implications for Missional Leaders from Richard Rohr's *Immortal Diamond: The Search for Our True Self*', *Colloquium* 46.2 (2014): pp. 242–54.

[14] Dietrich Bonhoeffer, *The Cost of Discipleship* (London: SCM, 1959).

[15] Rohr, *Immortal Diamond*, p. 110.

[16] Rohr, *Immortal Diamond*, p. 88.

[17] Shane Claiborne and Jonathan Wilson-Hartgrove, *Becoming the Answer to Our Prayers: Prayer for Ordinary Radicals* (Downers Grove: IVP, 2008), p. 50.

[18] Henri J.M. Nouwen, with Michael J. Christensen and Rebecca J. Laird, *Discernment: Reading the Signs of Daily Life* (London: SPCK, 2013), kindle location 616–23.

[19] Frederic Brussat and Mary Ann Brussat, *Spiritual Literacy: Reading the Sacred in Everyday Life* (New York: Touchstone, 1996), pp. 491–2.

[20] Miroslav Volf, *A Public Faith: How Followers of Christ Should Serve the Common Good* (Grand Rapids: Brazos, 1996), p. 74.

[21] Thomas Merton, *Conjectures of a Guilty Bystander* (New York: Doubleday, 1966).

[22] John Dillenberger, ed., *Martin Luther: Selections from His Writings* (New York: Doubleday, 1962), p. 226; quoted in Telford Work, *Ain't Too Proud to Beg: Living through the Lord's Prayer* (Grand Rapids: Eerdmans, 2007), p. 198.

[23] Kenneth Grahame, *The Wind in the Willows* (Ware: Wordsworth, 1993), pp. 84–6.

[24] J.R.R. Tolkien, *The Lord of the Rings* (Boston: HarperCollins, 2005); discussed in Wynand de Kock, *Out of My Mind: Following the Trajectory of God's Redemptive Story* (Eugene: Wipf and Stock, 2014), p. 95.

[25] Michael Polanyi, *Personal Knowledge: Towards a Post-Critical Philosophy* (London: Routledge & Kegan Paul, 1962), p. 54; discussed in Michael Frost, *Incarnate: The Body of Christ in an Age of Disengagement* (Downers Grove: IVP, 2014), p. 86.

[26] James K.A. Smith, *Desiring the Kingdom: Worship, Worldview and Cultural Formation* (Grand Rapids: Baker, 2009); reviewed by me in 'Review of *Desiring the Kingdom*', *Journal of Adult Theological Education* 8.2 (2011): pp. 199–200.

[27] Smith, *Desiring the Kingdom*, p. 126.

[28] Cronshaw, 'Review of *Desiring the Kingdom*.'

[29] Frost, *Incarnate*, pp. 78–9.

[30] Bertrand Russell, *The Autobiography of Bertrand Russell, 1872–1914*, vol. 1 (London: George Allen & Unwin, 1967), p. 13; Bertrand Russell, *The Autobiography of Bertrand Russell, 1944–1967*, vol. 3 (London: George Allen & Unwin, 1969), Postscript, p. 223.

[31] Philip Hughes and Darren Cronshaw, *Baptists in Australia: A Church with a Heritage and a Future* (Melbourne: Christian Research Association, 2013), p. 69; Darren Cronshaw, '"Lord Let Me Care": Glimpsing Back to Baptist Approaches to Social Justice', Baptcare-commissioned resource article; https://www.buv.com.au/documents/item/1744

[32] Tim Costello, *Streets of Hope: Finding God in St Kilda* (St Leonards: Allen & Unwin, 1998), pp. 126–7.

[33] Tim Costello, 'A Passion for Hope and Justice', in *Another Way to Love* (ed. Tim Costello and Rod Yule; Brunswick East: World Vision and Acorn, 2009), pp. 13–14.

[34] From funeral notes and Darren Cronshaw, 'Domestic Violence – Where Is God in the Grief?', *Baptists on Mission Blog (BoMb)* (24 November 2016) https://www.buv.com.au/news/domestic-violence-where-is-god-in-the-grief

[35] Michael Roddan, 'Domestic Violence: Telling It Like It Is', *The Citizen* (2013) http://thecitizen.org.au/features/domestic-violence-telling-it-it; Australian Institute of Health and Welfare Australian Government, Specialist Homelessness Services 2011–12 (Canberra: AIHW, 2012) http://www.aihw.gov.au/publication-detail/?id=60129542549

[36] Stephen Sondheim, 'Into the Woods – Any Moment Lyrics', *Metro Lyrics* http://www.metrolyrics.com/into-the-woods-any-moment-lyrics-broadways.html

[37] Ben Myers, 'Dr Ben Myers – Deliver Us from Evil', Common Grace [video], YouTube (uploaded on 24 March 2015) https://www.youtube.com/watch?v=1nZnquVyfJs or http://www.lordsprayer.org.au/and_lead_us_not. Used with permission.

Conclusion: Confident Celebration of the Mission of God

[1] Kevin Percival, 'Not Just the Task of the Church to Preach the Gospel, but to Serve Those in Need', final year thesis (Baptist College of New South Wales, c. 1976).

[2] Peter Lewis, *The Lord's Prayer: The Greatest Prayer in the World* (Milton Keynes: Paternoster, 2008), p. 232.

[3] Gerald Bray, *Yours Is the Kingdom: A Systematic Theology of the Lord's Prayer* (Nottingham: IVP, 2007), pp. 197–200.

[4] Steve Oedekerk, *Patch Adams* screenplay (1998), accessible at Patch Adams, 'Patch Adams Butterfly Omen' [video], YouTube (uploaded on 23 October 2011) https://www.youtube.com/watch?v=30rGicdlWm0; see also Darren Cronshaw, 'Reenvisioning Theological Education, Vocation and the Kingdom of God', *Zadok Papers* S195 (2012): p. 12.

[5] Malcolm Muggeridge, *A Twentieth Century Testimony* (Nashville: Thomas Nelson, 1978), p. 72.

[6] John H. Walton, *Genesis: The NIV Application Commentary* (Grand Rapids: Zondervan, 2001). Walton also pointed to the relevance of *Patch Adams*.

[7] Roger Steer, *George Müller: Delighted in God* (Tain: Christian Focus, 1997), p. 131; 'George Müller', *Wikipedia* http://en.wikipedia.org/wiki/George_M%C3%BCller#cite_ref-12

8 Annie Dillard, *Teaching a Stone to Talk: Expeditions and Encounters* (New York: Harper & Row, 1982), p. 40.

9 Taken from C.S. Lewis, *The Lion, the Witch and the Wardrobe*, The Chronicles of Narnia, Book Two (New York: HarperCollins, 2002), pp. 75–6, © copyright CS Lewis Pte Ltd 1950. Used with permission.

10 Helmut Thielicke, *Prayer That Spans the World: Sermons on the Lord's Prayer* (London: Lutterworth, 1988), p. 151.

11 Thielicke, *Prayer That Spans the World*, p. 153.

12 Shane Claiborne, 'Lessons from the Good Samaritan', *New Urban World*, no. 3 (2013): p. 39.

13 Greenbelt is a forty-three-year-old festival of arts, faith and justice held each August in England. It creates a space for acts of the imagination. http://www.greenbelt.org.uk/

14 Shane Claiborne, Jonathan Wilson-Hartgrove and Enuma Okoro, *Common Prayer: A Liturgy for Ordinary Radicals* (Grand Rapids: Zondervan, 2010), p. 193.

15 Bishop Ken Untener of Saginaw, 'Archbishop Oscar Romero Prayer: A Step along the Way' (1979). http://www.usccb.org/prayer-and-worship/prayers-and-devotions/prayers/archbishop_romero_prayer.cfm

16 Robert Chao Romero, *Jesus for Revolutionaries: An Introduction to Race, Social Justice, and Christianity* (Christian Ethnic Studies, 2013), p. 227.

17 Tim Costello, 'Rev Tim Costello – Thine Be the Kingdom', Common Grace [video], YouTube (uploaded on 31 May 2015) https://www.youtube.com/watch?v=8JcUE9nrLGs or http://www.lordsprayer.org.au/yours_is_the_kingdom. Used with permission.

Versions

1 Lord's Prayer in 'Night Prayer', *A New Zealand Prayer Book: He Karakia Mihinare o Aotearoa* (Auckland: The Anglican Church in Aotearoa, New Zealand and Polynesia), p. 181; http://anglicanprayerbook.nz/167.html. Adapted from Jim Cotter's prayer. Copyright © The Anglican Church in Aotearoa, New Zealand and Polynesia. Used with permission.

2 http://jmm.aaa.net.au/articles/12661.htm. Copyright © Roslyn Wright. Used with permission.

3 Jack Nelson-Pallmeyer and Bret Hesla, *Worship in the Spirit of Jesus: Theology, Liturgy and Songs without Violence* (Eugene: Wipf and Stock, 2004). Used by permission of Wipf and Stock Publishers. www.wipfandstock.com

Paternoster:
thinking faith

We trust you enjoyed reading this book
from Paternoster. If you want to be informed
of any new titles from this author and other
releases you can sign up to the Paternoster
newsletter by contacting us:

By post:
Paternoster
PO Box 6326
Bletchley
Milton Keynes
MK1 9GG

E-mail:
paternoster@authenticmedia.co.uk

Follow us:

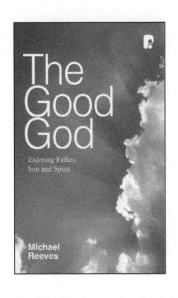

The Good God

Enjoying Father, Son and Spirit

Michael Reeves

In this lively and refreshing book, Michael Reeves unfurls the profound beauty of the Trinity, and shows how the triune God of the Bible brightens everything in a way that is happily life-changing. Prepare to enjoy the Father, Son and Spirit!

'At the heart of the universe is the passionate love between the members of the Trinity. Mike Reeves not only helps us grapple with a difficult doctrine but draws us to the magnetically attractive centre of all things. His light touch and theological wisdom combine to provide a truly helpful book which both clears your mind and warms your heart' – **Terry Virgo, Newfrontiers, UK**

'*The Good God* is a wonderful read. Reading it feels like you're eating candy floss – sweet, fun, easy. But in fact you're getting a nourishing, nutritious meal of real substance. This book will enlarge your view of God and increase love for God. You'll be blown away by the lavish love between the Father, Son and the Spirit that overflows to the world. If you want to enjoy God more then read this book – **Tim Chester, Crowded House, Sheffield, UK**

Michael Reeves is the Head of Theology for UCCF

978-1-84227-744-7

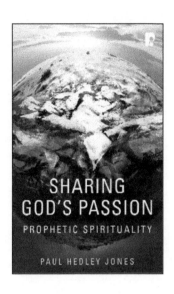

Sharing God's Passion

Prophetic Spirituality

Paul Hedley Jones

This book seeks to illuminate the critical role the prophets played in God's overarching purposes for his creation, and how we in the 21st century may also learn to collaborate with God. *Sharing God's Passion* provides a comprehensive overview of the various dimensions of a prophetic spirituality through a series of fifteen studies, each based on events in the life of the prophets, starting with Moses through to John of Patmos, including two chapters on Jesus, himself. The studies offer in-depth analyses of biblical texts, suggestions for life application, and questions for personal reflection or group discussion.

'Paul Jones has written a persuasive walk through the prophets. His interpretations are reliable, with an eye on the contemporaneity of these old texts. An interesting feature that commends the book is Jones's continuation of the prophetic trajectory into the New Testament' – **Walter Brueggemann, Columbia Theological Seminary**

Paul Hedley Jones is a doctoral student, working under Professor R.W.L. Moberley, at Durham University, UK.

9781842277454

Primitive Piety

A Journey from Suburban Mediocrity to Passionate Christianity

Ian Stackhouse

In *Primitive Piety* Ian Stackhouse takes us on a journey away from the safety and pleasantries of suburban piety and into a faith that is able to embrace the messiness as well as the paradoxes of the Christian faith.

In a culture in which there is every danger that we all look the same and speak the same, Stackhouse argues for a more gritty kind of faith – one that celebrates the oddity of the gospel, the eccentricity of the saints, and the utter uniqueness of each and every church.

Ian Stackhouse is the Pastoral Leader of Millmead, Guildford Baptist Church.

9781842277867